In Search of Harriers

Over the hills and far away

DONALD WATSON

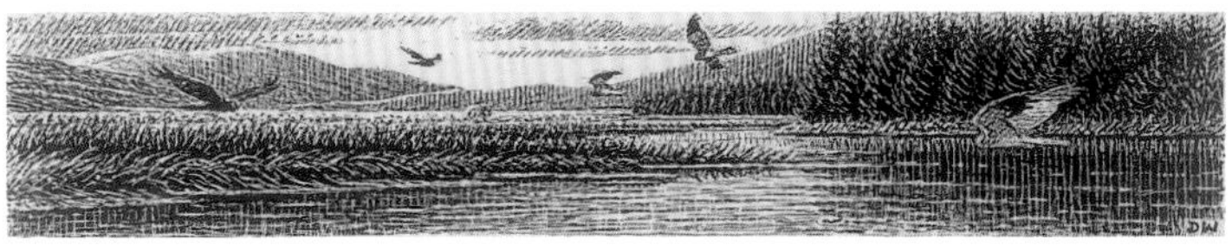

LANGFORD PRESS 2010

Acknowledgements

I am glad to acknowledge the huge amount of work that Ian Langford, as publisher, has put into the production of this book. I must also thank the support from my wife Joan and our daughter, Pam, for their interest. And especially the work that our daughters, Louise and Kate – both experienced editors – have done in coping with my terrible writing and producing immaculate print-outs of the text. I also thank our son Jeff for useful comments and for editing and improving the chapter on polygyny. As an aged writer I thank the many friends who have helped to sustain me in the making of the book.

The publisher would very much like to thank Dean Hearn at Healeys Print Group for his skill and patience in bringing the contents of the book together in such a wonderful way.

Both Donald Watson as author and artist and the publishers would very much like to thank the many owners of the artwork for generosity and help in providing the images used throughout the book.

First published 2010

Langford Press, 10 New Road, Langtoft,
Peterborough PE6 9LE
Tel / Fax: 01988 341132
www.langford-press.co.uk
Email: sales@langford-press.co.uk

Printed & Bound by Healeys Printers, Ipswich, Suffolk.
Origination by Dean Hearn.

A cip Record for this book is available from the British Library.

ISBN 978-1-904078-12-8

Contents

Unless otherwise stated all paintings within the book are gouache and approximately 60 x 42 cm (23 x 16 inches) for example pages 17, 24, 27, 43, 45, 46, 48, 64, 72, 78, 79, 86, 88, 89, 102, 110 and 112 are smaller.

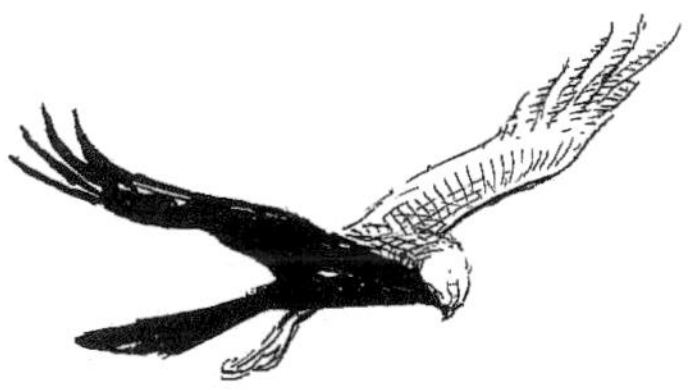 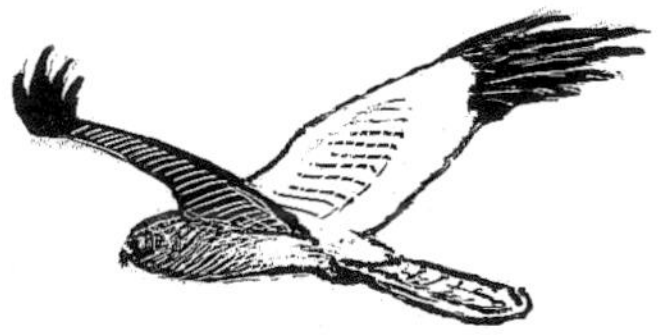

Dedication

In devoted memory of Joan, my loving wife of 54 years, who died on 10th September 2004.
Born 1919, died 2004

Donald Watson born 1918, died 2005

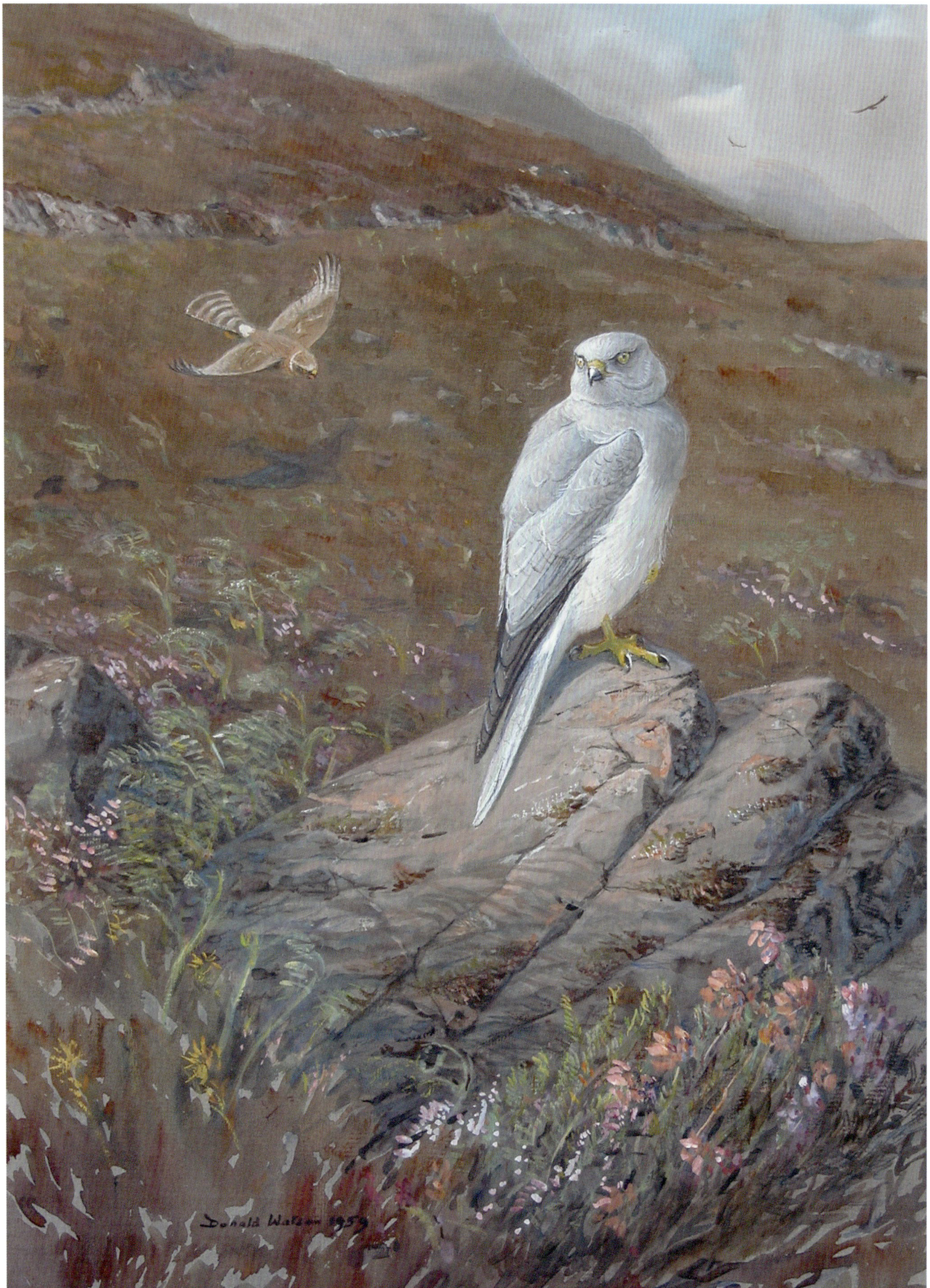
Donald Watson 1959

Introduction

I must have painted many hundreds of bird pictures in the last 50 years or so, including a large number featuring Hen Harriers. It was Ian Langford's suggestion that I should collect many of them in a book and write short chapters which could be linked to the pictures. Very many of my paintings are no longer in my possession, so it has involved getting them photographed to a high standard. Ian has been largely responsible for doing this and I am pleased with the quality of the reproduction.

Readers may well ask the question I have posed as the title of a chapter, 'Why paint Hen Harriers?' I have tried to answer this question on page 10. Briefly the answer must be that all harriers are beautiful, wonderfully graceful and a joy to watch in flight. The harriers in which the adult male is largely a light grey bird – Hen, Montagu's and Pallid – all exhibit the astonishing contrast in plumage colour between the sexes when mature, which for centuries made people believe that the male and female Hen Harrier, at least, were different species.

This is primarily a book of my paintings but each one has a chapter relating to it, which in most cases includes personal observations, many in Scotland – especially Galloway and the islands – but also abroad. There was some discussion about whether the book should be entirely one about harriers and the landscapes and habitats where they occur, or whether it should include some other species of birds which are associated with them. We decided to include a few of these to add variety, some obviously being frequent prey of harriers, others because harrier watchers can expect to see them in habitats frequented by harriers. I also had to find paintings or drawings of these other birds, a few having been published in earlier books, but most of these will not be familiar to many people now.

Writing the chapters of this book has meant that I have referred to works by many other authors. I had read most of the important books or papers before, but some were well worth consulting again. One scientific ornithologist who visited me was dismissive of Jacques Delamain's aesthetic approach in *Why birds sing*, but I have particularly appreciated his splendid account of a pair of Montagu's Harriers throughout a breeding season in his home countryside of Western France. That one of the pair was a melanistic bird – known as a 'dark morph' – added spice to his story. When I was younger and able to travel abroad I watched harriers in several countries, including the memorable Montagu's Harriers which are still plentiful in France, where enthusiastic protectionists save many nests from destruction by combine harvester. I still vividly recall the splendid Pied Harriers I saw often in the Arakan region of Burma during the 1939–45 war, and the fine Pallid Harriers that I saw in Hyderabad state in India in 1945.

Apart from the brief attempts to colonise parts of Scotland by Montagu's Harriers in the 1950s, the Hen Harrier has been the only harrier breeding regularly in Scotland. Although it is still persecuted on some grouse moors, it is a well-established bird nowadays and can be seen widely at all times of the year. This book contains many paintings of breeding and wintering birds in my home district of Galloway.

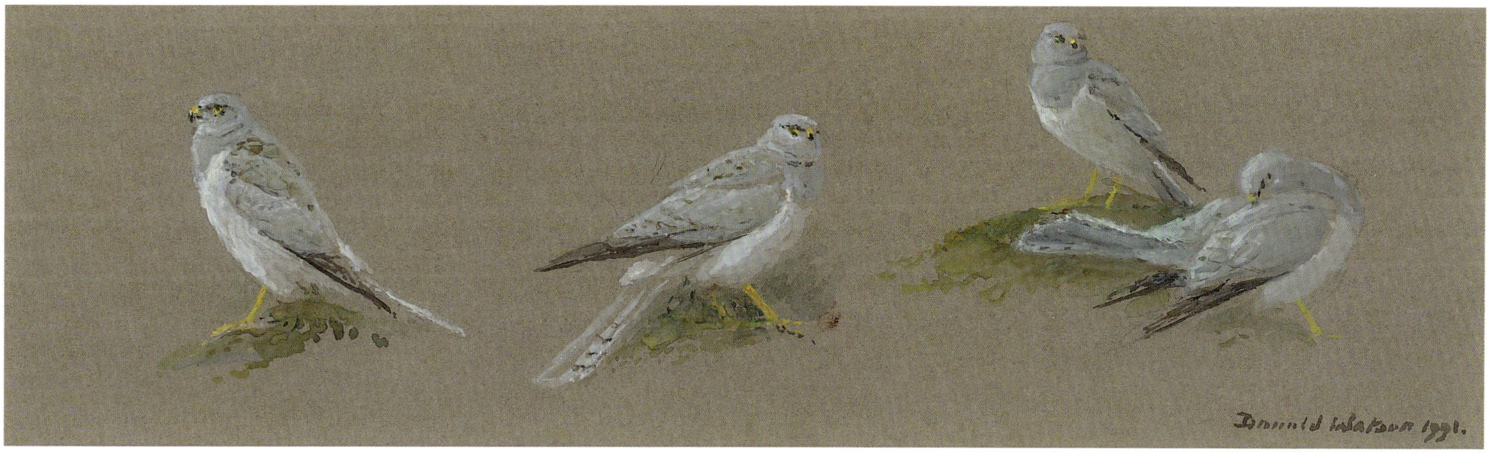

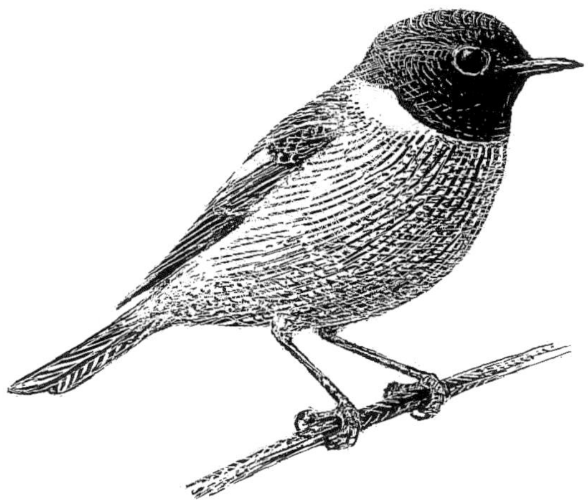

Harriers and other species

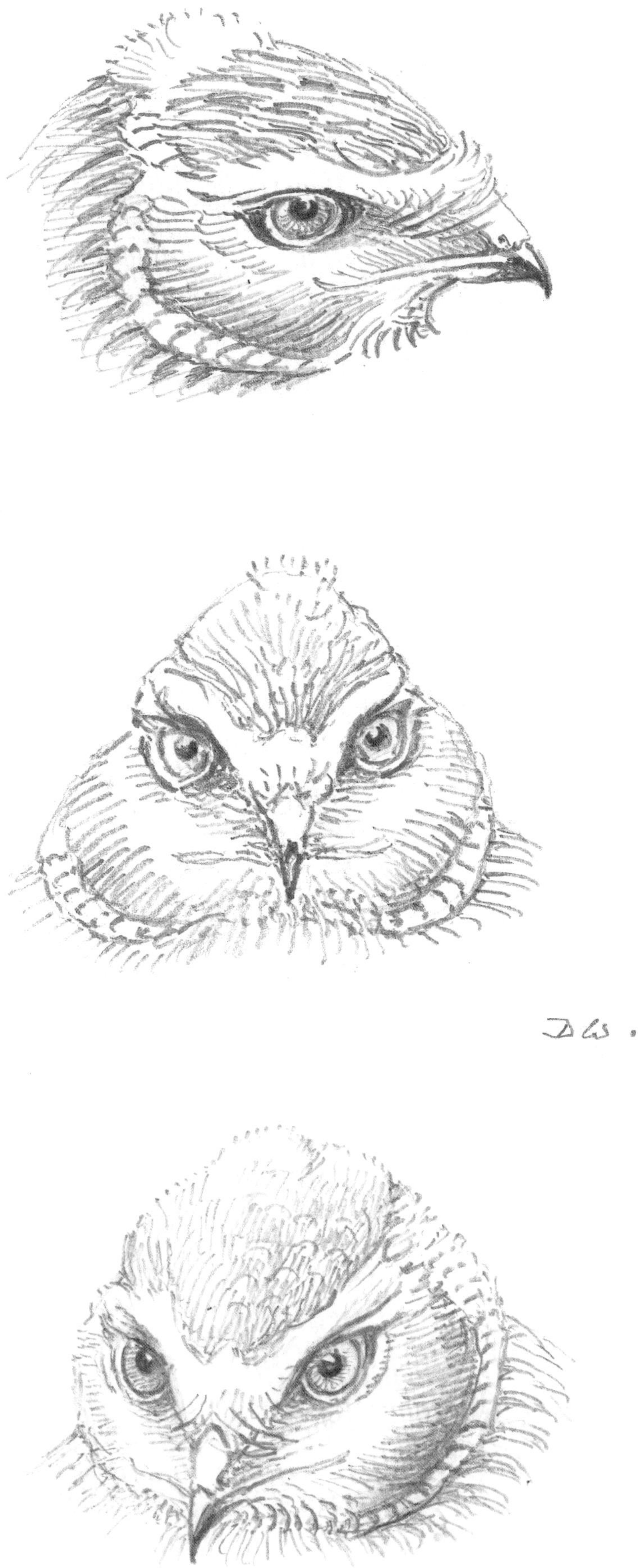

Field sketches in pencil.

Why paint Hen Harriers?

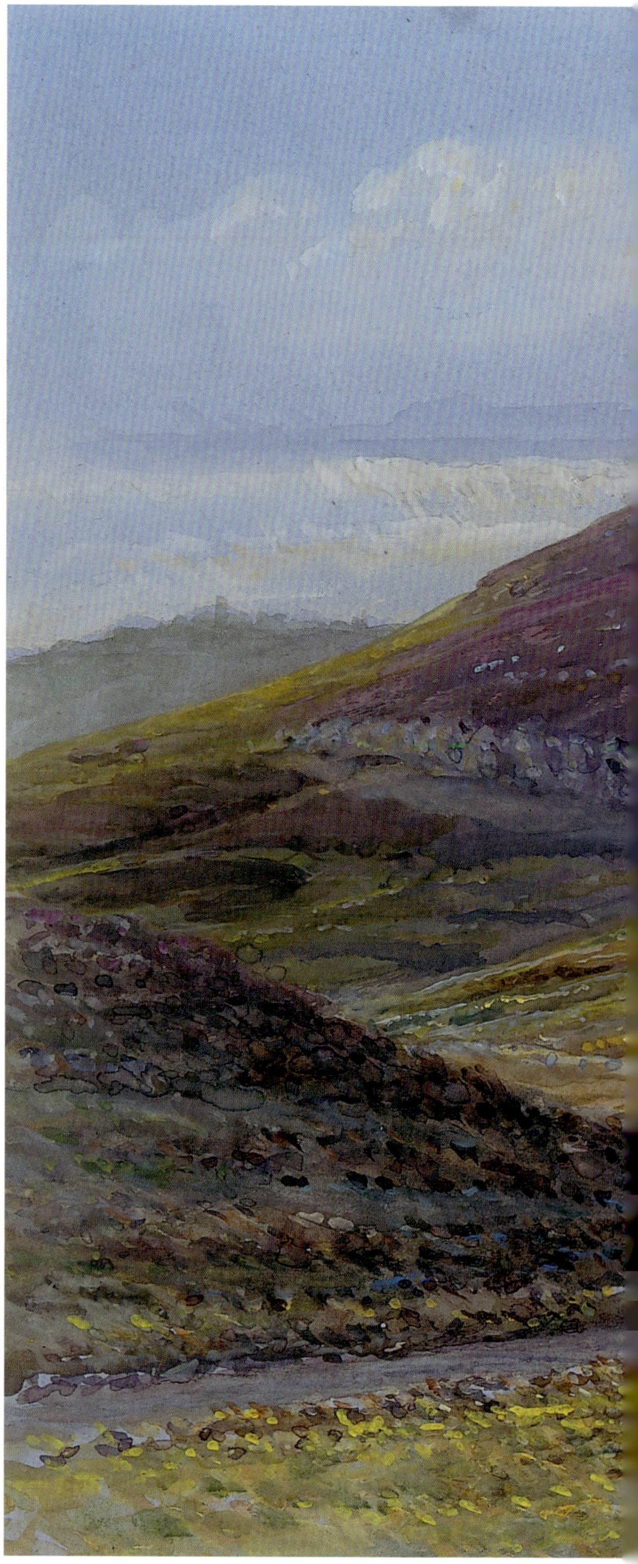

It was the Hen Harrier in flight that inspired me to attempt to draw and paint it. I should perhaps qualify this statement by saying that finding Montagu's Harriers in France preceded my ever seeing more than occasional Hen Harriers, because of their rarity in Britain when I was young. I had begun drawing birds as a child, but it was many years before I grasped that drawing moving birds from life was what I must try to master. In early days my artist uncle scorned my own and my brother's admiration for Archibald Thorburn's paintings, reproduced in our bird books. Thorburn's work is still much sought after and fetches high prices. I still admire much of it but I came to realise that his flying birds were particularly criticisable. A gift from a friend of a book crammed with Bruno Liljefors' pictures opened a new world for me. I realised that his great paintings of wildlife in landscapes were unequalled. He was also a great hunter himself.

I came to understand that my uncle's favourite, Joseph Crawhall, was also a great animal artist of a very different kind and that other artists in my own

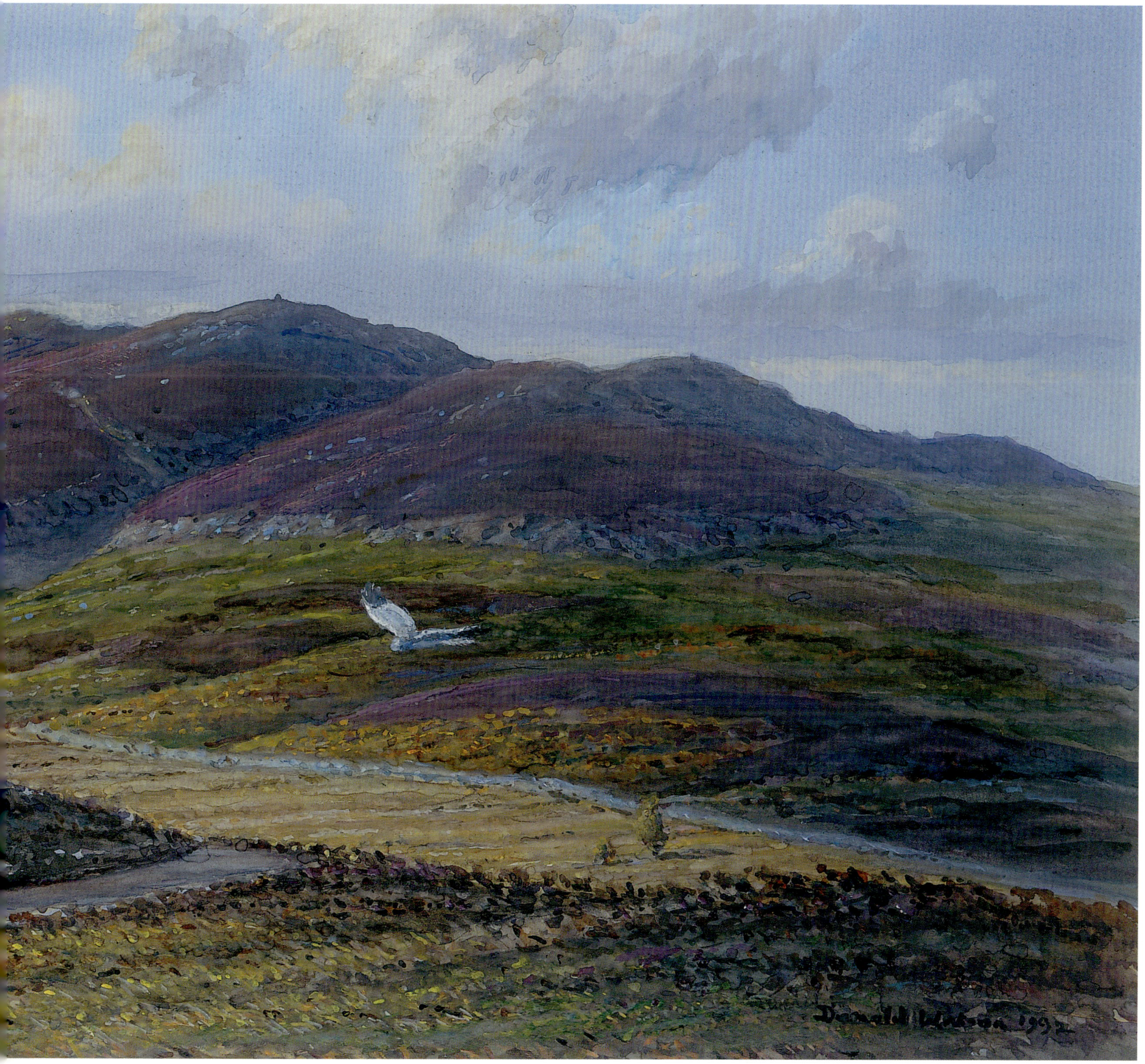

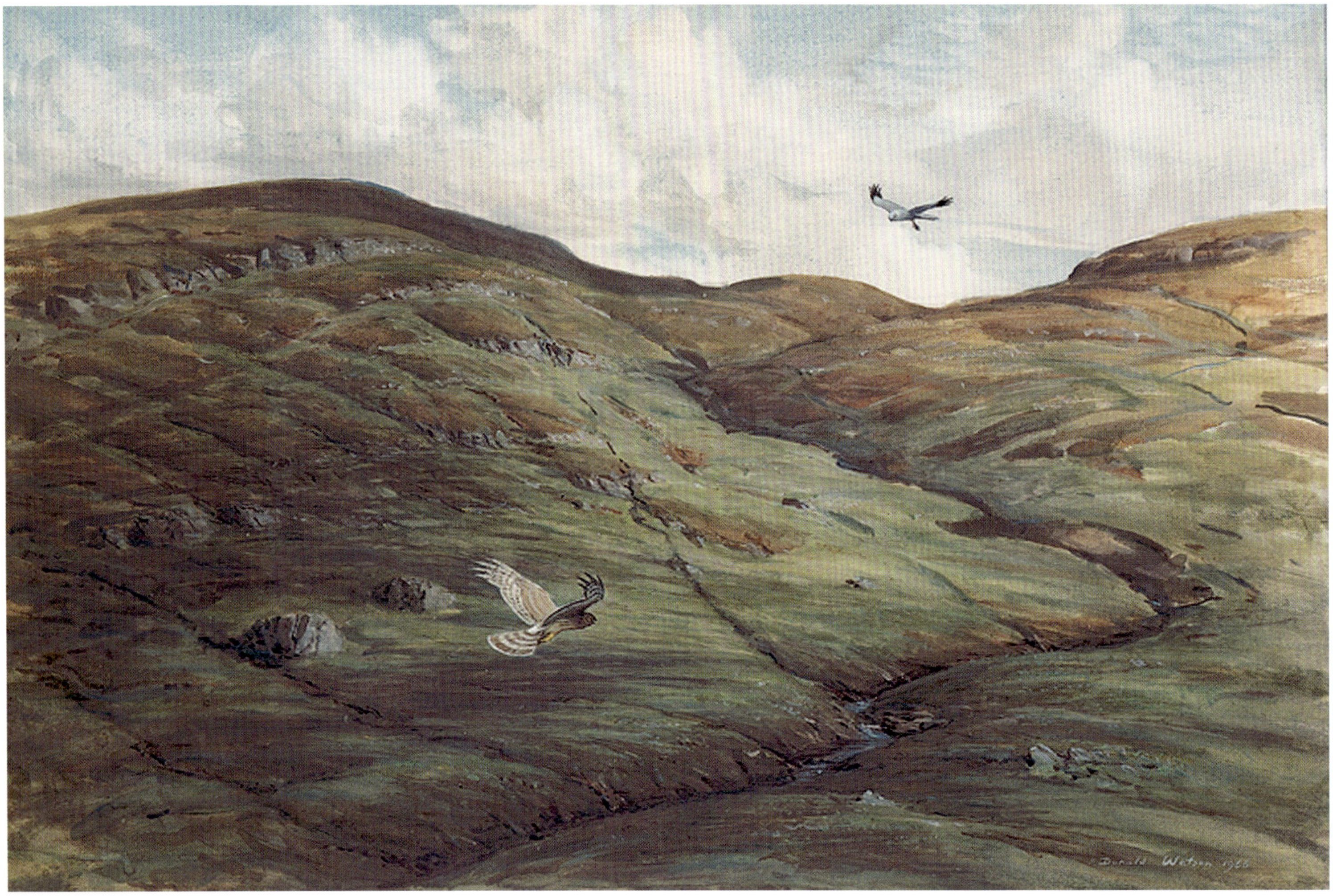

country, like Edwin Alexander (who was greatly admired by Thorburn), could be an inspiration. When I saw a whole gallery full of Eric Ennion's work, it made a great impression. In his early work I saw a strong Thorburn influence, but later Ennion painted much more freely in a more personal style which put him at the highest level.

Studying Hen Harriers, which some people still class as vermin on grouse moors, I re-read Hemming Weiss' touching account of the Montagu's colony he wrote about long ago in Denmark. 'It provides the enlivening element to its surroundings,' he wrote, 'and has brought life to places that were waste and desolate before.' I am not sure I can quite agree with 'waste and desolate' but a cock harrier of either species can certainly bring an arresting focal point of life to a spacious landscape and sky. Pictorially, it is the harrier in apparently leisurely flight that most often adds the spark of life to such surroundings. Many years ago I said apologetically to an established Scottish Academician that I doubted if my paintings were 'real art' because I only painted what I saw, but he encouraged me to have self-belief and continue on my own path. I recognise that painting in gouache or oil gives the freedom to introduce the almost white form of a cock Hen Harrier against the dark but varied tones of hill or forest. I do also paint in pure watercolour but am too impatient to attempt many large landscape or foreground settings for my birds in this medium, such as Charles Tunnicliffe could manage so beautifully. His big watercolours must have been the result of very precise preparation.

The cryptically coloured females of Hen and Montagu's Harriers present different problems to the artist from the adult males.

Harrier people

The late Jimmy Campbell (Dr J. W. Campbell) wrote a good account of the return of the Hen Harrier to the Scottish mainland after 'the lean years before 1939.' It was he who drew attention to the efforts that George Arthur had made to protect the few remaining Hen Harriers in Orkney when egg collectors were arriving there to rob nests of their eggs. George Arthur was very well known in the islands, being the owner of a big store in Kirkwall, and he would alert the police when a known collector arrived.

George Waterston introduced me to George and his wife, Jean, in Kirkwall in 1946. Sadly George Arthur died a few years later, but Eddie Balfour soon became the doyen of harrier protection and study in Orkney until his sudden death in 1974. Jimmy Campbell lived in Perthshire, so was well placed to record the spread of nesting by Hen Harriers on Perthshire grouse moors and the hostility they soon began to receive from gamekeepers and grouse shooters. He noted that the return of Hen Harriers to nest on grouse moors was being slowed down by the late 1940s, when the spread of young forestry plantations provided a safe haven for them.

Dugald Macintyre, himself a keeper, had written admiringly about Hen Harriers in his books. I have noted elsewhere that he knew of Hen Harriers still nesting successfully in Kintyre in 'the lean years.' There does seem to be sound evidence that extinction on the mainland of Scotland was never quite so complete as generally believed, at least in Kintyre and Arran. Campbell also wrote that an increase in Norway was likely to have contributed to the resurgence in Scotland.

Although persecution of harriers was intense in most European countries, such beautiful and interesting birds were bound to have their defenders, notable among them Jacques Delamain in France, Henning Weiss in Denmark and Laszlo Studinka in Hungary. In his short life Weiss studied a colony of Montagu's Harriers in young forestry on heather moor between 1913 and 1918. His book, *Life of the Harrier in Denmark*, was illustrated with fine photographs. It was published posthumously.

Delamain's *Pourquoi les oiseaux chantes*, published in English as *Why Birds Sing* in 1932, demonstrated what an exceptional field ornithologist he was, while his writing had a strongly aesthetic approach; his appreciation of all the birds of his native countryside was delightful. Montagu's Harriers were a special interest for him, nesting colonially in western France, some of his field observations bringing new facets of their breeding behaviour to light.

Studinka was a large landowner in pre-war Hungary. He made a close study of Montagu's Harriers on his own estates. His large collections of skins of birds he shot are still in the British Museum (Natural History). He threw much new light on plumage changes. As a callow youth, with no particular interest in harriers, I attended a lecture he gave in Edinburgh in 1934. I imagine that his estates were broken up in the Communist era.

In 1947 the animal artist John Murray Thomson told me that when fishing in Sutherland he had seen nesting Hen Harriers.

I wish now that I had met Fran Hamerstrom, the American expert on Northern Harriers, considered to be con-specific with Hen Harriers. I was fascinated by her book about her study of them in Wisconsin. She had teams of young scientists working for her.

'Harrier people' with widely differing interests in them have existed down the ages. The Scots poet William Dunbar was familiar with the male Hen Harrier early in the 16th century, calling it 'St. Martin's fowle' from its appearance in France about Michaelmas, and I'm sure that the hawk which he called 'the mytane' must have been the ringtail Hen Harrier. He wrote of St Martin's fowle and the mytane in the same context as though he had seen them together.

> *"The mytane and St Martin's fowle*
> *Wend he had been the hornit howle*
> *They set upon him with a yowle*
> *And gave him dint for dint."*

Dunbar travelled to France and knew the names of at least eight kinds of birds of prey. His knowledge was obviously gained from falconry. It could shame many people today who claim to be knowledgeable about the countryside.

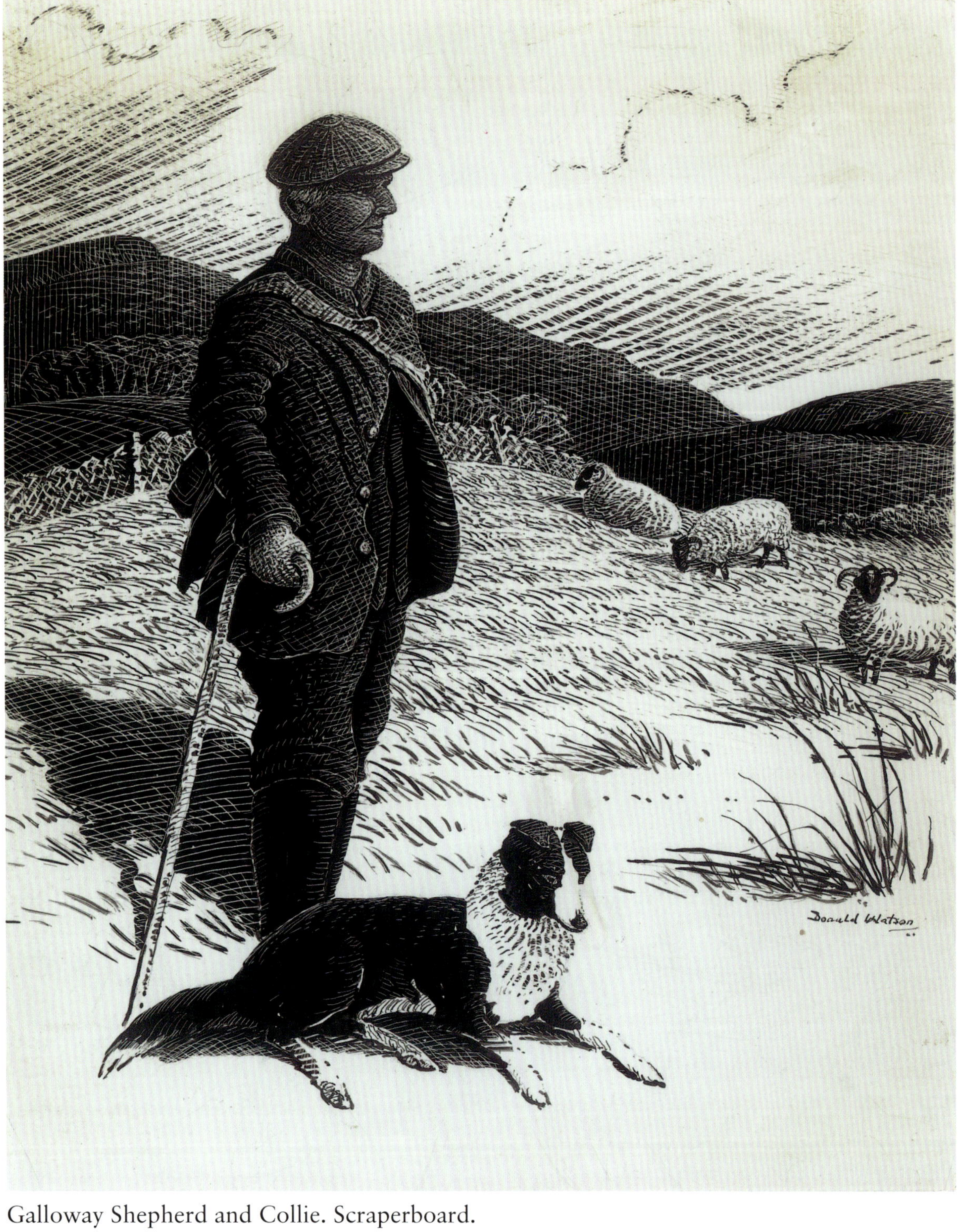

Galloway Shepherd and Collie. Scraperboard.

William Turner wrote of the 'Hen Harroer' in 1544 that 'gets its name among countrymen from butchering their fowls.' It was John Heysham at Carlisle who first recognised incontrovertibly that the grey male and the brown female were of the same species. By taking young from the nests and rearing them in captivity, he proved that young males in first-year brown plumage began moulting into the grey plumage when about a year old. It was, however, the much more famous naturalist George Montagu who discovered in 1802 that the Montagu's Harrier was a distinct species, from his studies in southwest England.

A mass of references to Hen Harriers occurs in 19th-century writings. Most of them are by collectors, who gave accounts of shooting Hen Harriers which often ended up as stuffed specimens in grand houses. The wonderful poetry of John Clare stems from a different outlook, of delight in its beauty.

"A hugh blue bird will often swim
Along the wheat when skys grow dim
Wi clouds – slow as the gales of spring
In motion wi dark shadowed wing
Beneath the coming storm it sails."

This could equally apply to a Montagu's Harrier and perhaps more likely it does, as Clare may have seen them more commonly than Hen Harriers in his native fenland.

Today birdwatchers enjoy sighting any harrier, and a sighting of a grey male is always a highlight of a day. Roger Clarke has written an excellent book on Montagu's Harriers which is a mine of information. He once told me that he was first enthused about Hen Harriers when coarse fishing in East Anglia.

Dick Roxburgh, from Catrine, Ayrshire, who had been a miner, had an immense knowledge of the countryside and its wildlife, inspiring many younger men, such as Chris Rollie, Ricky Gladwell and Charlie Park, with his passion for birds, particularly Peregrines, eagles, harriers and Merlins. He was a dedicated hill walker and said that in the Galloway hills a mile equalled three anywhere else he knew. His letters, written in his inimitable style, were, like his conversation, laced with his dry humour. He was also a very serious person. Every summer he paid his respects at the site, high on the Rhinns of Kells, where a young shepherd had died in a March blizzard in 1954.

Don Scott made the startling discovery that Hen Harriers had begun to nest in trees in Northern Ireland and has become a leading authority on them in the last decade.

I cannot conclude this long chapter without paying tribute to several shepherds who have been so helpful in my quests for Hen Harrier nests in Galloway, particularly the late Jimmy Stewart at Grobdale and Will Dalziel, his predecessor there.

I gladly acknowledge the many kindnesses I received from the late Sir Arthur Duncan, a Dumfriesshire farmer and landowner who for many years encouraged my painting of birds in landscapes and to whose wide knowledge of natural history I am so greatly indebted. He was a brilliant chairman of the former Nature Conservancy and great company on the many walks we enjoyed together in the Galloway hills. He was one of the very few friends to whom I divulged the discovery of my first Galloway nest of Hen Harriers.

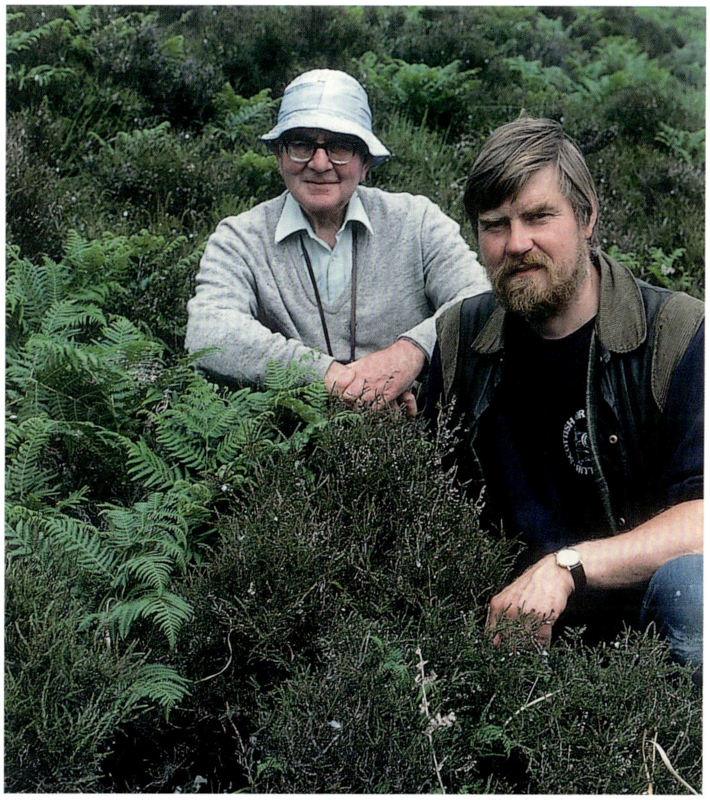

Donald Watson (with hat) and Geoff Shaw at a Galloway Hen harrier nest 1988. Photograph: I. Langford.

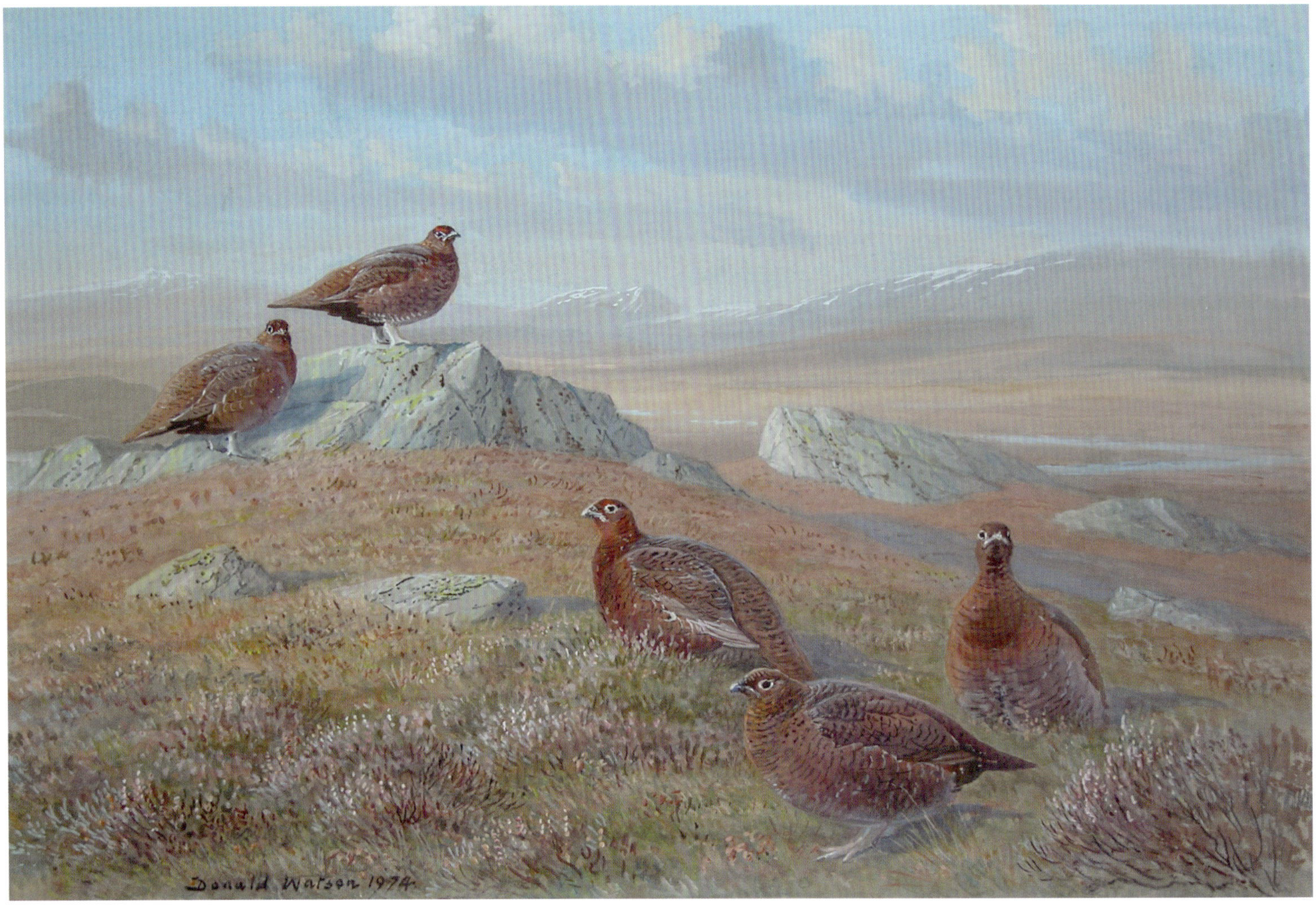

Hen Harrier prey

Field Voles, Meadow Pipits and Skylarks are the main prey of Hen Harriers in many regions. Field Voles are called Meadow Mice in North America, where the Hen Harrier is known as the Northern Harrier. Field Voles are well known to be subject to cyclical fluctuations in numbers, with peaks every three or four years. The large Orkney Vole, an important prey there, does not have such marked fluctuations.

In Europe generally a variety of birds and small mammals are taken as prey. On grouse moors in Britain, Hen Harriers take Red Grouse, mainly chicks, but also some adults, especially females when they are carrying eggs in spring and cannot fly very fast.

In the long-running study on Red Grouse and Hen Harriers carried out by Redpath, Thirgood and their team on the Langholm moors, supplementary food was provided for harriers: dead poultry chicks and rats were placed near harrier nest-sites to reduce predation by harriers on Red Grouse chicks. At Langholm, Hen Harrier nests increased substantially in the 1990s but have declined substantially in numbers since. Buccleuch Estates consider grouse shooting no longer viable.

Redpath found that on the Langholm moors, Hen Harriers took mostly voles in the early weeks of the breeding season. This change may be being brought about by the replacement of much heather by grasses: this is detrimental to Red Grouse, which are dependent on heather for food and nest-sites.

On my home ground in Galloway, southwest Scotland, Hen Harriers prey on Whinchats, Stonechats and Wheatears, mostly young; and harriers that nest in conifer forests hunt the numerous Siskins breeding there. Crossbills, when they are in good numbers, are taken but they are unlikely to be frequent prey except

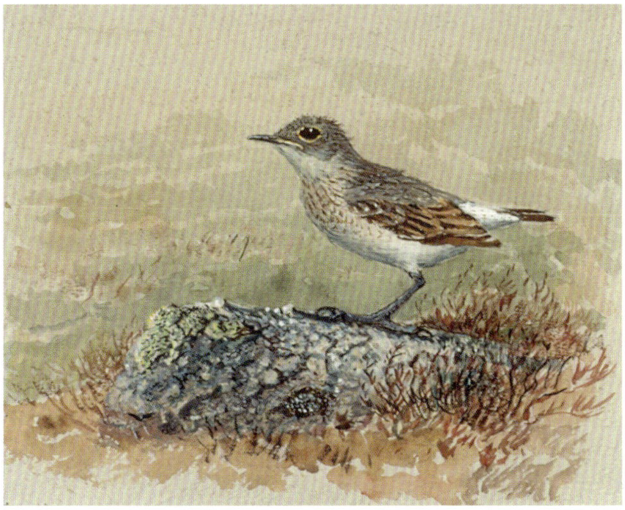

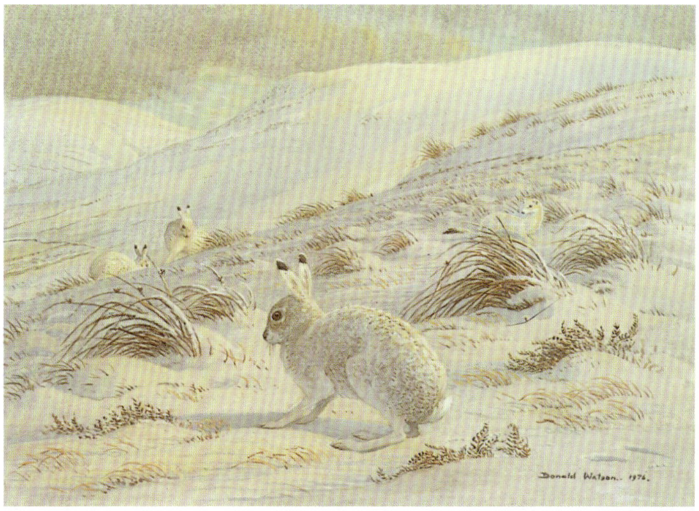

in big invasion years. In high summer, when flocks of juvenile Starlings come on to the higher ground, they may become prey to Hen Harriers and particularly Merlins.

On open moorland, waders, especially young birds, are targets for hunting harriers. Golden Plover chicks are caught, as are young or juvenile Curlews. On Hebridean moors, particularly in the Outer Isles, small waders are hunted most on the machair, where the greatest concentrations of breeding waders are found. Hen Harriers nesting on the moors on the eastern side of the Uists and Benbecula are often seen hunting over the machair to the west.

Black Grouse, formerly abundant in Galloway, have declined so greatly that they are unlikely to be prey any more; the story from a ranger's wife that she had seen a Blackcock killed by a male Hen Harrier seems most unlikely. Perhaps it referred to a young cock moulting into the black plumage of an adult, or perhaps it was an old bird in heavy moult.

In the early years of afforestation in Kintyre, Redpolls were found to be an important prey of Hen Harriers; they have become much scarcer recently and do not seem to be taken often now.

In high summer when Wood Pigeons have large young in the older conifers, Hen Harriers kill some and may drop the large young in forest rides before taking them to nests.

Where rabbits are plentiful, the young are killed by Hen Harriers, and the leverets of Brown and Mountain Hares are taken at times. The young of thrush species and warblers, mostly Willow Warblers, are brought as prey to forest nest-sites.

On the Isle of Man, which now has many Hen Harriers nesting, I am told that rabbits are frequent prey at nests and Hen Harriers kill full-grown rabbits, which they dismember before taking to nests.

Hen Harrier prey is more diverse in winter. When large flocks of Fieldfares and Redwings arrive from Scandinavia, many alight in the uplands of Galloway; according to Chris Rollie they feed initially on the seeds of rushes (Juncus spp.), and Hen Harriers often hunt such upland sites and take a toll on the flocks. Chris Rollie has told me that once, when waiting to see harriers go to roost, he startled a male harrier that had plucked most of a Fieldfare. It was still alive and scuttled into cover but was unable to fly; meanwhile the harrier stayed overhead, obviously waiting to return to its prey.

Winter flocks of finches and buntings are visited and hunted by Hen Harriers. These flocks contain a mixture of species, often including many Greenfinches, Linnets, Reed Buntings and Dunnocks. They gather in weedy fields where they take a variety of seeds, which have been found in quantities in the pellets of harriers. Roger Clarke has analysed large numbers of harrier pellets and found that they contained an abundance of seeds. In his paper in 'British Birds', he writes of the likely effects on the seed-eating small birds of GM crops being grown commercially, postulating that this could havc important adverse effects on the numbers of seed-eating small birds and indirectly on the abundance of food for harriers in winter.

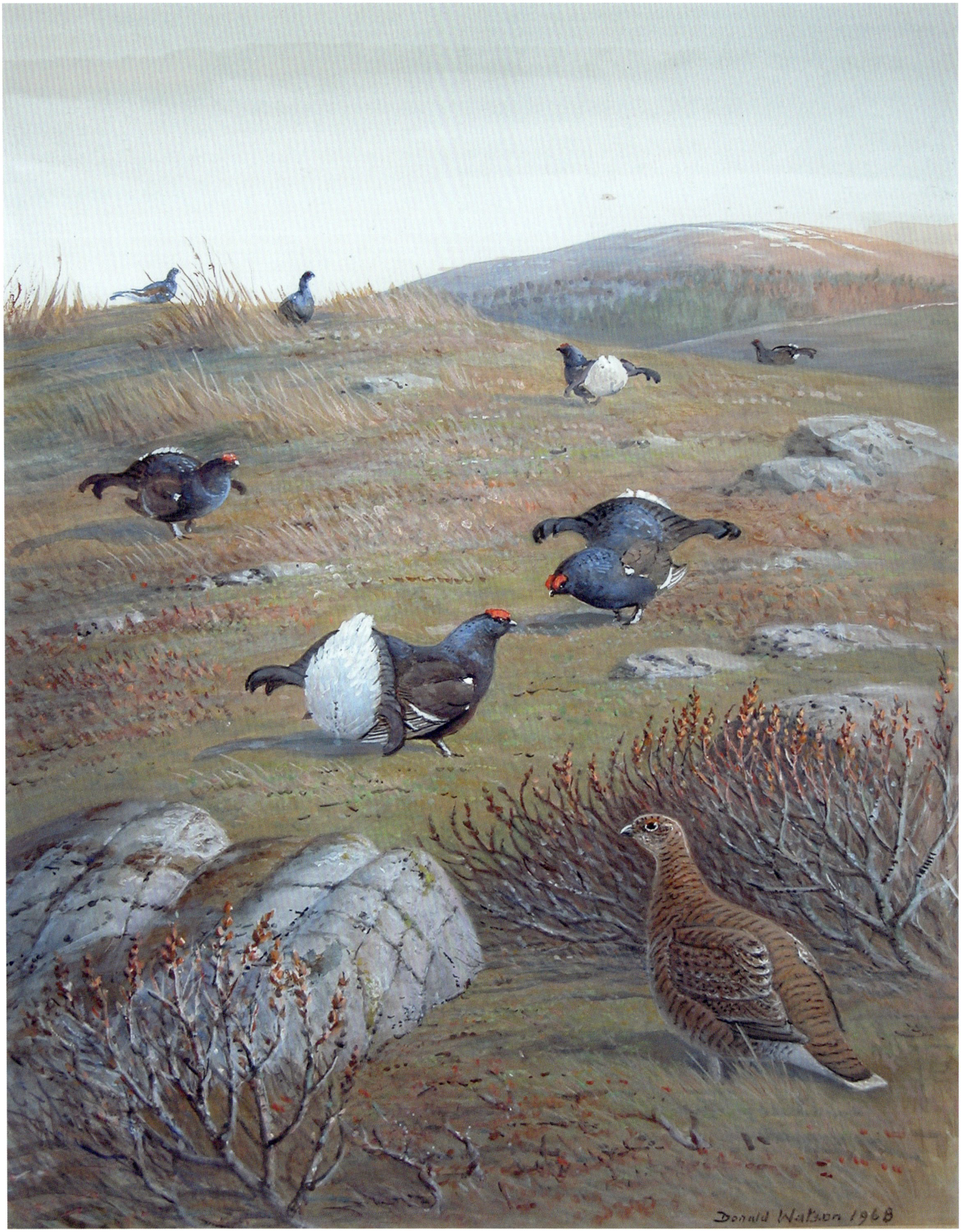
Donald Watson 1968

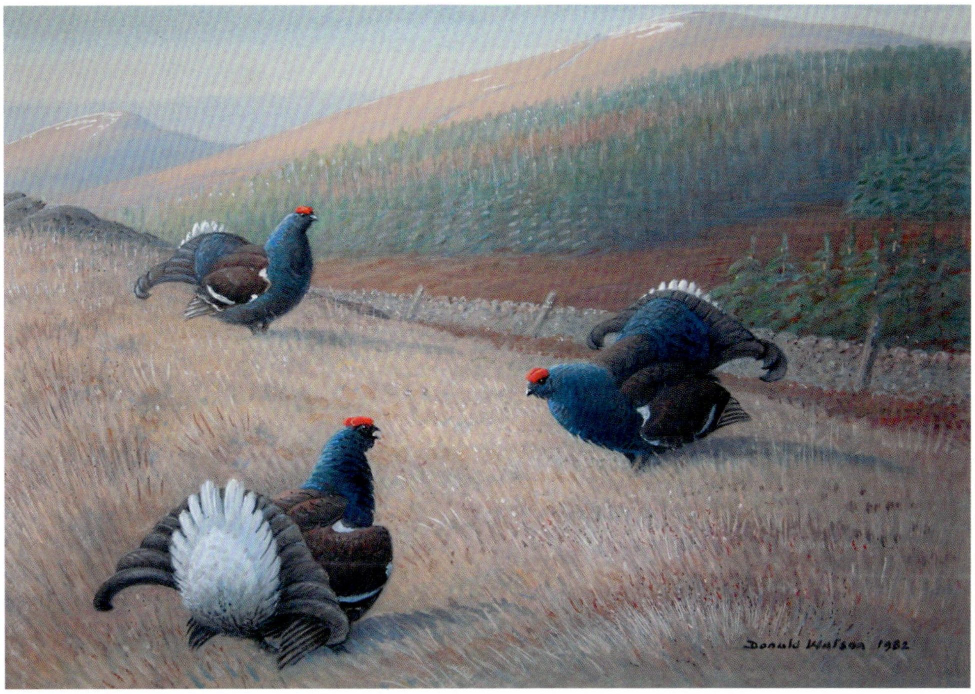

Black Grouse

I once stumbled over a nest with a large clutch of eggs, deep in Polmaddy forest when that vast area of conifers was very young. It was beneath a small tree where the ground vegetation was a mixture of heather and grasses. I don't remember finding any more nests, but at that time, in the late 1960s, Black Grouse were very plentiful in Galloway. In early spring I used to see up to 60 or 70 together, feeding on willow buds in the sauchs (willow scrub) in the upper Ken Valley. Some of these gatherings were unisex, males or females (greyhens), but often the sexes were mixed. I must have known 20 or 30 leks in Galloway in the 1960s–70s. The magnificent Blackcocks, with an ultramarine sheen on their glossy black plumage, gathered to fight each other and display in competition for hens. The big leks were on heathery or grassy unplanted ground within or close to the forest and the bubbling calls of the cocks could be audible from a great distance. So could their other call, like an aborted sneeze. Leks were at their best in spring into early summer, at dawn or dusk. There was some recurrence of 'lekking' in the autumn.

In later years, as the numbers of Black Grouse declined, leks have been much smaller. In spring a cock attended by a single hen can be found displaying deep in forest plantations or there may be small gatherings at a lek site. One of the best traditional leks was on the moor at Craigengillan in the High Ken valley, and there was another very big one in the Fleet valley, south of Loch Grannoch. Even in the 1980s a lek near Loch Dee and another in the Black Water valley numbered almost ten cocks, and others on the Deer Range and near Lochinvar Loch had nearly as many. It is still something of a mystery why Black Grouse have decreased so much but a researcher found that in parts of their range heavy grazing by deer or sheep seems to be responsible for reducing availability of their main food plants.

The extraordinary 19th-century story of a Peregrine carrying a Blackcock to an eyrie on the Bass Rock from the Lammermuir hills is mentioned by Macgillivray. And not long ago Chris Rollie watched a Golden Eagle in Galloway fly about 7–8 kilometres to kill a Blackcock, which it had presumably spotted.

The lyre-shaped tail feathers are moulted after the breeding season, when parties of cocks in their drab eclipse plumage can often be seen feeding on rowan berries.

Greyhen does not seem to me the most appropriate name, since the predominant colour is much warmer than grey, and beautifully mottled. They are not uncommonly at risk from traffic when they take their chicks on to roads in the forests for grit. Now and again there have been claims that Capercaillie have been seen in Galloway, but the only reliable records are of single females found at the head of Glentrool by my friend Geoff Shaw on 29 September 1977 and 2 November 1982.

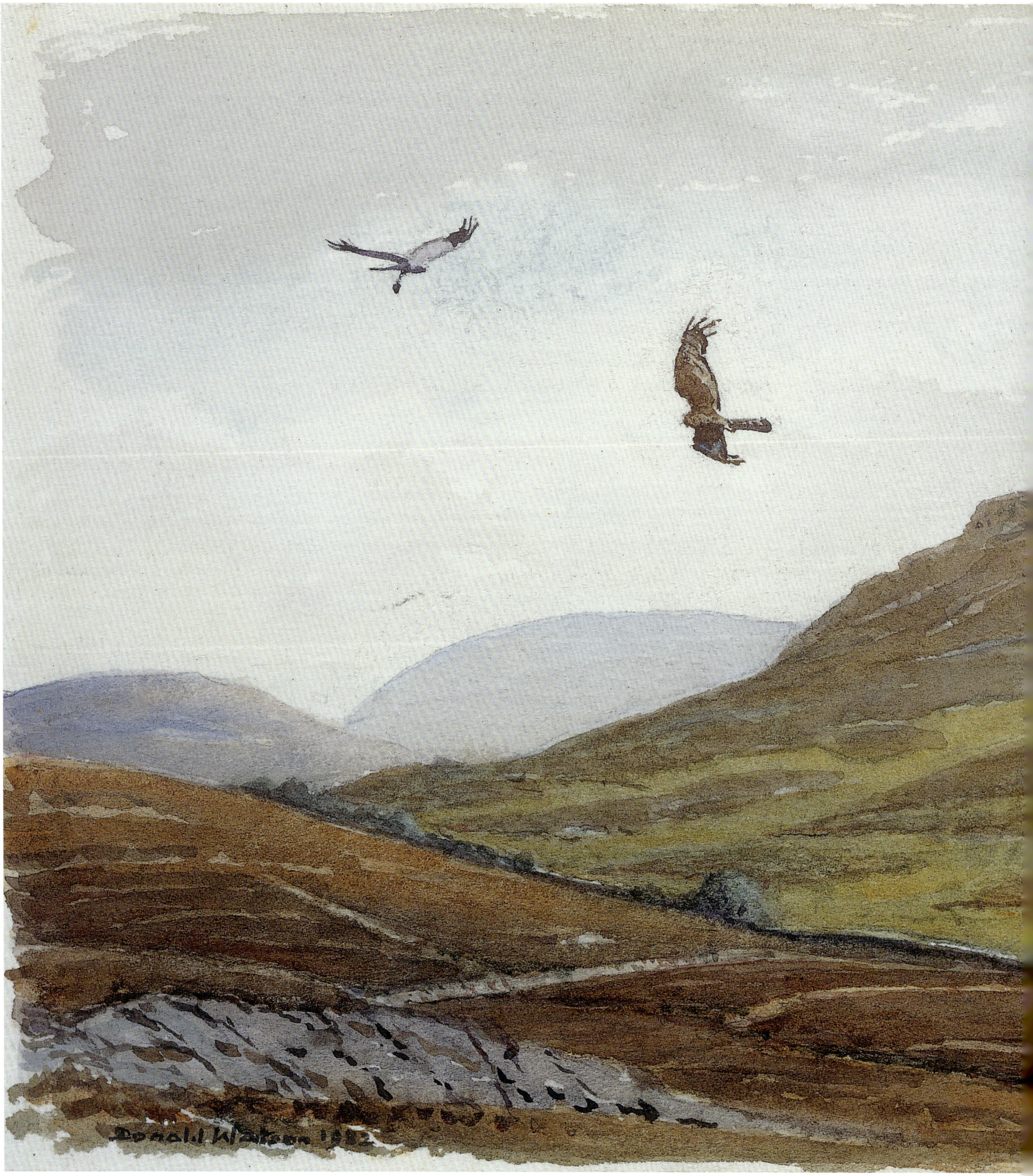

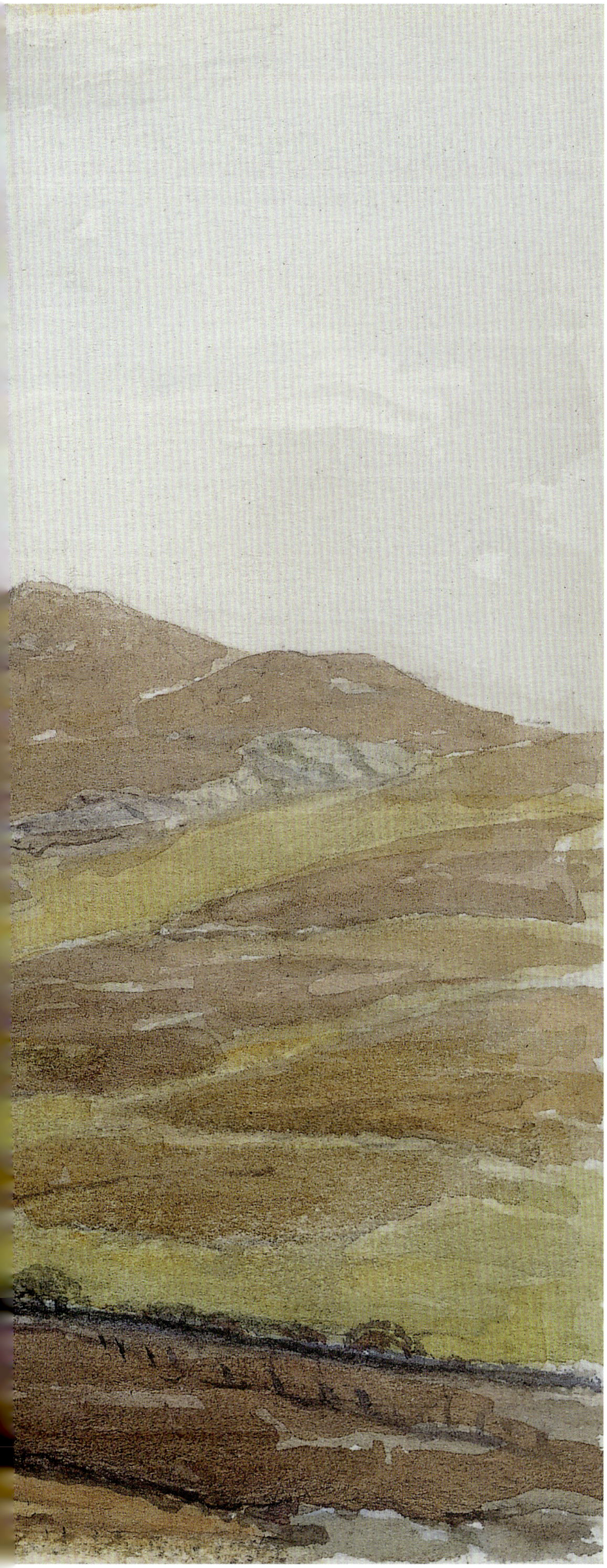

The first Hen Harrier nesting in Galloway in the 20th century

This painting is one of my earliest paintings of Hen Harriers, in 1959, when I spent so much time watching my first nesting pair in Galloway. Both were fully mature birds, the male looking as light as a gull when he crossed the dark red-brown heather and the female clearly several years old from her brilliant yellow eyes. The male would often perch on a fence-post below the nest after a food-pass, when the female usually flew a few metres to pluck and eat the prey on the ground before returning to the nest. From their ages I was sure that it was not the first year they had bred, but they may not have bred together before. In the 1950s Hen Harriers were still rare in Galloway, and the site was too near a much-used road to give any confidence that the nest would be successful. I, often with my friend Alan Mills, watched from below a small knowe, out of sight from passing traffic. When after a couple of weeks we thought it safe enough to walk up to the nest to discover its contents, I was so anxious about disturbing it that we stopped a few metres below it and turned back without flushing the sitting female. When we did go to the nest, a week later, I had my first experience of a very aggressive female harrier. The eggs had hatched; there were four small downy chicks. They all fledged successfully in July. By that time, ewes with large lambs coming near the nest often received a buffeting on the nose from

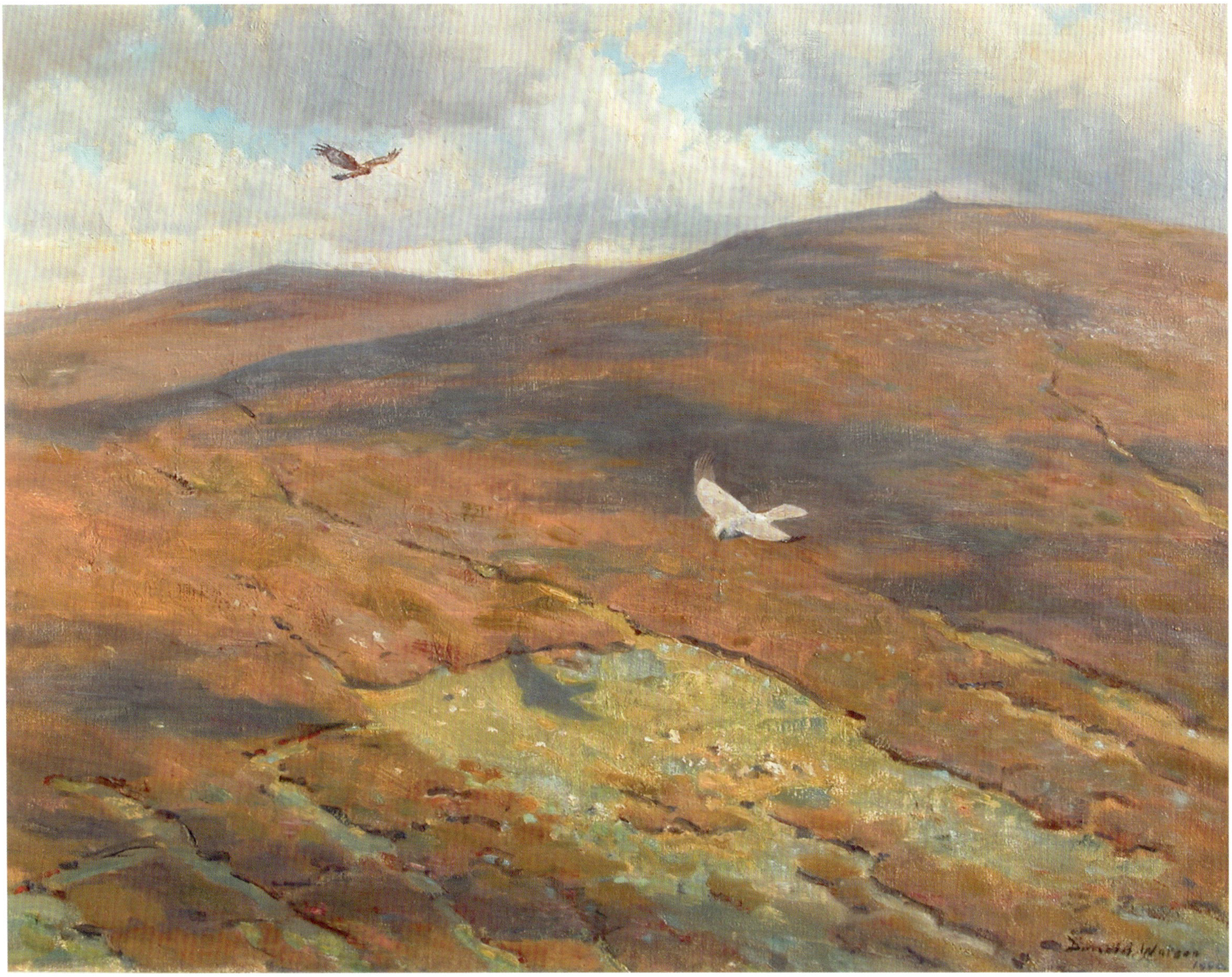

Oil painting of Harriers over moorland.

the female harrier. On the flatter ground below, two or three pairs of Whaups (Curlews) had their young, the parents boldly diving at the harriers. Throughout the early summer Cuckoos called all day but were at their most active in the early mornings.

The lowest ground in front of the Craig, where the harriers' nest was, had once been a loch and was still known as the Corbie loch to the shepherd. Hardly more than a small burn remained, but odd willow trees grew beside this where Whitethroats and Reed-buntings sang. A few pairs of Wheatears and Stonechats are still to be seen in this once enchanted place but so much has long gone – Red and Black Grouse and Golden Plover, for instance, and there is scarcely a Whaup to be heard.

Higher on the cliffy side of the Craig a pair of Kestrels still nest where long ago there was always a pair or two of Ring Ouzels. Merlins are still not far away but Whinchats are far fewer than they used to be.

The heather on the Craig is still luxuriant and has not been burned for about 40 years. It still looks perfect for harriers, which are seen from time to time but have never returned to nest on the Craig – although there were nests in the hills nearby for the next 10 years until they moved into the forests.

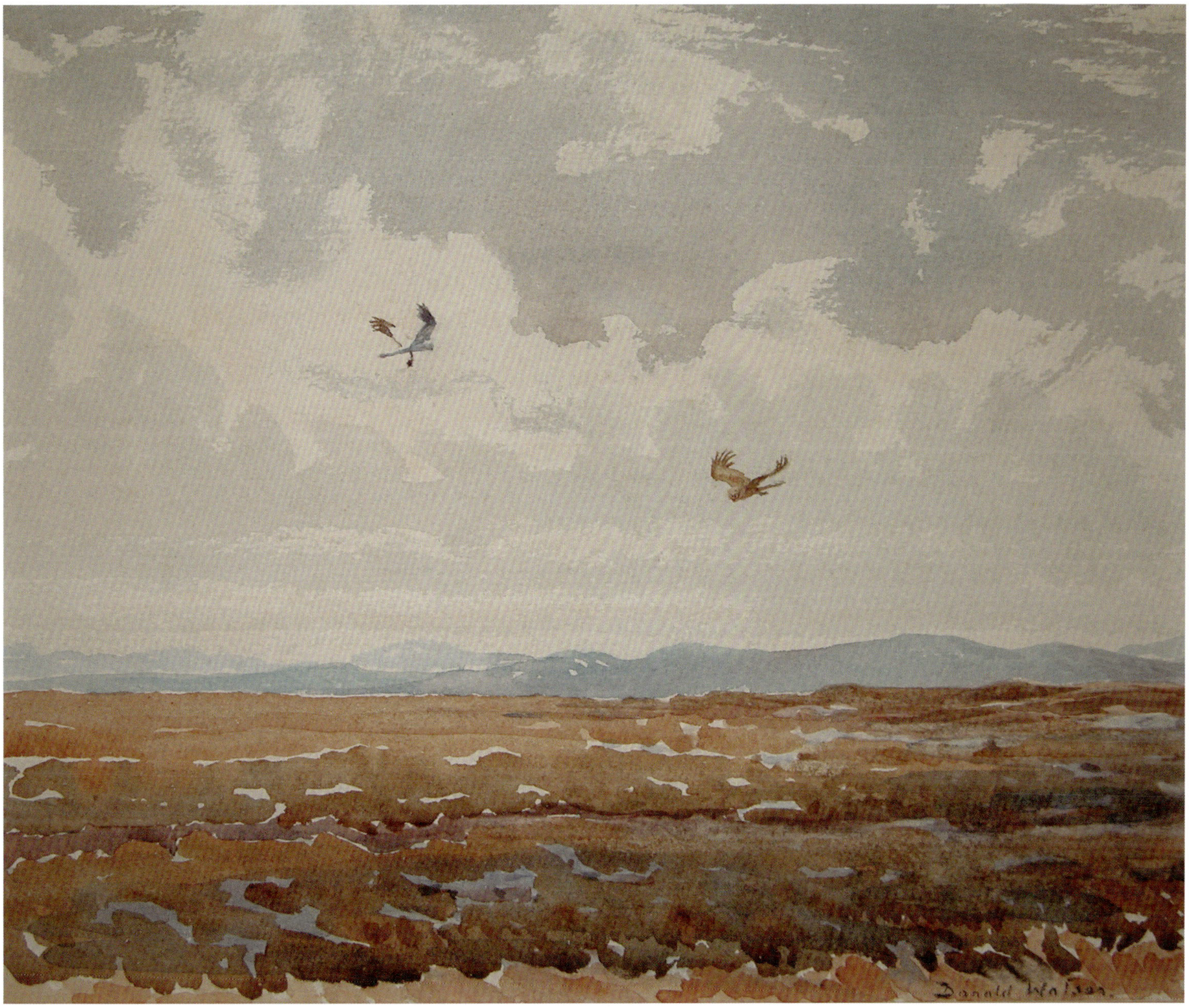

Studies of male and female Hen Harriers, 1959

After my 1959 season attempting to make sketches of the pair of Hen Harriers I had been watching for so long, I painted this study of them. I am well aware that the results have varying success, but they made quite a striking decoration and I thought it was worth including in this book. I hung the picture in our house for a while but sold it to Margaret and Michael Williams from Cumbria later. It now hangs in their house in Curthwaite. It certainly owes its existence to an obsession with harriers.

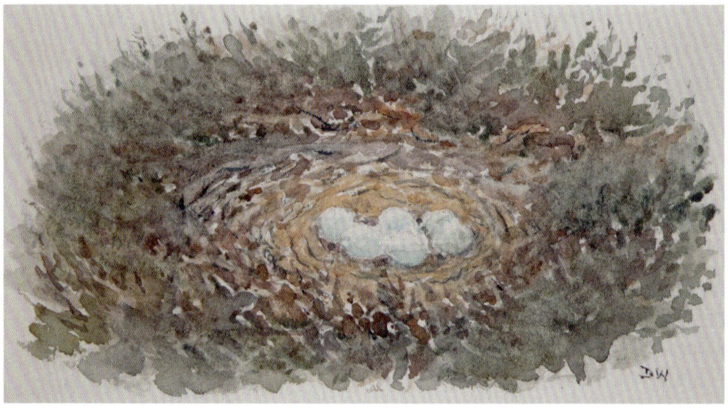

A brood of young Hen Harriers, 1959

The story of the successful Hen Harrier nest in 1959, the first definite nesting in the south of Scotland in the 20th century, has been told in detail in my book *The Hen Harrier* (Poyser, 1977). I will not repeat it here except to comment on the painting of the almost fledged brood of young. This nest was unlikely to be the first, as the shepherd at Grobdale in Girthon told me that he had seen a brown Hen Harrier for eight years and a grey male had been reported in 1958. As the 1959 nest was in fairly deep heather on the open slope of Craig of Grobdale, any previous unknown nests were most likely to have been in similar situations. The great number of hours I spent watching and guarding this nest taught me a lot about Hen Harriers and the difficulties of making convincing sketches of them in flight.

On the early morning in July when three of us (Bobby Smith, Lars Svensson and myself) ringed three of the young – by special dispensation of Bob Spencer, then the head of the BTO ringing office – one young male had flown from the nest as we approached. The adult female had been very bold on previous visits but was less so this time. Handling the fully feathered young was a memorable experience. We knew that we must not stay long at the nest and I only had time to make quick sketches and notes. The painting was done at home from them in the next two or three days. It was helpful to do this on dark brown Canson paper, working in gouache fairly rapidly. This was made possible by using the toned paper which approximated to the actual tones of the subject, working from dark to light, bringing the brighter colours and highlights up in an impasto technique. The colours have stood the test of time well. It has of course never been exposed to direct sunlight.

Twenty-five years later I found a brood at almost the same age: the painting was of a forest nest and was perhaps a more accurate picture of young harriers. By then I had seen a great many nests. I still think that the 1959 painting has a certain immediacy from the excitement I felt at a first discovery.

Bobby Smith is still one of the best-known ornithologists and photographers in Dumfriesshire. Lars Svensson was 18 in 1959 and was spending a month over from Sweden, where he has since become famous as an expert taxonomist and author.

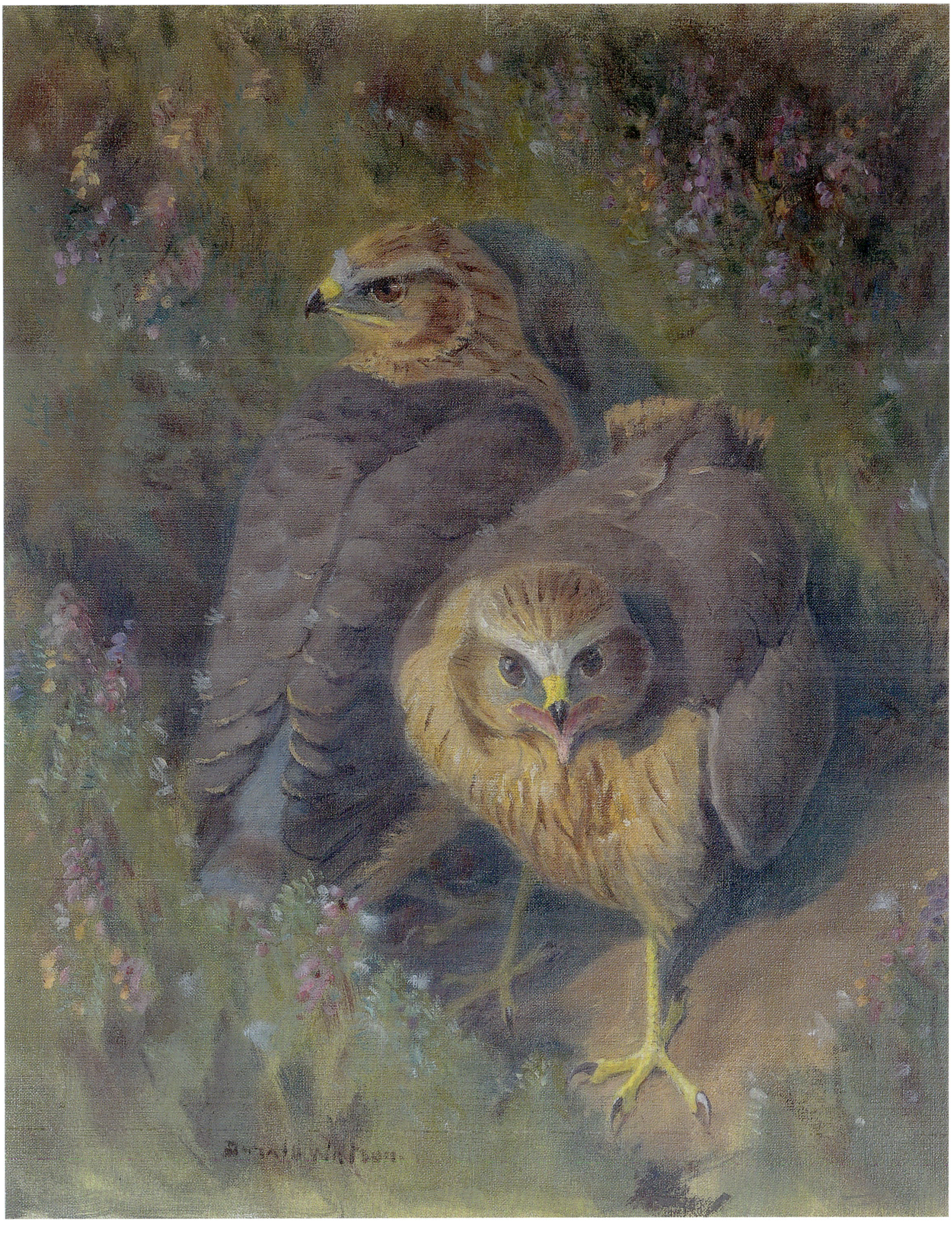

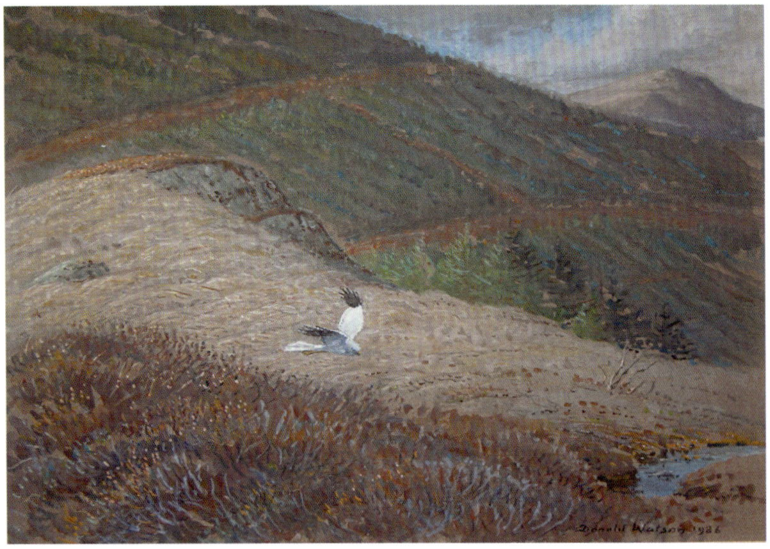

The increase of Hen Harrier nests in Galloway in the early 1960s

In 1961 I was very confused about what the harriers were doing in the Craig of Grobdale area. The 1959 pair had returned and fledged a brood on Castramont Hill in the summer of 1960. They may have been settling on the Craig again in April 1960, but the heather there was burned in early spring. They had made a striking picture mating on the blackened slope of the Craig but finally soon chose a site at a lower elevation on Castramont Hill, which was much more difficult to overlook. In 1961 confusion arose when there were at least two males around. One was certainly a younger bird, partly in brown plumage becoming grey. This male and his mate attempted to nest on the flat ground of the 'Corbie Loch' where the vegetation was a damp mixture, mostly bog myrtle and a little heather. It was the male of this pair that performed the most dramatic display flights I had ever seen, over several kilometres, apparently still undecided where to select a nest-site. The Corbie Loch site was much too near the road, though one or two eggs were certainly laid there. They may have been harassed by a Goshawk and an inquisitive couple from a small Austin car who kept asking the shepherd where the nest was. Jimmy Stewart had succeeded Will Dalziel as the shepherd at Grobdale in Girthon and on 7 June his wife wrote me a letter to say he had found the Hen Harrier nest on Culreoch on 30 May, with three eggs. I found two sucked eggs at Corbie Loch, presumably eaten by Crows after being abandoned. Only three chicks fledged from the large clutch of seven eggs at Culreoch. The male may well have been the same one as in 1959 and 1960. I was more doubtful about the female.

I observed this nest from a sheep stell with an ancient larch growing over it, three to four hundred metres from the nest. Interestingly there was a colony of Linnets feeding young in the tall bracken nearby. I never found any evidence that the harriers preyed on them. They took mostly young Meadow Pipits and a few young Whinchats, but some grouse chicks were taken when the harrier young were nearly fledged. This was not the first nest I had seen with more food being brought than was required. Here the male left many partly plucked carcasses of small birds on a knowe, a few metres from the nest. From the top of Culreoch there was a wonderful outlook down to Loch Skerrow and the railway, which in 1961 still had trains running.

Hen Harriers were showing signs of increase by 1962, but keepers were becoming aware of this. Louis Urquhart and I decided to call on Mrs Murray-Usher, the formidable land-owner at Castramont. She listened to us patiently and later gave her keepers orders not to kill harriers.

A decade later most Hen Harriers in Galloway had taken to nesting in the lush growth beneath trees in conifer plantations and few local moors had many grouse for shooters.

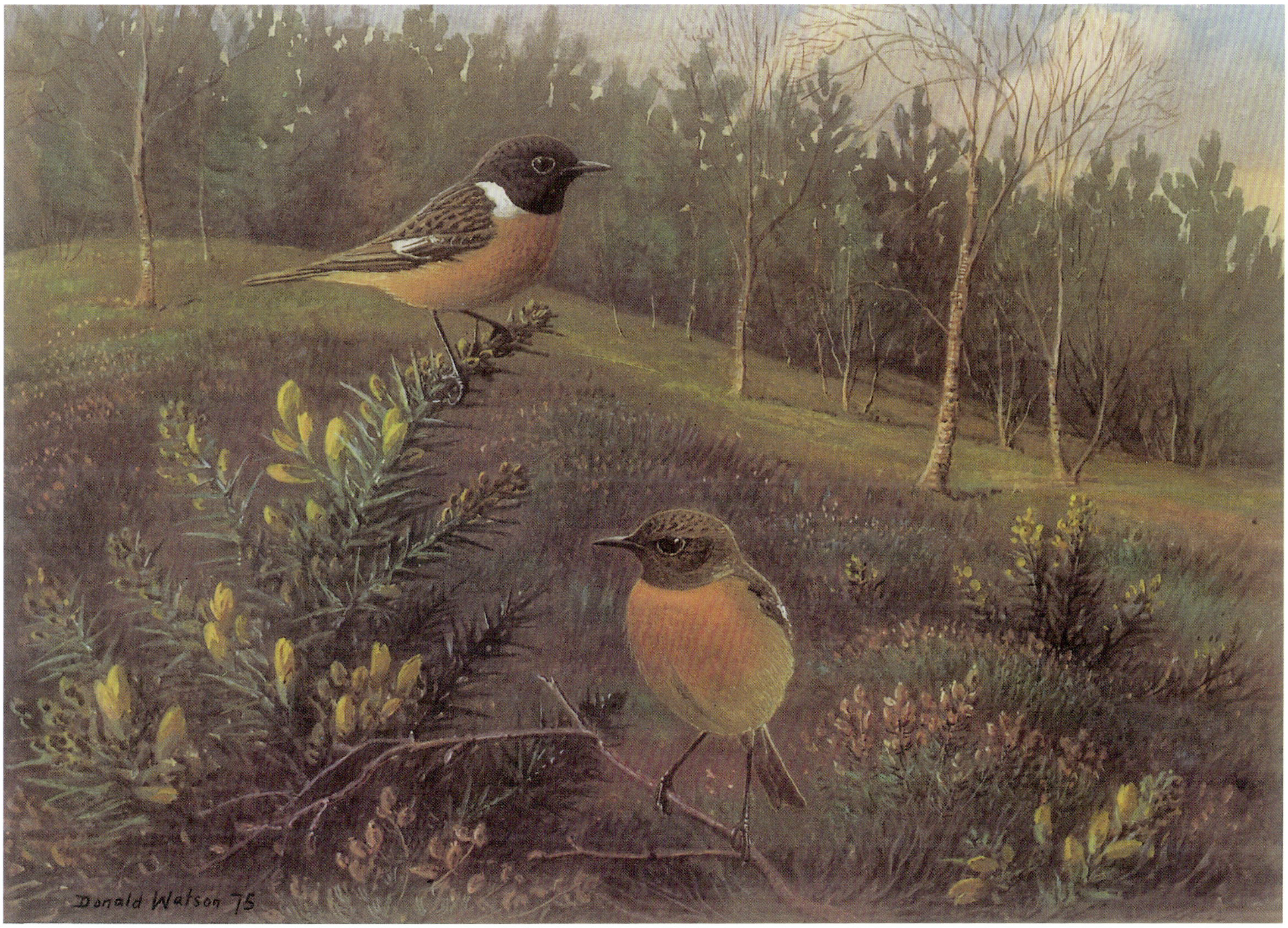

Whinchats and Stonechats

In June 1935 I camped with two school friends among the beautiful deciduous woods beside Loch Voil in Perthshire. I was probably trying to show off when I pointed out a pair of Whinchats to one of them, saying it should be easy to find their nest. I cannot now remember how long we spent with our eyes on them, naively thinking that they would surely disclose their nest if we sat quietly watching them, but their continued alarm calls never ceased because we had not been well enough hidden. Of course they could see us all the time, until they shamed us into giving up. Years later, when Whinchats had become favourite birds, I realised that the best way to find their nests was to watch the birds from a car, which made a good hide. Many Whinchats build their ground nests close to roads in Galloway. If cock Stonechats are more strikingly coloured, cock Whinchats are more subtly marked with their pale stripe over the eyes and peachy-buff underparts. They are of the essence of spring when they return from migration in late April or early May. Seeing a few in the Gambia in drabber plumage in 1990, I had to speculate that they could have come from Scotland. Being much attracted by young conifer plantations, they, especially the newly fledged juveniles, are at risk of falling prey to predators such as Hen Harriers.

Milder winters have allowed the resident Stonechats to increase in Galloway. They may have three broods, while Whinchats, which start to breed later, usually have only one. Stonechat nests are more difficult to find than those of Whinchats and may be very well concealed, especially in gorse. (See Bruce Campbell and I. J. Ferguson-Lees, *A Field Guide to Birds' Nests*.)

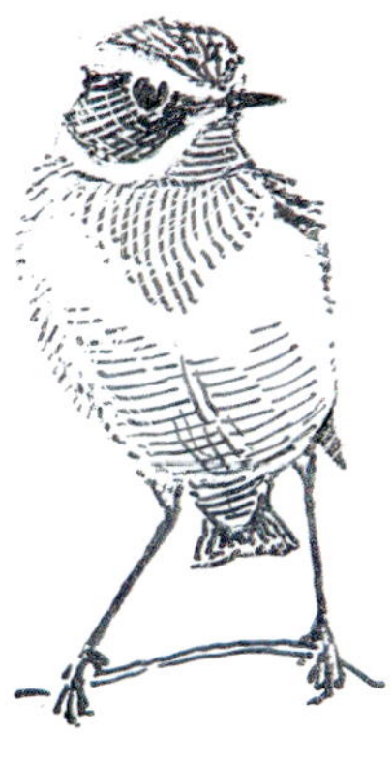

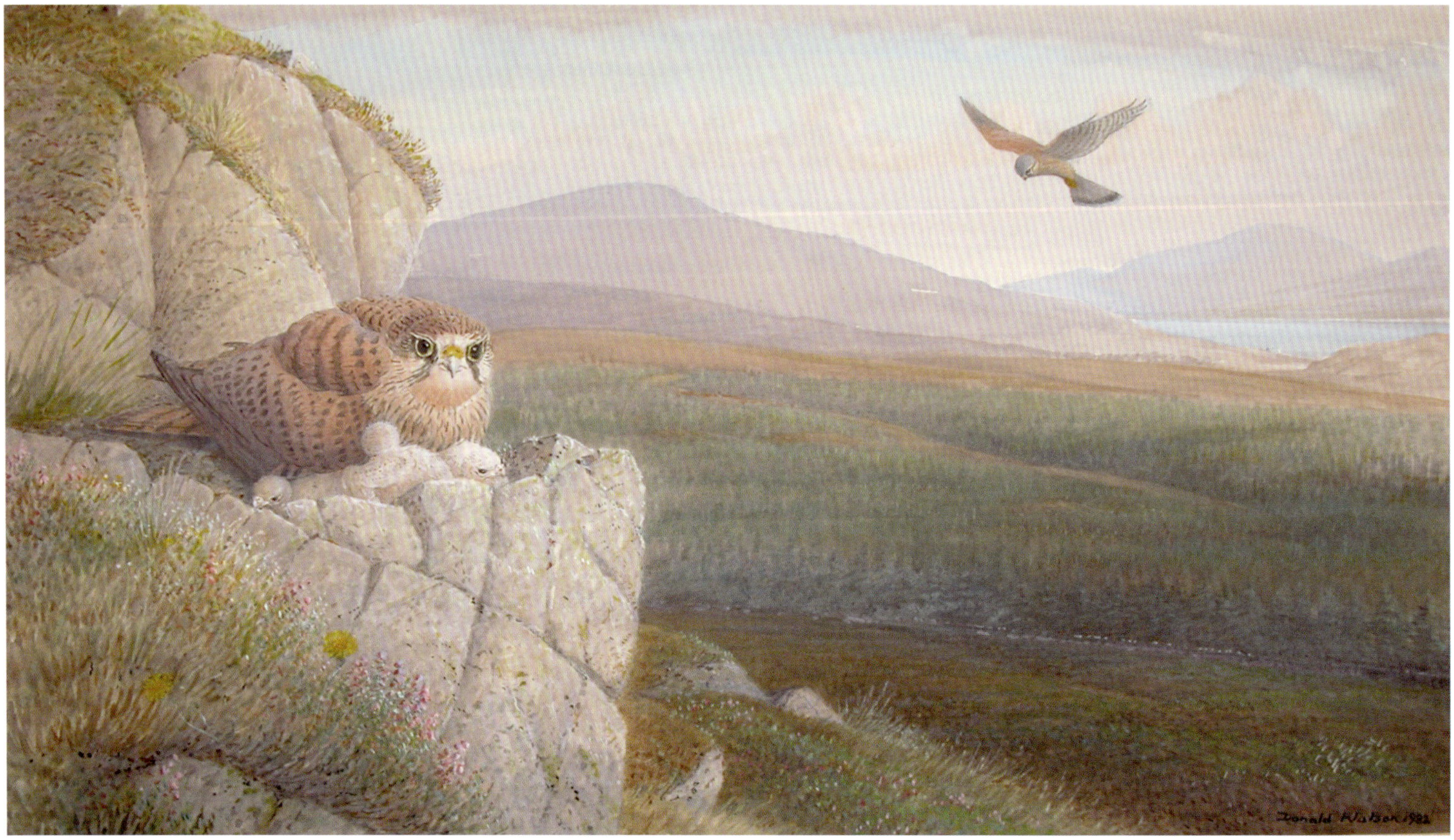

Kestrel, a fellow raptor often encountered in similar habitat to Hen Harriers.

Black Harriers

Van der Merwe (1981) said that it is not clear what governs the restricted distribution of this harrier in South Africa. The African Marsh Harrier is the only other harrier breeding south of the Sahara. The Black Harrier is found mainly in drier areas, especially the Karoo. Langley Roberts found that it was not aggressive to humans at nests he found in the Cape. It has been suggested that it may have evolved from ancestral stock in the Karoo, once more widely distributed. In his interesting paper, Van der Merwe discusses the possible reasons for its restricted range and estimates that its population may not exceed 1,000 pairs, but that it is clear that it is not as rare as formerly supposed.

In this harrier the sexes are alike in the striking black and white adult plumage.

Overleaf: Painting of Pied Harriers based on observations in Burma.

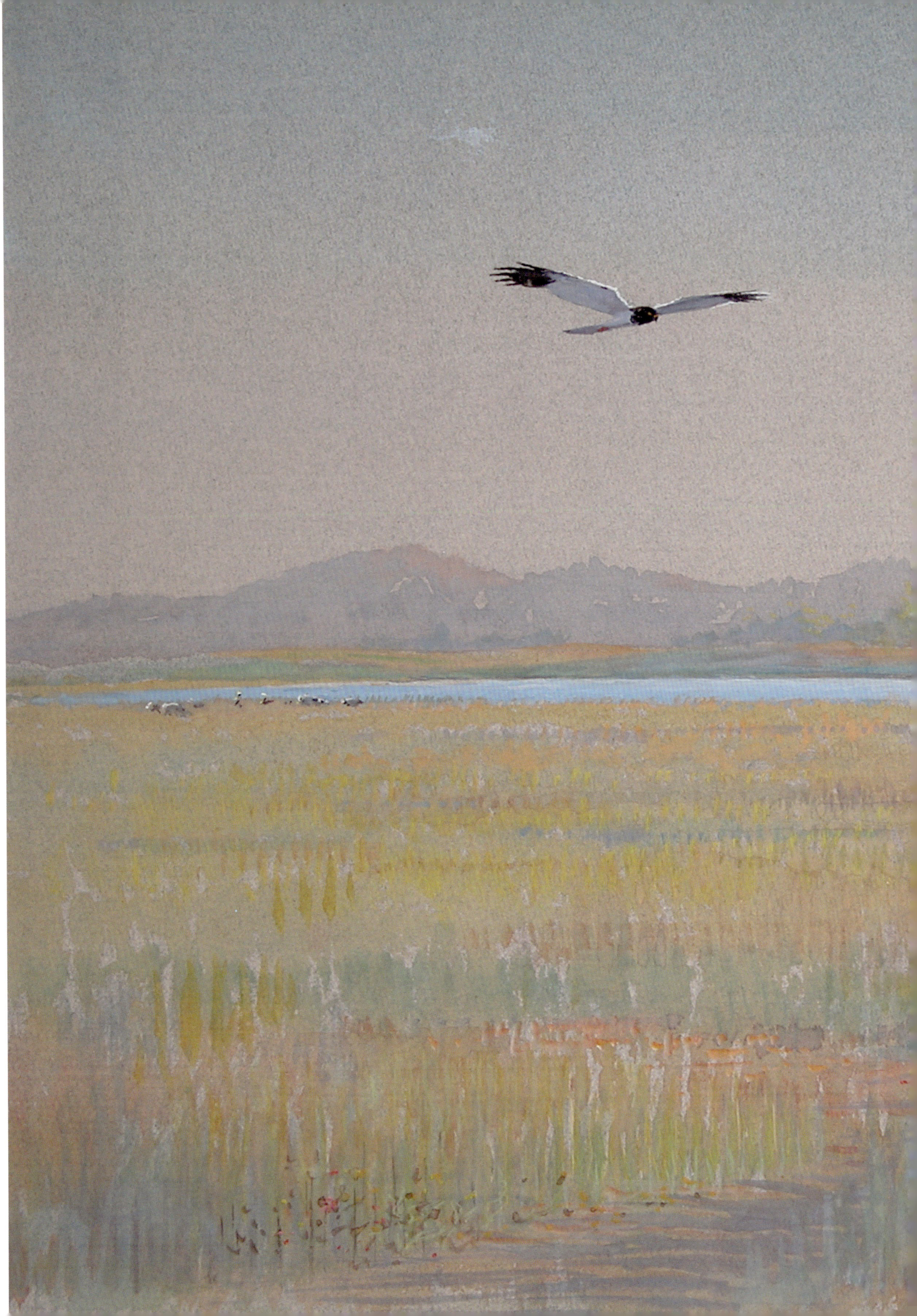

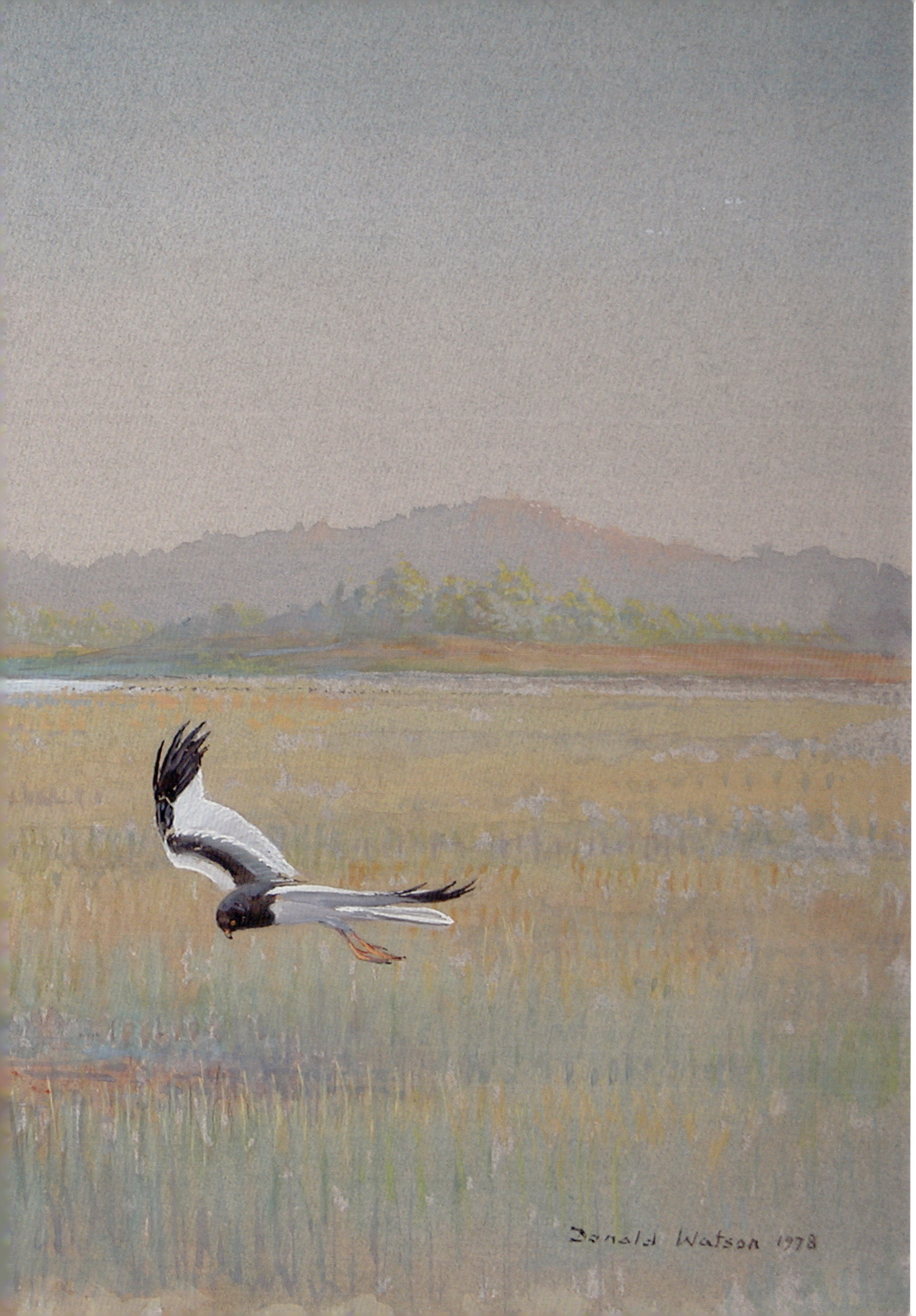
Donald Watson 1978

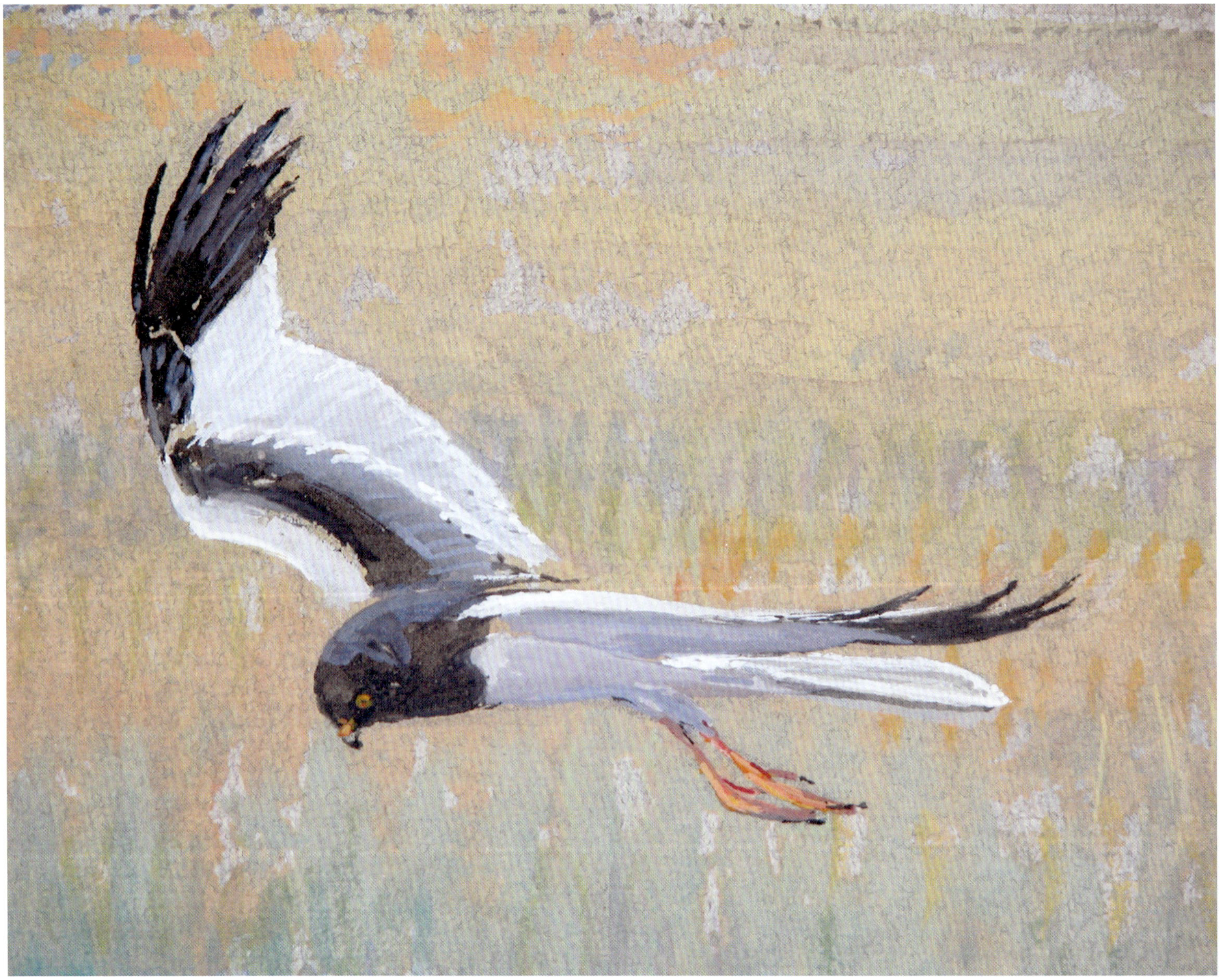

Pied Harriers

This is an eastern Asiatic bird. I was lucky enough to see it often in Burma, where it is mainly a winter migrant, in 1944–45. It is the most beautiful harrier I have seen, though I have not seen the Black Harrier of southern Africa.

I made sketches of Pied Harriers in the Arakan, Burma, but the painting was done much later. Sometimes one would alight in the marshy ground near the Kalapanzin River, but mostly it would be seen in typical harrier flight. Stanford said that when soaring, males held their tails tightly closed but females held them fanned out. A male which I saw closely on the ground appeared to have pink legs but all the books say they are orange-yellow. Perhaps my impression might have been because the bird's legs were a bit bloodied from prey. Ali and Ripley say this harrier does not often prey on birds, preferring frogs, lizards, mice or grasshoppers. The beauty of the male lies most of all in its pied plumage and manner of flight, but the tail is shorter than in the Pallid Harrier and similar to the Hen Harrier's.

The Pied Harrier has been found roosting communally with other harriers and is now known to breed sparsely in Assam and Burma, but more commonly in China and Mongolia. Unlike in the Black Harrier the sexes are dimorphic, so that the ringtails of Pied, Pallid, Montagu's and Hen are confusable at a distance.

Pallid Harriers

In 1945, when I was still in India, I saw many Pallid Harriers while I was in Hyderabad, one of the then old princely states. The country there was mainly open Savannah where Pallid, Montagu's and Marsh Harriers wintered. Although my medium Royal Artillery regiment was expected to take part in the landings in Malaya, we had time to explore some of the countryside in the meantime, after sailing south from Rangoon to Madras in the spring. Not far from where we were stationed lay the big lake of Nizamsagar, where thousands of ducks gathered, including large numbers of Pintail and Garganey. The most enjoyable times were when my friend Mike Lewis and I drove miles from our base into the countryside, spending a night in a dak bungalow. One weekend, George Arbuthnot came with us, hoping to shoot some duck. He knew nothing about birds. One day a splendid male Pallid Harrier happened to land on a knowe quite near us. George saw no harm in shooting it, much to my disgust. It was dead when we collected it. Later in the mess I was much mocked for showing my distress. Mike and I made a very indifferent skin of it. Many years later, in the 1980s, a young Indian ornithologist wrote to me that he was studying harriers near Secunderabad and finding communal roosts with a mixture of Pallid and Marsh Harriers. More recently my son, Jeff, found many Pallid and Montagu's breeding in Kazakhstan, bringing fine photographs of them home.

As its name implies, the mature male Pallid is the palest of the grey male harriers and the wings have only narrow black tips. Juvenile Pallids have rusty-cinnamon unstreaked underparts, like in the Montagu's, but paler. An observer should look closely at the head and neck marking of the ringtails (females and immatures), all confusable, but they are well-described in detail by Lars Johnsson in his superb book, *The Birds of Europe with North Africa and the Middle East*.

In the last few years, British records of Pallids in autumn–winter have slightly increased. Roger Clarke's Russian friends have reported some spread in the breeding range, which probably accounts for this.

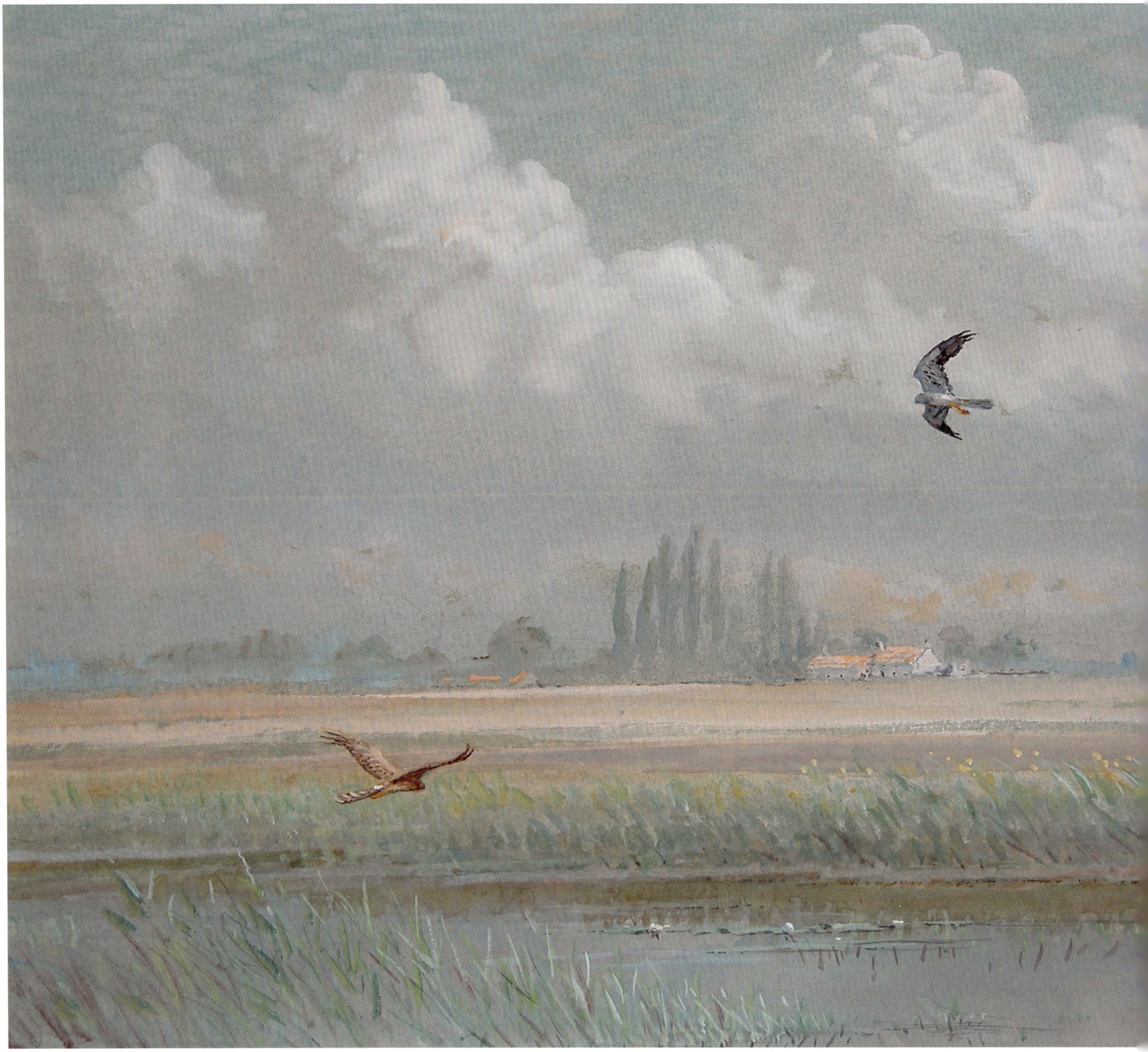

Montagu's Harriers in La Vendée, 1971

When I visited France in 1937 with my friend Bernard Richardson, both of us still teenagers, it was by chance that we arrived at La Pallice on the west coast, which was swarming with French sailors. We walked with our heavy rucksacks to La Rochelle. We had a good dinner at Chez Simon and found we could stay the night there. This turned out to be very noisy, the sailors and their girls coming and going upstairs with much giggling and squealing. We speculated that the poker-faced patron kept a brothel above his restaurant. One or two of the girls mocked us, calling out 'Vous êtes clahunes,' which seemed to mean 'clowns.' Next day we met some of the sailors in the town. They were friendly enough.

The weather was very hot as we started to walk westward out of the town in the morning. Seaward the land was flat and untended, intersected by watery ditches. Here many pairs of Montagu's Harriers must have been nesting. All the brown females were evidently still on nests but the beautiful blue-grey males were widely dispersed, hunting in wavering flight, doubtless for voles or small birds. I thought they looked a little like big butterflies. Later as we made our way into the Auvergne mountains we saw both Montagu's and Hen Harriers but never again in such numbers as the Montagu's on that July morning near La Rochelle. It was a revelation to find Goshawks, Red Kites and the harriers evidently breeding successfully in France when so many rare birds of prey were still being persecuted to near extinction in Britain. Although French hunters even used a stuffed owl as a decoy when shooting harriers, persecution cannot have been as ruthless as it was on grouse moors in this country.

In the summer of 1971, I was back in western France with my wife, Joan, and two of our young daughters. The girls enjoyed themselves at Les Sables d'Olonne, a name on everyone's lips when Ellen Macarther became a famous yachtswoman more than 20 years later. Les Sables had long been a holiday destination for young French people when towns and cities were almost deserted in their holiday month of August. Memories of Montagu's Harriers at La Rochelle, south of Les Sables, were much in my mind from over 20 years earlier. It was a delight to find them still plentiful along the low-lying countryside of La Vendée. In mid-August the harriers with their flying young circled playfully above the tall tamarisk trees and squat red-roofed farmsteads among cultivated fields. I sat with my sketchbook beside a stream, making many quick sketches of flight postures. It is hard to remember now how much of the painting was completed on the spot.

Marsh Harriers

In the summer of 1954, Willie Austin drove me to Norfolk in his smart car. The warden at Hickling Broad was a large, red-faced man appropriately called Piggin. He agreed to take us to see a Marsh Harrier nest in the reed-beds. There was also a cock Montagu's Harrier around, and after Willie had slipped Piggin a five-pound note we asked if he would show us a Montagu's nest, one of the last known in the Broads. In his inimitable Norfolk brogue he answered 'no,' saying if he did 'there wouldn't be nuffin' for us to come back for next year.' Of course we were not in Norfolk the next year.

We did however boldly call on Anthony Buxton, the famous protector of harriers on the Norfolk Broads. He had two of my wildfowl paintings hung in his house, and gave us a warm welcome. One of the paintings he had of mine was of Goosanders in Dumfriesshire. He was not quite happy about a distant Goosander I had put into it up-river and asked me 'to make it dive,' which I was happy to do for him. As a landowner he was ahead of his time in protecting harriers, writing admiringly about the Norfolk Montagu's in his fascinating book *Fisherman Naturalist*.

In 1960 Arthur Duncan and I were surprised to find a male Marsh Harrier in summer hunting the Ayrshire moors near Cairn Table. Reading some of the 19th-century bird books, I realised that Marsh Harriers, referred to as 'Moor Buzzards,' evidently may have bred on upland bogs in Scotland but over time were probably exterminated at such sites for the usual reasons.

In recent decades Marsh Harriers have been recorded increasingly often and at various seasons in Scotland. In 1992 a pair nested unsuccessfully at a lowland loch in Ayrshire, and in 1994 two young were reared at a Kirkcudbrightshire loch with extensive reed-beds. I had the good fortune to see them when fully feathered on a few occasions and observed many food-passes by the male. With their creamy-white crowns and chocolate bodies, the young harriers were very beautiful, one with its crown more creamy orange. On 1 September the adult female was not seen, the male dropping small prey to the large flying young, which made no attempt to hunt for themselves. The loch was very secluded and peaceful, calm blue water reflecting the tawny autumnal colours of the reed-beds.

One or two of the adult Marsh Harriers did visit the Galloway loch again in 1995 but nesting was not repeated. Although it appeared an ideal nesting site I much doubt whether it was a safe place for birds of prey, as it was on the neighbouring farmland that three of the introduced Red Kites were illegally poisoned a few years later.

I have seen many Marsh Harriers in France, where they are much commoner than in Britain. In 1971 Joan and I spent a little time in Les Solognes, the complex of lakes that Leonardo da Vinci planned to drain when King Francis I was his patron. Fortunately, this was never done and today it remains an area of exceptional ornithological richness. Later that summer we visited La Brenne where Marsh, Hen and Montagu's Harriers were breeding, and we watched a Short-toed Eagle carrying a snake in its talons.

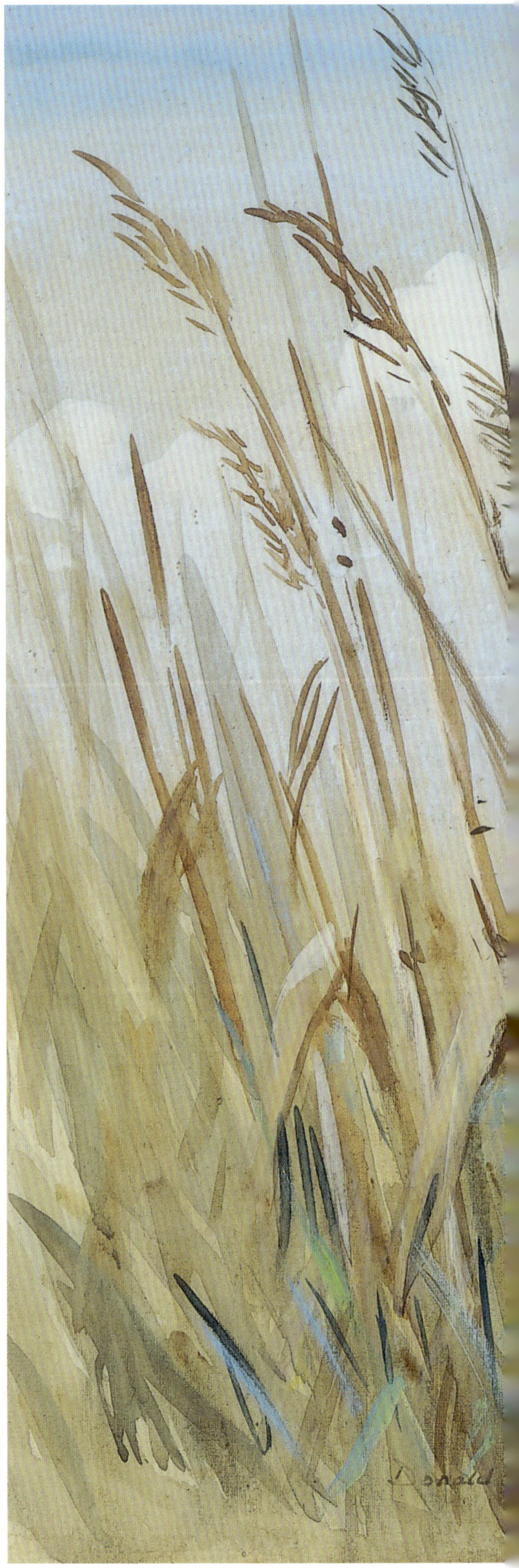

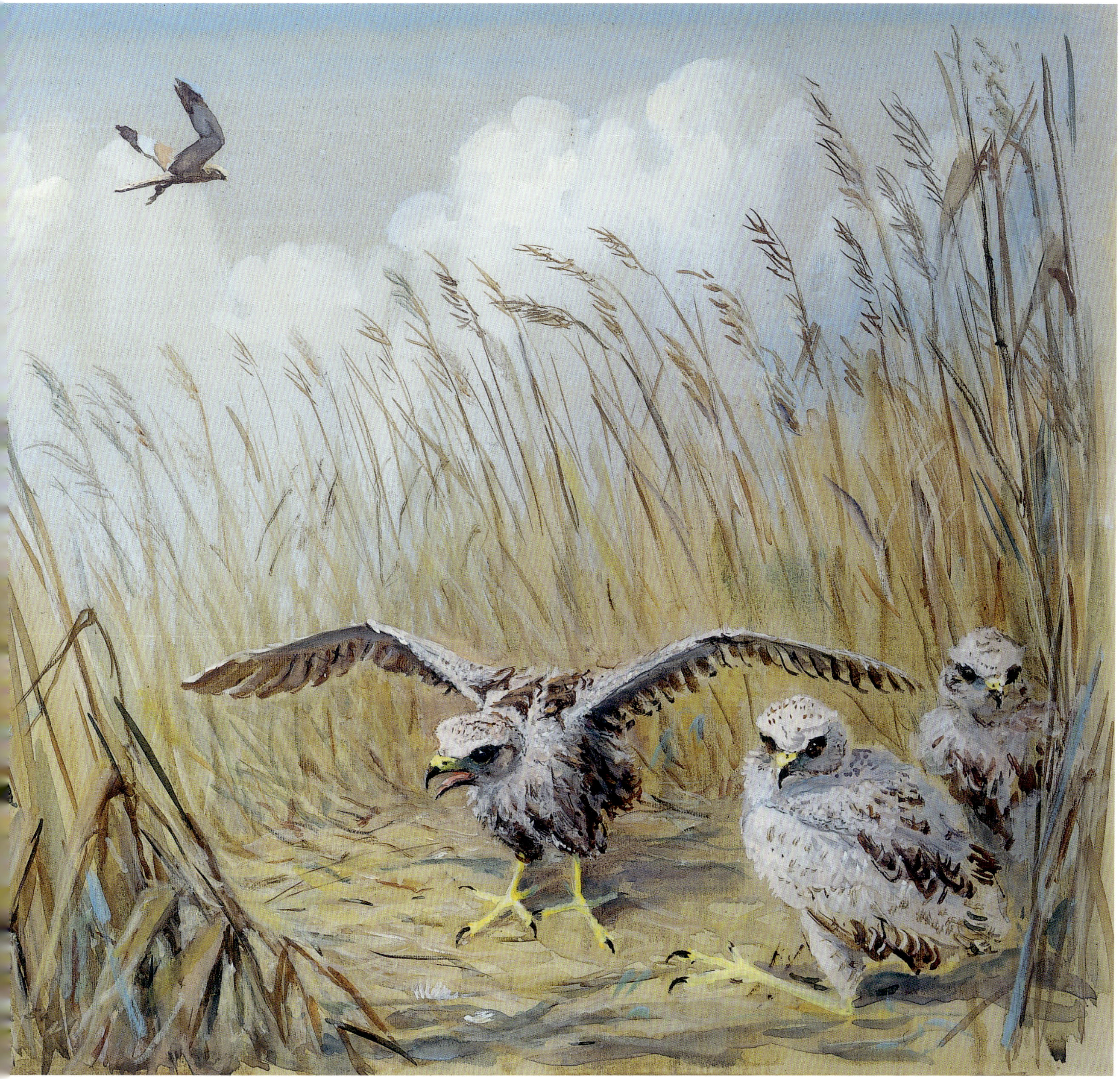

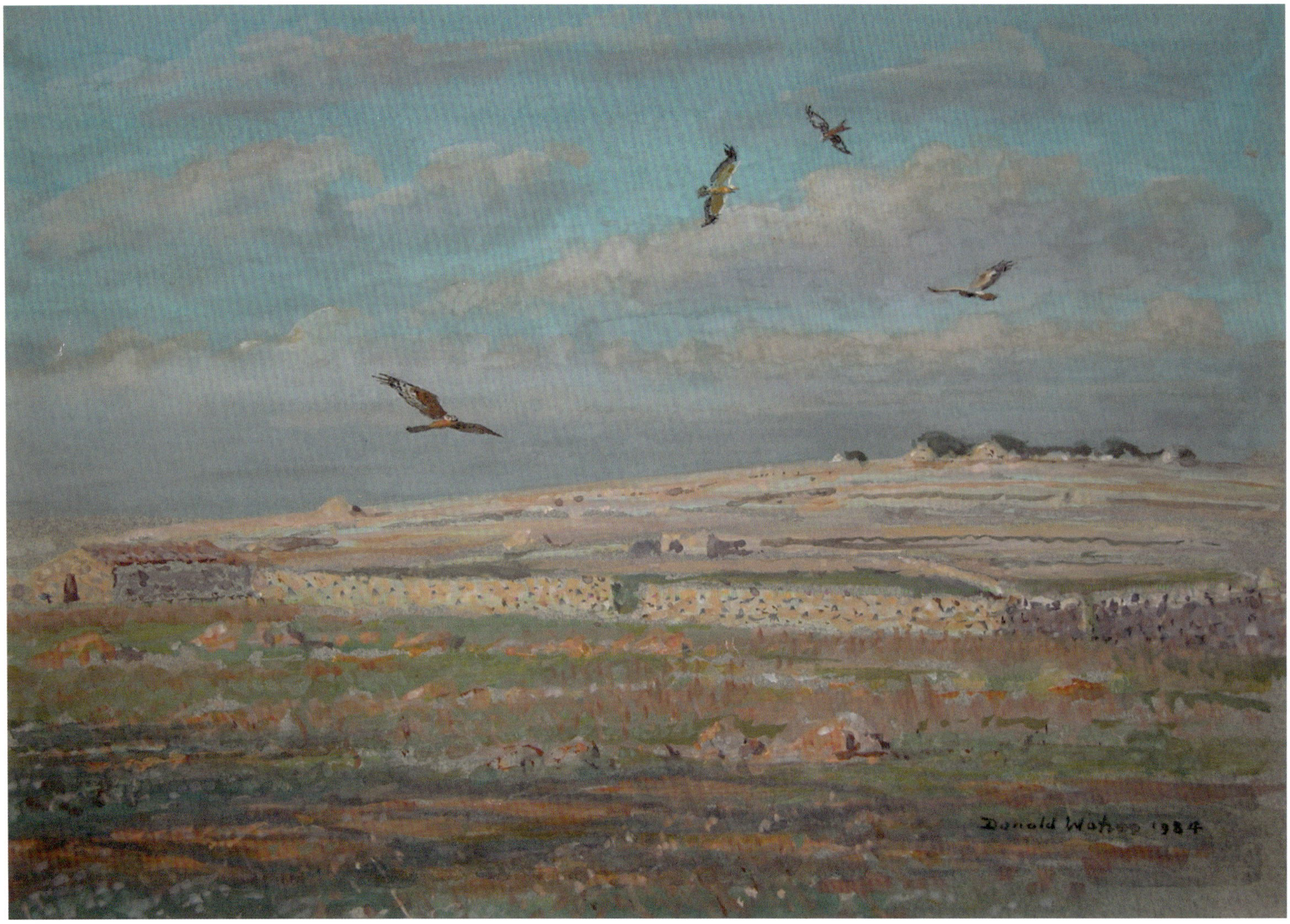

Red and Black Kites

The re-introduction of Red Kites to Britain has been much publicised. Long ago this beautiful raptor was a common bird here, protected in Mediaeval times as a useful scavenger in the filthy streets of London.

A 'puttock [Red Kite] riding high' in the fenland sky was a familiar sight to the poet John Clare when he was writing 'The Shepherd's Calendar' in the 1820s. But by that time it was no longer a protected scavenger in cities, and had become a target for the gamekeeper's gun or trap in the countryside.

Kites became extinct as breeding birds in England in about 1879 and in Scotland soon after. The small number of pairs hanging on in mid-Wales continued through the efforts of a few dedicated people. However, in the 1920s–30s there was so much distrust among members of the 'Kite commitees' that there was continued concern that the Welsh nesting might cease. It was only a handful of people, like the Vaughans, Peter Davies and Colonel Morrey Salmon, who bore the brunt of kite protection in the 1920s–60s.

The story up to 1990 is told in Roger Lovegrove's RSPB book, *The Kite's Tale*. Ian Carter's *The Red Kite* brings the story up to 2001.

After experiments from 1989, the year 1994 saw the introduction of young birds from the healthy populations of south Sweden and Spain, and later

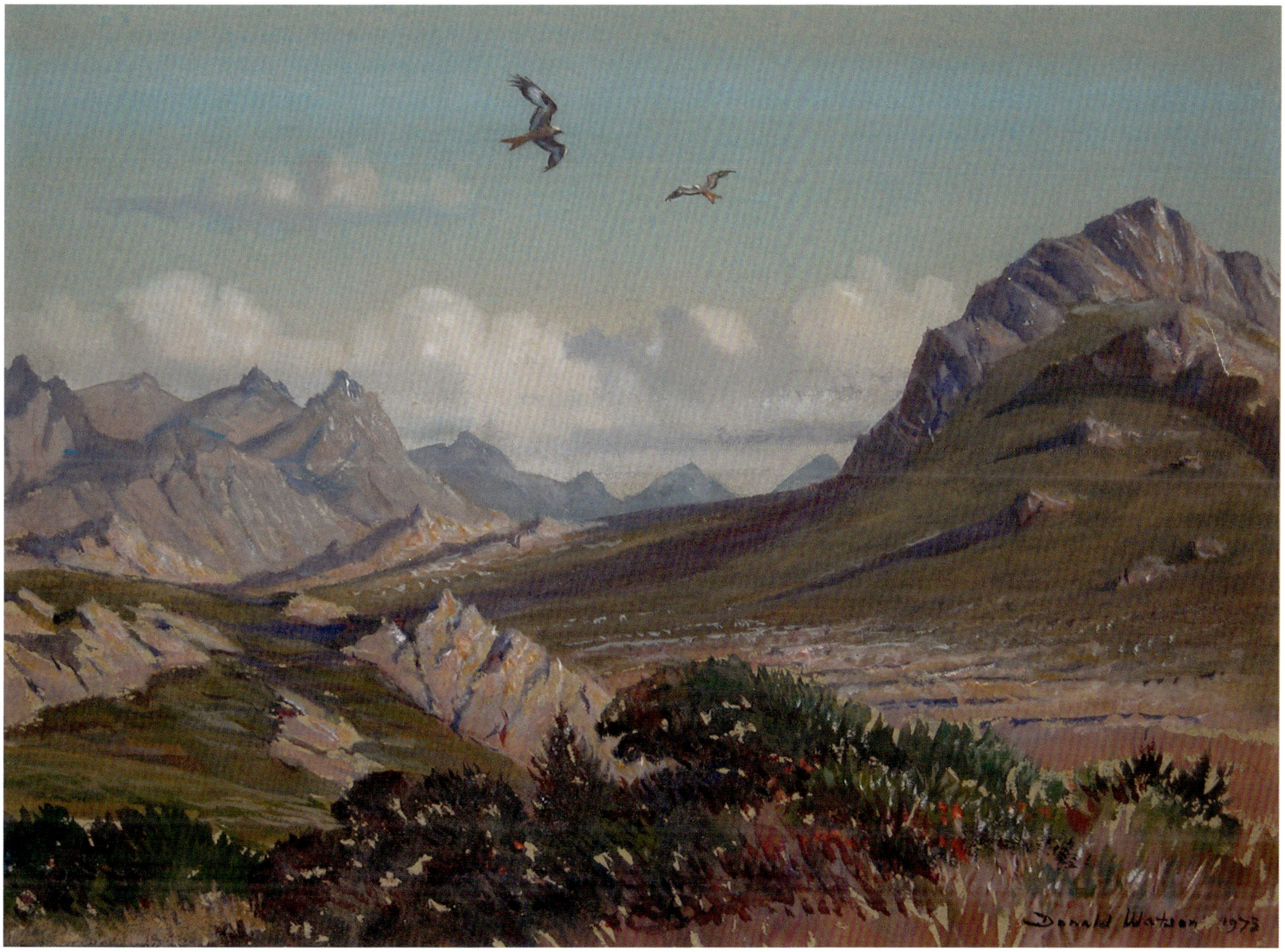

from Germany also. The introduction programme has been so successful at sites in southern England, the Highlands and Central Scotland that a number of young have been brought to Galloway and released near my home, one chick having fledged from a nest near there in 2003.

On arrival at the release site, the young kites are placed in aviaries in secluded woodland and fed through hatches so that human providers are not visible to them. After some weeks they are released into the wild, where food dumps are quickly found by them.

Old habits die hard in some places and kite deaths from poisoned baits still occur.

The Black Kite, which has a more sombre plumage and much less deeply forked tail, has for long been widespread on the Continent and is most plentiful near water. It has always been a scarce migrant visitor to Britain. It was certainly the Red Kite that became a resident scavenger in London during the Middle Ages.

A sadder story comes from the island of Menorca, where I saw large numbers of Red Kites in 1984. Recent reports say that there has been a catastrophic decline to about 8 breeding pairs, and 27 pairs in Mallorca (Carter, 2001).

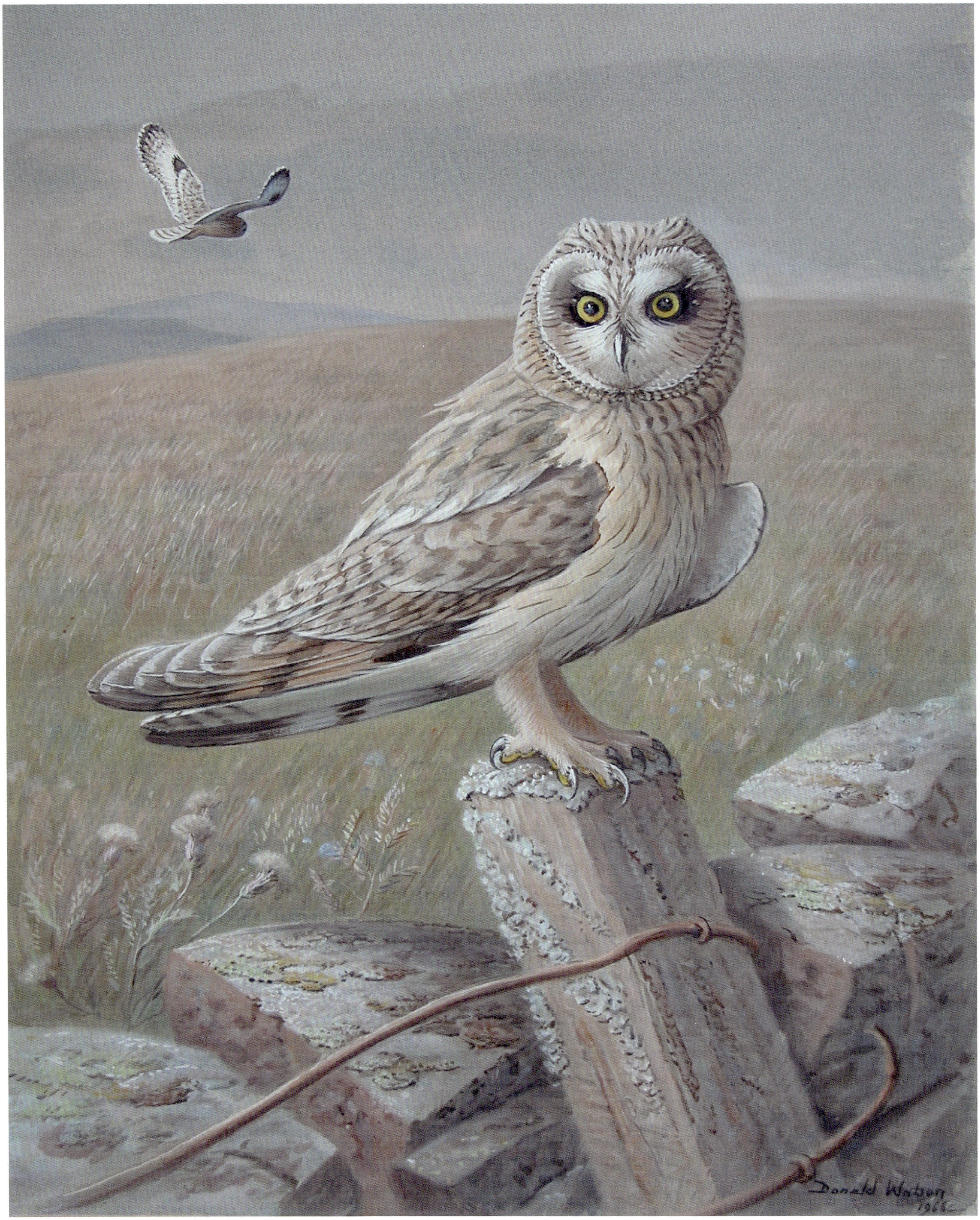
Donald Watson
1966

Short-eared Owls

More than 40 years ago I was walking with a friend in the Dumfriesshire hills when we came upon a Short-eared Owl on its nest. It must have been terrified by the sudden appearance of two pairs of human eyes gazing so closely down at it. It was brooding small downy owlets in a nest in deep heather and showed not a flicker of movement. Its entire head shrank, ear tufts raised to points and the normally large, brilliant lemon-yellow irises became narrow circles round the inflated dark pupils. This I understood was the threat posture, which was successful in causing my companion to say quietly, 'I am rather frightened of Short-eared Owls.' Very gingerly he lifted the bird's breast feathers with the point of his stick, half revealing the owlets below. The brooding female had no escape route through the dense growth of heather at its back. Forward it would have to fly at our faces, which I think my friend feared it was about to do. We had an unforgettably close encounter with it and soon continued on our way. It had perhaps tried to make itself as invisible as possible, and at the same time as threatening. Over the years I have found a number of Short-eared Owl nests but never again had such an experience with a sitting bird. Generally I have thought nests were quite difficult to find, needing a fair amount of careful watching of a bird's flight lines to a nest.

Seen in the distance, hunting over young forest plantations or moorland, Short-eared Owls can look quite harrier-like. In spring the males rise high into the sky in display flight, calling a resonant 'boo, boo, boo,' suddenly losing height and clapping their wing tips together below the body, a spectacular performance. Short-eared Owls nest on open moorland in Galloway and Ayrshire, but many more nest in young conifer plantations or clear-felled areas, where a nest-site may be in an unsightly pile of brash. Good years for the owls are when voles are in peak numbers. Locally, there have been few such years recently, so the owls are in low numbers. The winter of 1990–91 was remarkable for the number of Short-eared Owls, Buzzards, Kestrels and Hen Harriers which concentrated in the High Ken Valley feeding on voles.

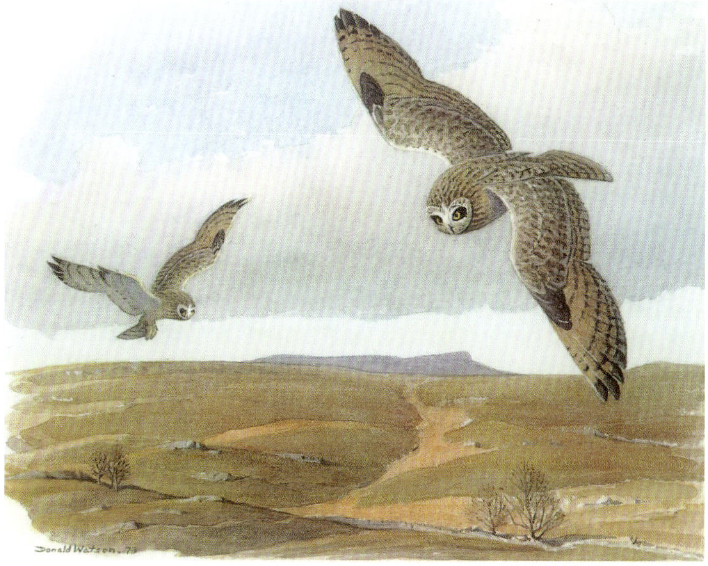

Most famously, when vole populations reached plague proportions on open hills in the Scottish Borders in the 1890s, Short-eared Owls homed in on them in huge numbers. Even in my own time, when peaks in vole numbers have been lower, it has not been difficult to tell from the numbers of predators in the sky where voles are plentiful.

In Europe, Short-eared Owls hunt both diurnally and nocturnally but they hunt most in late afternoons and early evenings. In their book *Hawks, Owls and Wildlife*, the Craigheads wrote that in Michigan, U.S.A., they were nocturnal hunters, roosting communally during the day. At one site some owls did not leave until after the nocturnally roosting Marsh Hawks (now called Northern Harriers) began to come in to roost in the evenings.

When I visited the Isle of May in the Firth of Forth, Short-eared Owls arrived there on autumn migration from Scandinavia, preying on passerine migrants on the islands, where Baxter and Rintoul found that the owls made caches of prey.

In the absence of field voles in Ireland the Short-eared Owl breeds only sparingly, preying mostly on brown rats.

Short-eared plumage is variable in colour, most adults being greyer brown than younger birds, which are rich buffy-fawn in general colour. The mostly nocturnal Long-eared Owl is shorter winged and darker coloured, especially on the underparts.

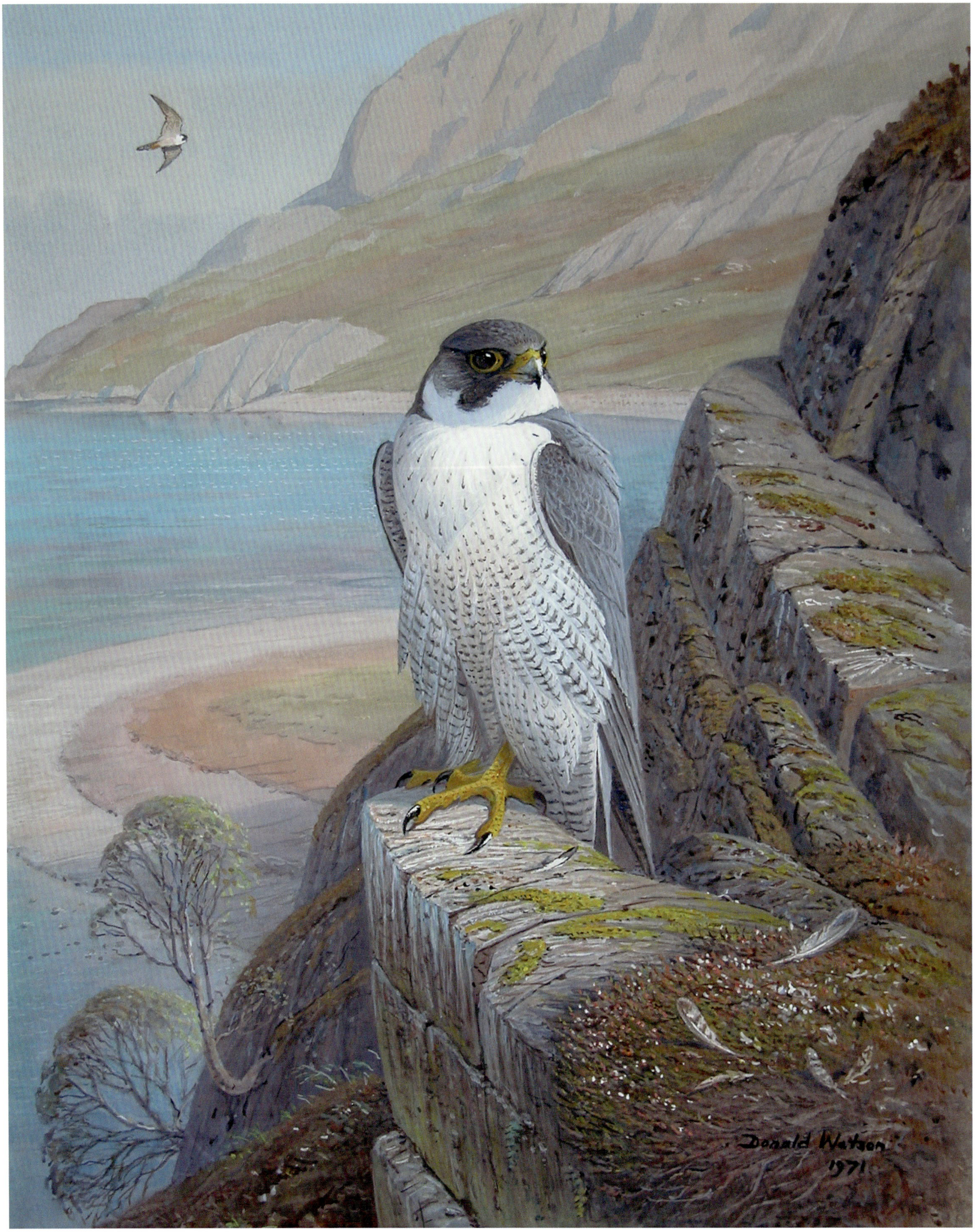

Peregrine at sea cliff.

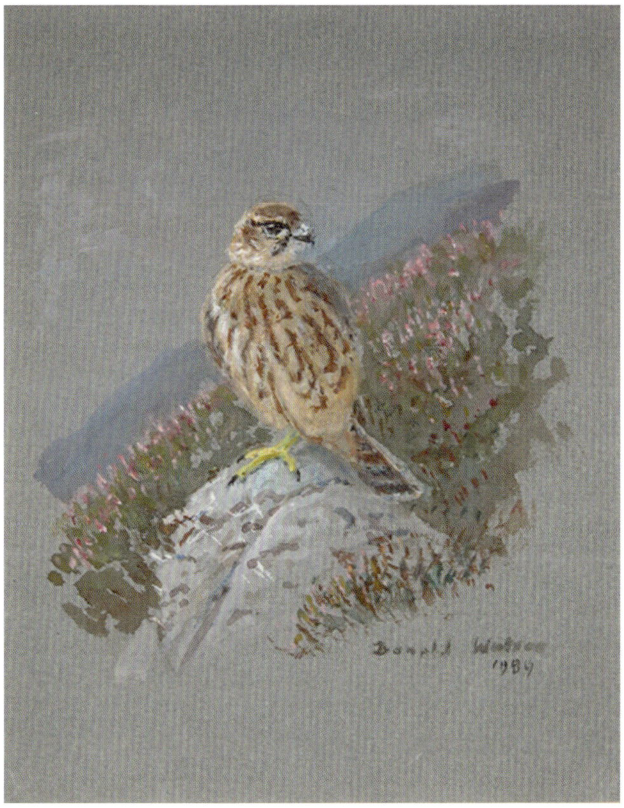

Merlins

My most memorable experiences with Merlins were in the mid-1970s when Jeff came down from Aberdeen and we spent many rewarding hours observing several pairs nesting in Galloway. One July day in 1973 he was watching a recently fledged brood of five young Merlins when a Hobby flew over, and they all took wing and mobbed it. Hobbies are still rare to see in Galloway. Most of our Merlin nests were in similar situations, craggy outcrops arising out of forest plantations and considered unplantable by the foresters. One site was very close to a forest road – a gamekeeper turned keen photographer was able to reach it from the roadside with his stick. Others were less accessible. One brood of young fell victim to a fox at another easy site. Yet another nest was on a mini cliff which could be reached by walking through young conifers for a few metres from a forest road. There could have been many more nests than we ever found, but I doubt if Merlins had then begun nesting in the trees as they did in later years, becoming much more difficult to locate. At some sites the young, when well feathered, could be spotted from a long distance as they clambered about on some little ledge; but when the female was incubating eggs, nest-finding could be very frustrating. I recall one hot and sweaty climb through dense forest to a high point where we had believed the nest must be, only to find we had been misled. These little falcons could be most elusive. Later, when tree-sites, usually in old crow nests, became usual, a searcher might be put on the right track by finding pluckings on posts in a fence line at the forest edge.

Years ago the first nest I found was mostly by luck. A pair had been noisy around a rocky summit, which I decided to climb. I walked down just below the long line of cliff face through the rather steep heather slope, close enough to have a chance that a bird would fly out, which rather fortuitously for me it did. It was thrilling to look down on the clutch of four richly marked, purplish-red eggs. Prey at Galloway nests included many young Starlings and large moths such as Oak Eggars. Their bitten-off wings could be found scattered around plucking places. Coming down the hill I sat among a jumble of boulders unobserved by a vixen and her cubs for an hour or more, while they played on a big flat-topped rock.

The slightly longer-winged Icelandic race of Merlin is a regular winter migrant to Scotland. At that season I have more than once seen a Merlin shadowing a hunting Hen Harrier. When the harrier flushed a Skylark, the latter towered to escape the harrier only to fall prey to the Merlin's high, twisting pursuit. Can this be called hunting 'in tandem'?

I was once brought an injured first-winter Merlin which wing measurement showed to be Icelandic. Although not as beautiful as a blue adult male, it was a most attractive little hawk.

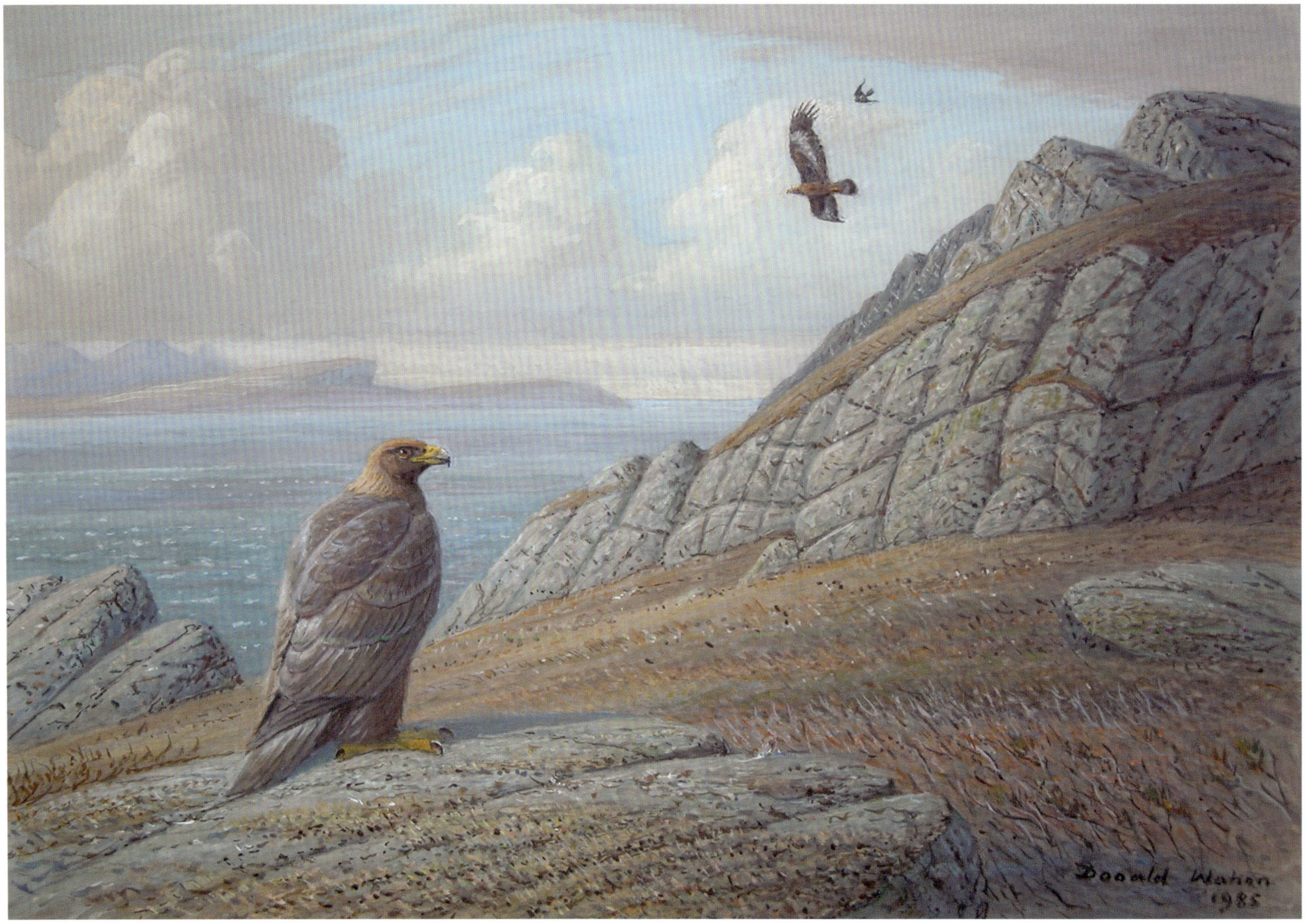

Golden Eagles and Hen Harriers in Galloway

In 1965 the pair of Hen Harriers at Grobdale nested in 'the Fleshmarket,' a name given to treacherous ground, in this case because much of the terrain was boggy and dangerous for sheep. 'Fleshmarket' was equally applied to precipitous places where sheep might be killed by a fall, like on Craignelder, where at that time one of four pairs of Galloway eagles had an eyrie. I suppose that the name Fleshmarket arose because historically there was a chance that a free meal of mutton or lamb might be there for the taking. In that year the nearest pair of eagles to the harriers was on Shaw Hill, not far across the railway from the Fleshmarket. It was the start of a long period of conflict between the local Golden Eagles and Hen Harriers. One of the young harriers reared in the Fleshmarket was the female I found dead, presumed to have been fatally wounded by an eagle, in 1968, not far away.

Afforestation had begun on the slopes of Shaw Hill in 1965, and certainly this work there led to the eagle eyrie being abandoned after a chick was fledged on Shaw Hill in 1965. By 1968 the eagles had moved to a different site, no further away from the harriers, and by 1970 a long series of successful nestings by the eagles started there. They continued to hunt frequently over the harriers' territory.

My son Jeff Watson in his book *The Golden Eagle*, writes that it is not usual for Golden Eagles under five years old to breed, so it was remarkable that in 1965 the male of this pair had conspicuous white in the tail and at the new site where the first chick fledged in 1970 the female had much white both in tail and wings. I was told that nests had been partly built, not far distantly, in two other sites between 1966 and

1969, presumably by the same pair of eagles. Jeff Watson strongly suggests that for two different birds not in fully adult plumage to have bred successfully indicates that there must have been a scarcity of older birds in Galloway at that time. There was at least one instance of a fully adult eagle being found poisoned, but it seems unlikely that there was much persecution. The first nest in Galloway in modern times was in 1945, found by Derek Ratcliffe in 1946. It had contained young in 1945.

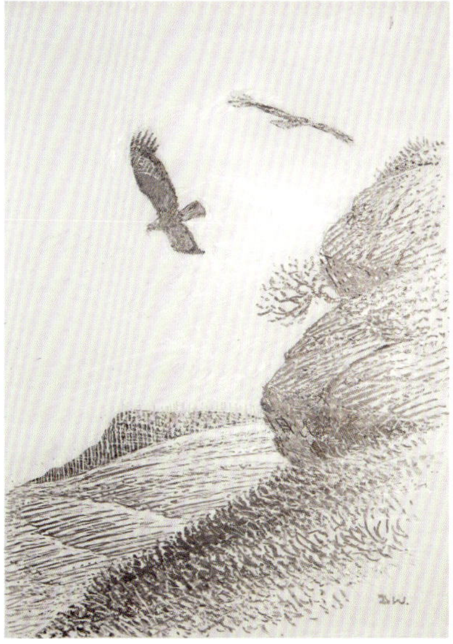

Many times I saw the Hen Harriers diving intensely aggressively at the eagles and even striking one, and it did not surprise me that they might have been too bold for their own safety. The persistence with which smaller raptors usually attacked the eagles when the latter flew at all near their nest-sites was frequently the best pointer to the approximate whereabouts of Merlin nests. The little falcons could easily be spotted from a long distance diving steeply at an eagle. Once, when I had been watching a Hen Harrier attacking an eagle, the latter flew through the arch of Little Fleet viaduct. In winter the Grobdale pair of eagles often landed in the in-by fields near the shepherd's house, probably looking for sheep carrion. They killed many blue (mountain) hares on Craig of Grobdale, where few now remain. The wide range of prey taken by Golden Eagles is well documented, from voles to deer calves, fox cubs and Blackcock. I have found a Short-eared Owl killed at a Galloway eyrie.

In 1852 White-tailed Sea Eagles still bred on Cairnsmore of Fleet. A young bird was taken from the nest and kept at Cairnsmore House for 50 years. The old keeper, Nicholson, told me years ago that when he was a boy it was his job to feed the eagle in its old age, when it was blind.

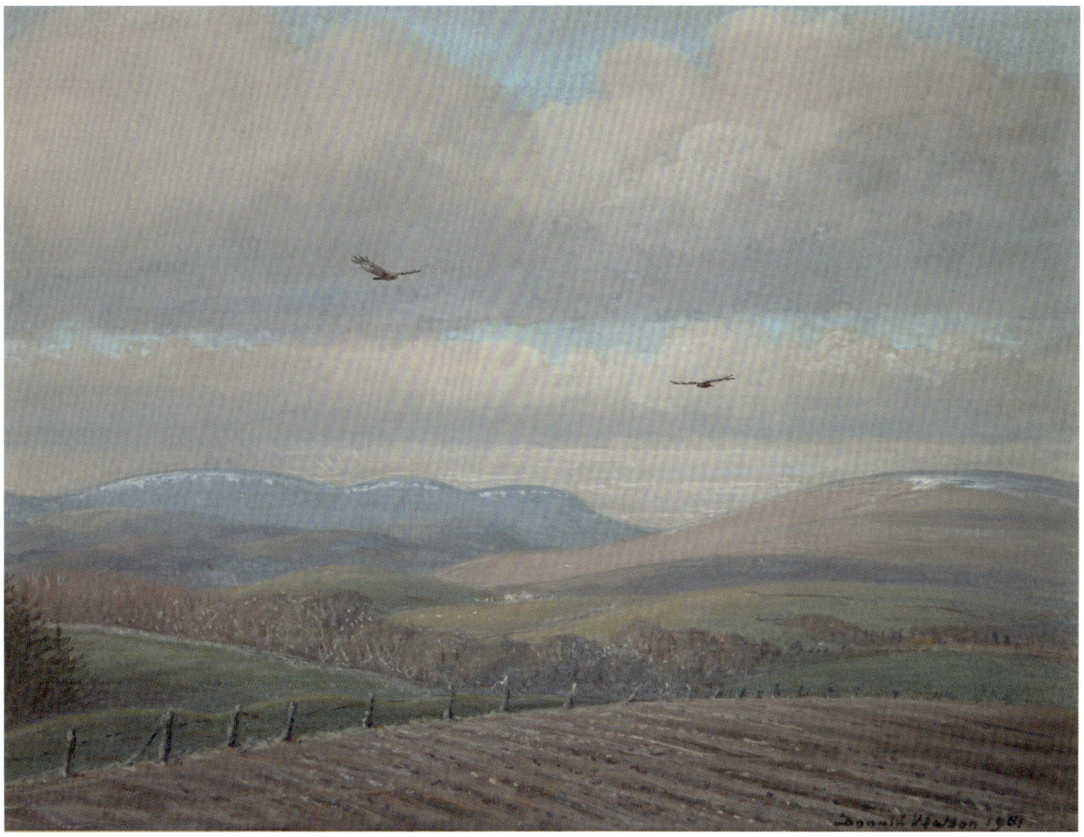

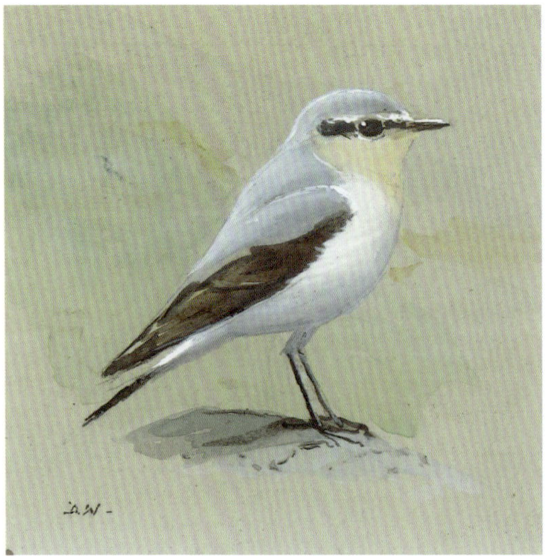

Hen Harriers in the breeding season

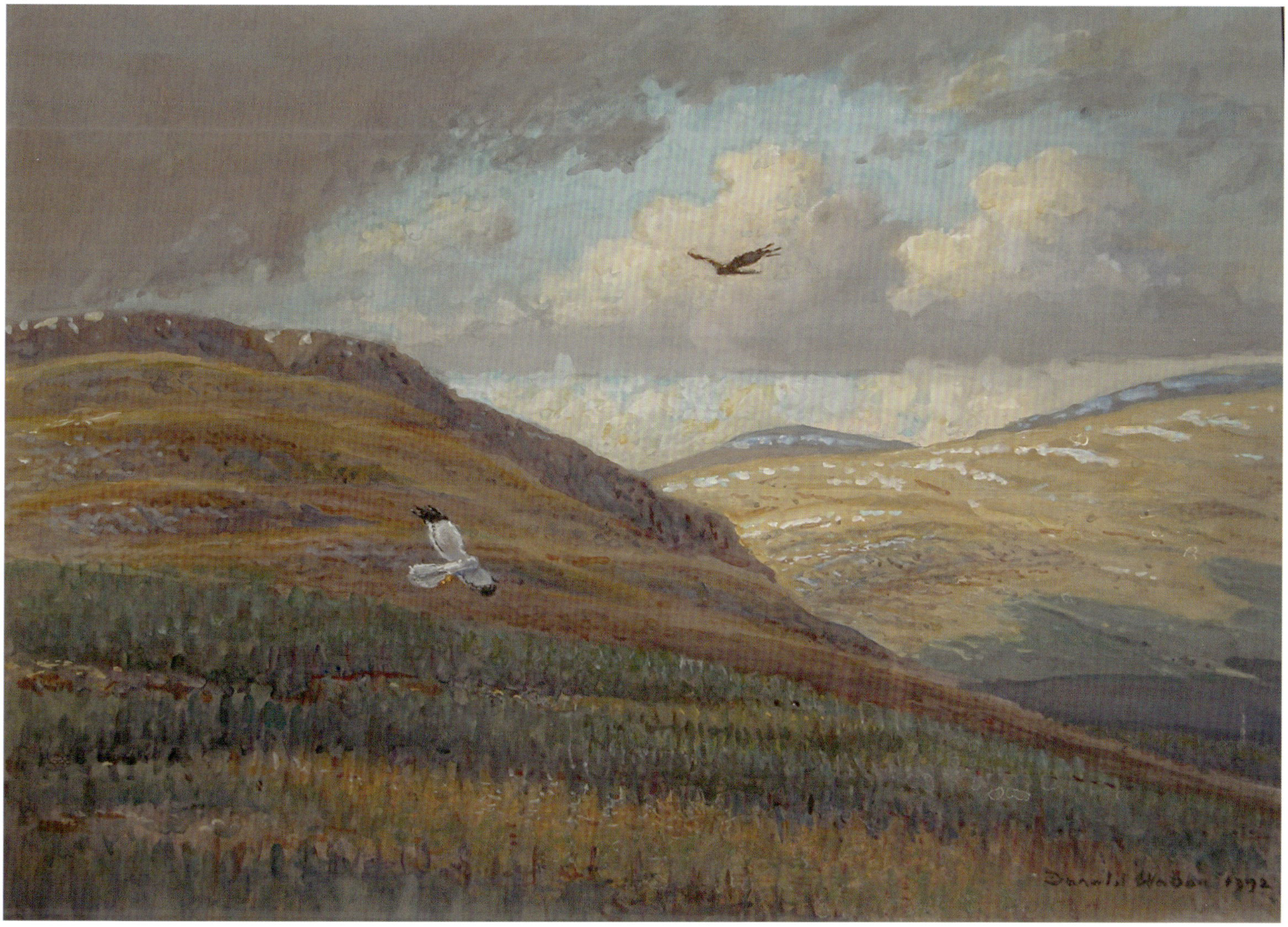

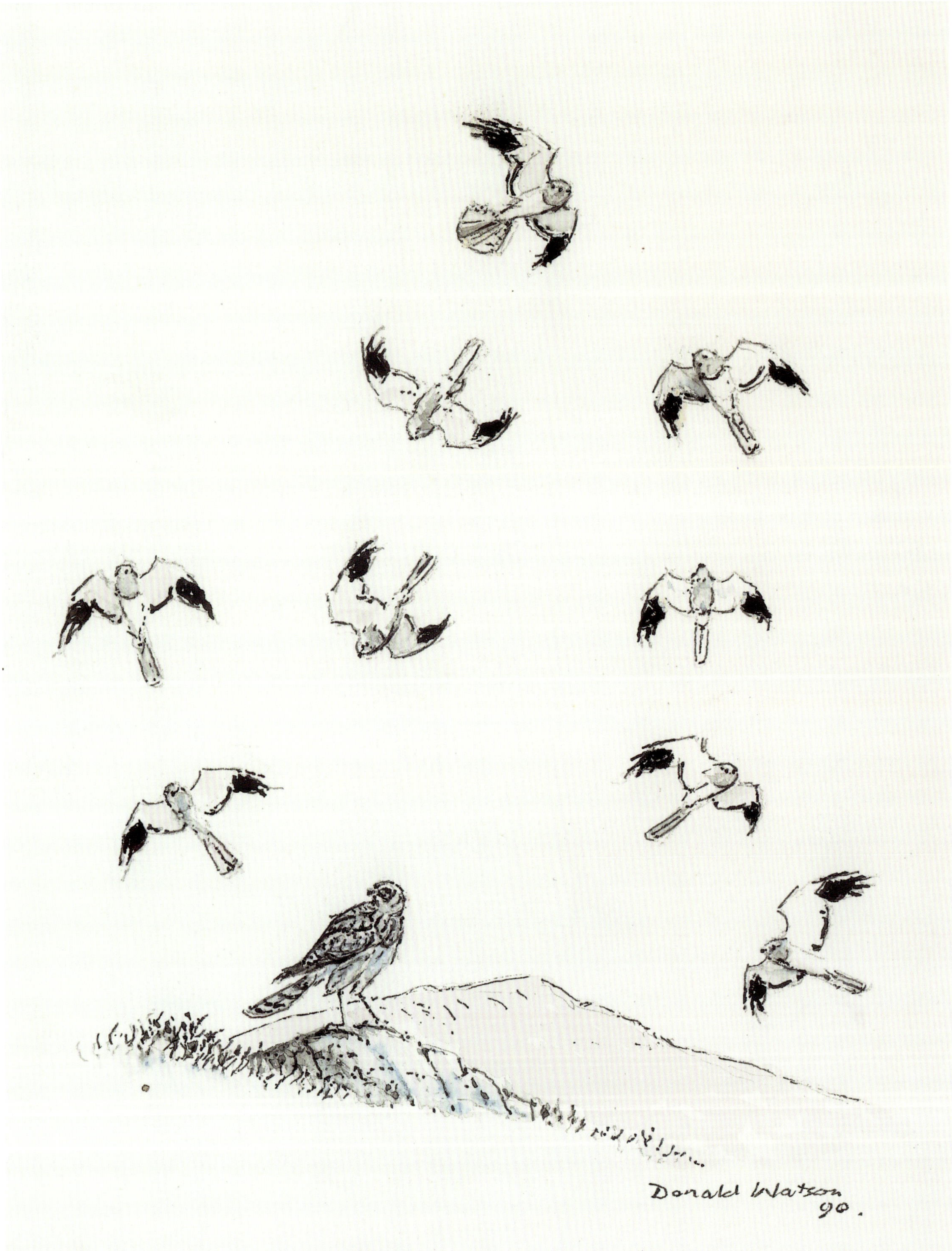
Donald Watson
90.

'Skydancing'

It seems that the term 'Skydancing,' which so aptly describes the Hen Harrier display flight, was coined by Fran Hamerstrom, the American ornithologist who studied harriers in Wisconsin.

Both male and female Hen Harriers perform aerial displays in spring, but it is the male's skydancing that is one of the most arresting of avian spectacles. I have never been able to convey in a drawing the sense of total abandon that this performance suggests. It seems an entirely different bird from the Hen Harrier which at other times glides and flaps over the landscape. The skydancer is 'a bird possessed' – I once thought that no bird could look like this unless it was attacked by a swarm of bees or midges. A male may at times perform over 100 skydances in succession. It no longer seems a bird of prey but is transformed into some strange wading bird that can ascend to a great height and turn on its back at the top of its climb. Even the body-shape seems to change as it flings itself about apparently uncontrollably. On a fine sunny day the brilliantly white underparts and jet-black wing-ends compel the eye to follow every twist in its tortuous flight. The only other bird I know which can assume such a frenzy of flight is the Lapwing in spring.

Intense skydancing may not always be seen where there is a single pair of harriers. Where there are more within sight there is a competitive element. If a younger male appears in a territory that is already occupied by a pair, the younger one may skydance over several different possible nesting sites. In Orkney, where there was much polygyny, skydancing was a frequent sight, neighbours never being far away.

Females usually perform a more undulating flight over their nesting grounds.

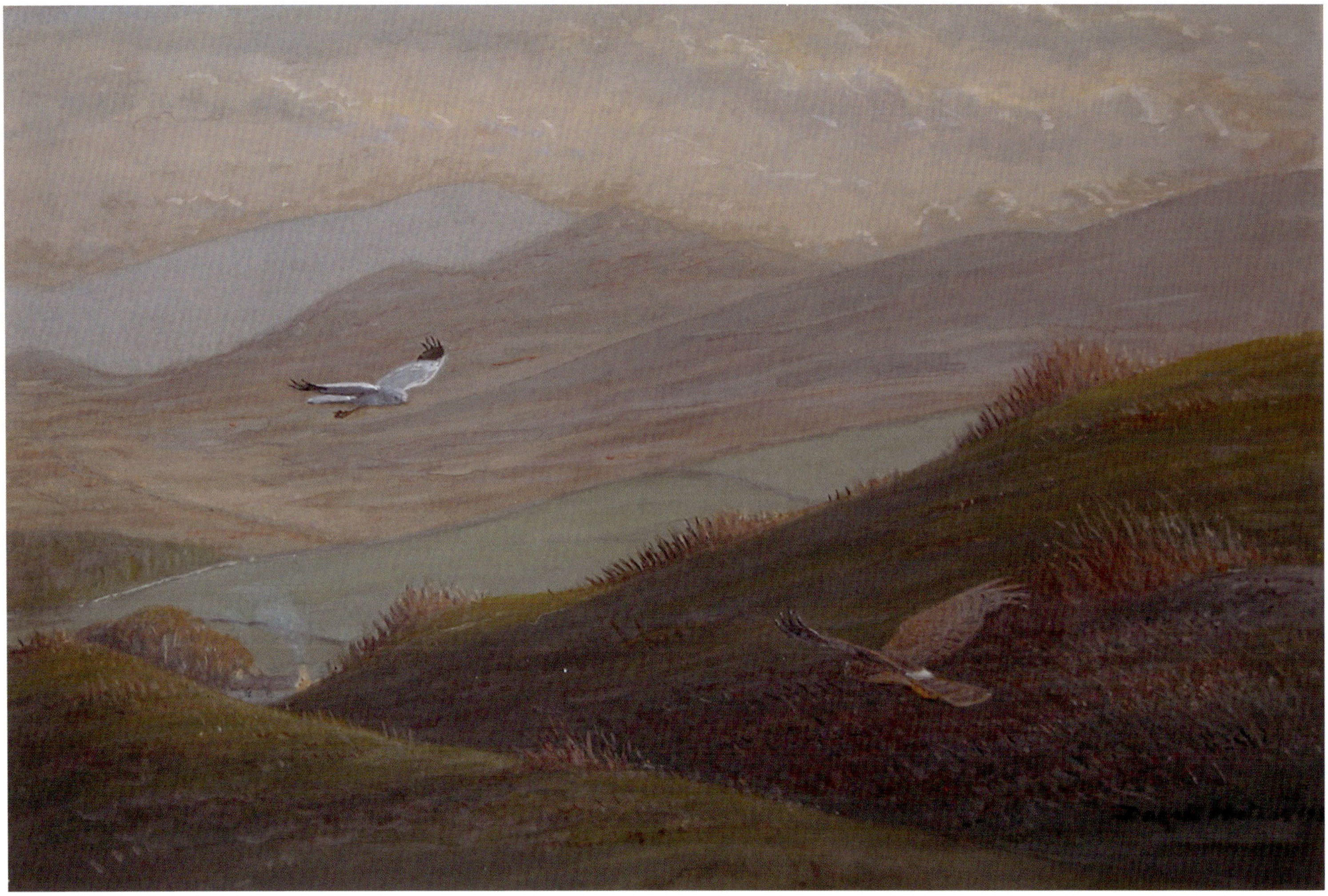

Nursery nests

Alfredo Noval, a noted Spanish ornithologist, and one of his sons, were photographing Hen Harriers near Guigon in Asturias, and told me the following story.

They were photographing a nest with five chicks when a farmer came by. They knew that the local farmers destroyed harrier nests, but they rarely found them as they were usually in dense gorse (Ilex europea). The farmer had obviously seen and heard the parent harriers, as they were being very active and noisy in defence of their brood.

So Noval removed the young from the nest and he and his son took them 50 metres away and hid them in dense gorse there. On their next visit the Novals found that the chicks had been fed and were flourishing – one of the parents, probably the male, had built a rather flimsy stick-nest which had become a 'nursery nest.' The young survived and fledged there.

Alfredo Noval wrote to me several times and told me about the harriers in Asturias. He sent me copies of the fine books he had written about the fauna of the Asturias. Although he and his family came to see us in 1980, we were never able to return the visit. Sadly, I am told by Ken Brewster that Alfredo has died.

I have seen occasional nursery nests in Galloway, always close to the original nest, but probably built in reaction to disturbance of it. 'Cock' nests, built by a male which has no mate, are not rare in Galloway and are known elsewhere. They seem never to be lined.

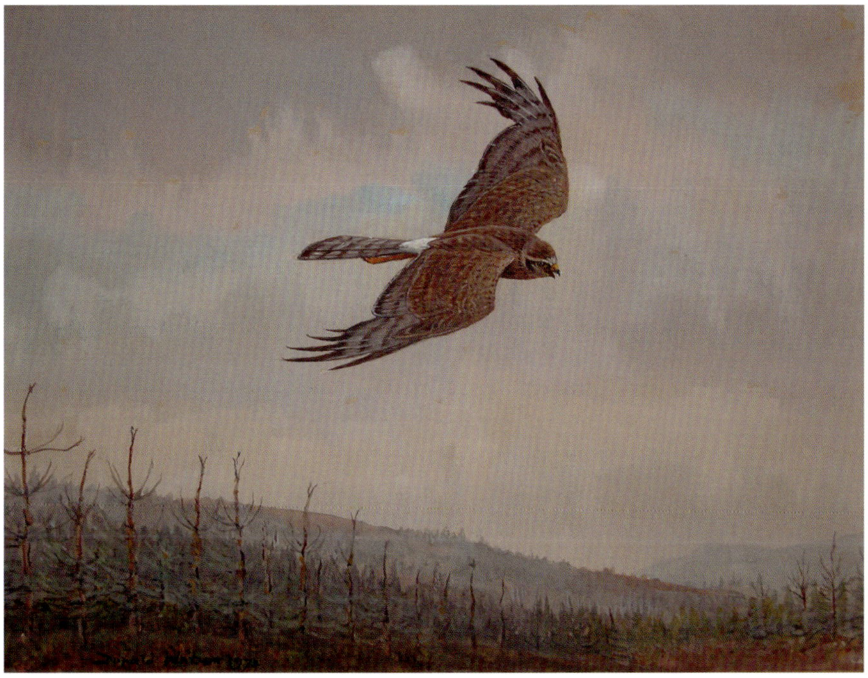

Behaviour of adult Hen Harriers at nests

Most accounts describe Hen Harriers as very defensive of nests, especially those with young. Females are often very aggressive but some hardly react at all when the nest is threatened. Ricky Gladwell, who has been to as many nests as anyone I know, believes that lack of aggression to humans at nests in localities where many nests have failed because of persecution has enabled nests where the female leaves quietly to survive. He thinks that keepers rely on aggressive females giving away the location of nests as soon as they are approached, while keepers may not find a nest where the female flies off silently. Are these birds adaptive? Most keepers are reluctant to spend time searching large tracts of heather or other dense vegetation where they have no reason to believe there is a nest.

The first nest I ever found, on open heather at Grobdale in 1959, had an intensely aggressive female and I came to think it was wise to wear a hat to save my head from her attacks with lowered feet and claws. A neighbouring keeper was in this case scared off by her attacks, but he was inexperienced on harriers. During the next few years I never found a moorland nest where the female was not aggressive. Eddie Balfour in Orkney told the story of how a friend with him had only been attacked when he put Eddie's hat on his head. When I began to find nests in forests, most of the females were less bold, but one male attacked me persistently at a nest. Again in the early 1990s I encountered two more very fierce males. One, which had a nest on an open heather and bracken hill outside but near the forest, pursued me for about a kilometre down the hill back to the car, never ceasing to be vocal. He would start 'whickering' at me or anyone else as soon as they appeared on the hill. Some males do not come at all near, though most are vocal at a distance. This, fairly certainly, results in more females being killed at the nest than males on keepered moors.

I have found young shot in the nest in Galloway but their greatest danger there comes from foxes. In 1992 a brood of six was taken by a fox, apparently one at a time.

Females may be less bold during incubation of the eggs but may continue to be aggressive as long as young remain in the vicinity after leaving the nests. Ricky Gladwell tells the memorable story of a female in Glenn App whose nest he had found (it was a bird which had been wing-tagged in Galloway the previous year) which flew about a kilometre from its nest to dive at and attack him. Both males and females from a Galloway nest I had found and revisited used to come almost as far and 'whickered' at me over a hill which was my favourite observation point. The painting was done from a rough sketch drawn when a female was attacking me.

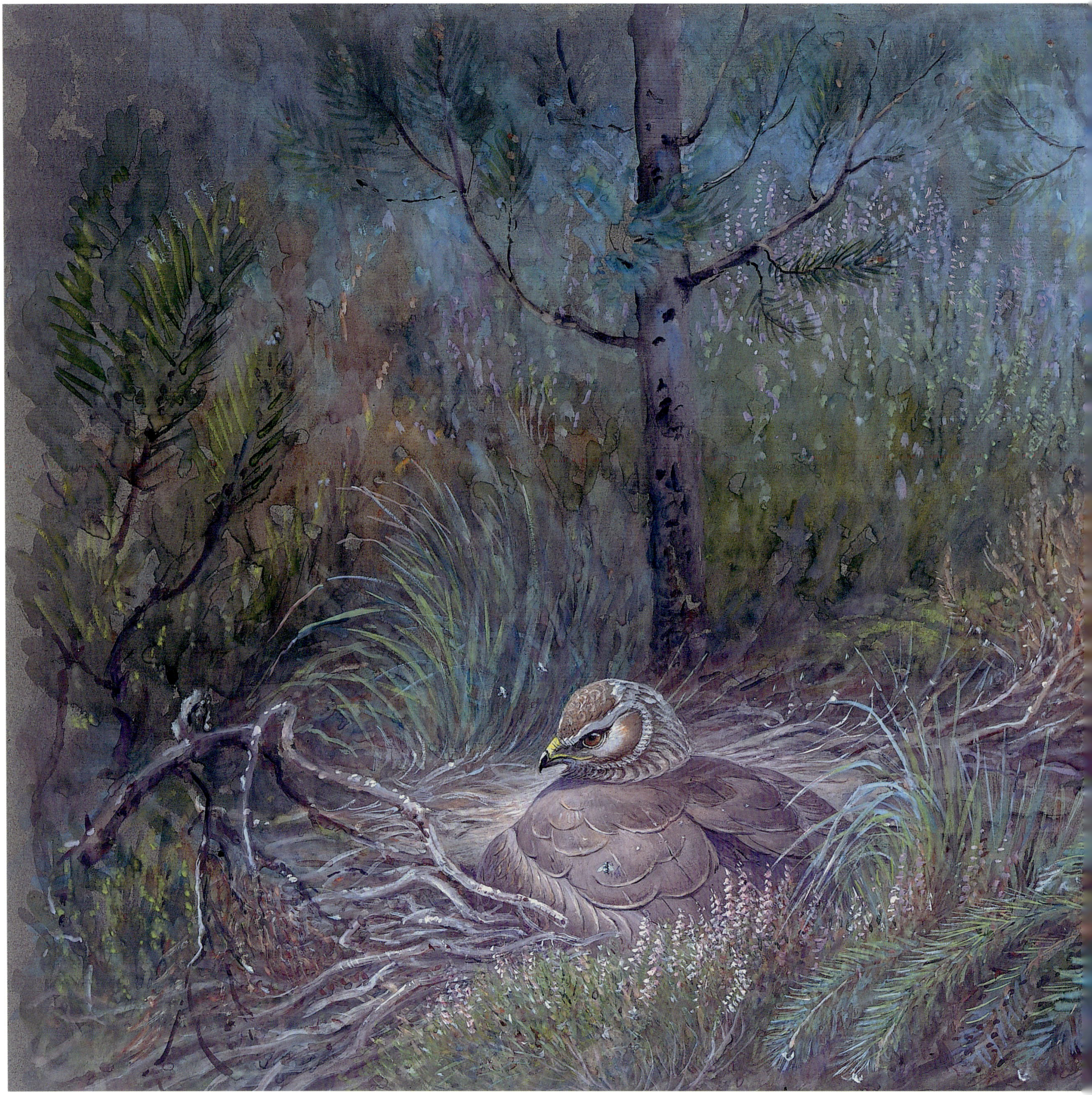

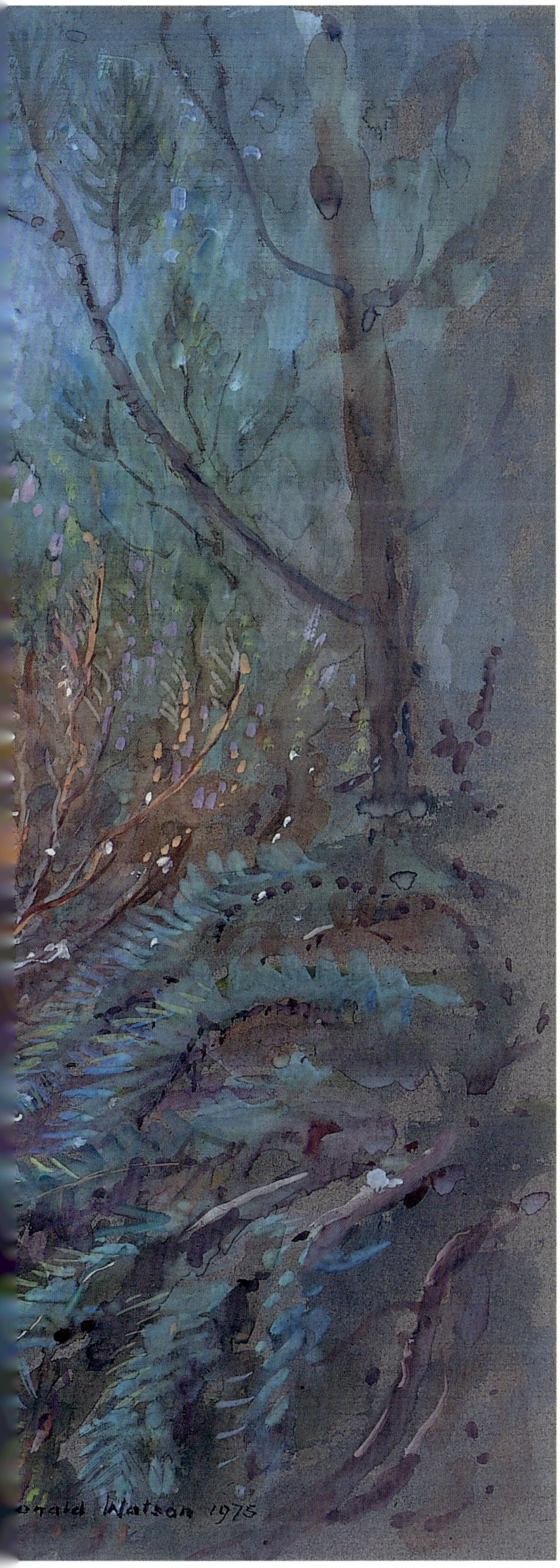

A hide at a forest Hen Harrier nest, 1975

Two well-known photographer friends, Jim Young and Brian Turner, put up a hide at one of the three nests in Laurieston Forest in July 1975. I was able to take advantage of this several times. It was the only nest I watched from a hide; I have described this experience in my 1977 book, *The Hen Harrier*. It was a late nest with a young female, probably one year old. The same older male had three mates and the female at this nest was no longer being brought prey by the male. Not surprisingly only one of the three chicks survived to fledge.

I made many sketchbook studies. Prey included young Wood Pigeons and Pheasant poults, the latter released in forest rides and feeding on grain supplied by a ranger or keeper. The young Wood Pigeons may have been taken from a nest but plumage suggested they were fledged. The weather was very hot with thunder showers. When I relieved a photographer at the hide, I had to walk a fair distance along a forest ride where the female sometimes spotted me, and she was at first reluctant to settle at the nest.

While much of the prey brought consisted of the usual small birds, such as Meadow Pipits and Skylarks, the larger items were important as much the heaviest prey. When a Wood Pigeon was dropped at the nest two metres away from the hide, it made quite an impact. Sometimes it would be lifted by the harrier and dropped in a ride, only to be brought back later. The painting of the parent sheltering the chicks illustrates the almost jungly surroundings deep in the forest. The remarkable patterned appearance of the plumage on the mantle is caused by moult being in progress, the new dark feathers contrasting with the old lighter ones. A closer view of the tail showed the shorter new ones were still growing. The fly on the female's back was just one of the myriad which were always around, especially when prey had been brought in. My hope of having some close views of the male were of course not realised.

The other two better-provisioned nests produced good broods but were too closely surrounded by trees to allow hides to be set up. In any case visits to the hide caused a great amount of crushing of the vegetation, which we did not care to repeat at other nests.

The only small bird taken among the Robins, Willow Warblers, Grasshopper Warblers, Wrens and Chaffinches nesting close to the harrier nest was one juvenile Robin, indicating that most of the hunting for prey was more distant.

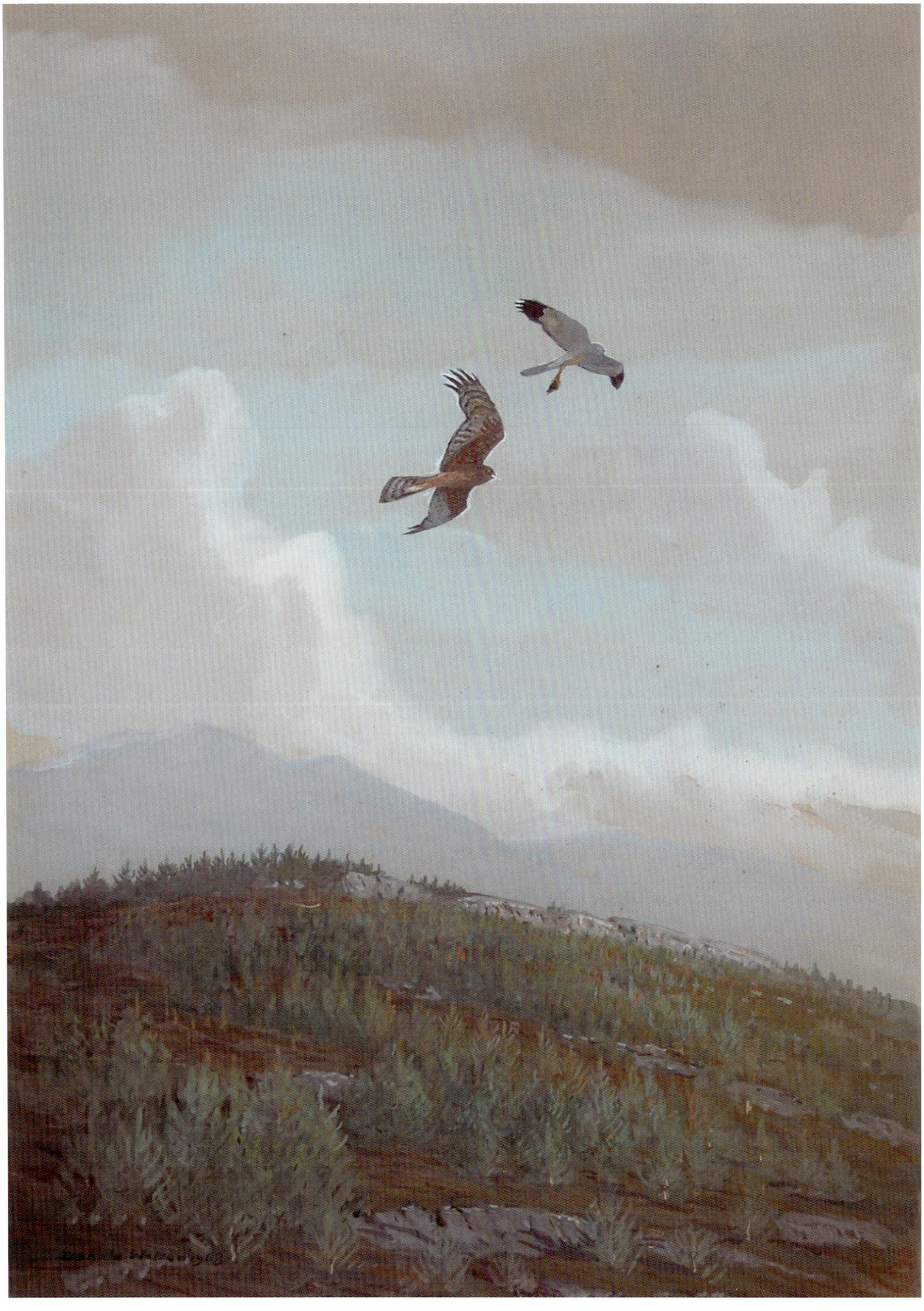

The food pass

'Courtship feeding' by the male to a female is a common feature of the breeding season in the lives of birds. It is said to cement the pair bond. In raptors it may take the form of 'food passing,' by aerial exchange at or near the nest, or on the ground near it. In harriers a pair may perform a food pass especially beautifully either from foot to foot or by a drop in the air by the incoming male, the female rising to catch the prize in a foot. Early in the breeding season she may sometimes attempt to snatch the prey from her mate in the air, or she may even bowl him off it on the ground. Very soon food passes are mostly perfectly executed. Much later, when young are fledged, attempting to secure prey which has been dropped to them by a parent, they often fail to catch it in an aerial pass, siblings competing for it on the ground. Making a clean catch is obviously a learning process for the young. Food-passing by adult harriers is closely linked to copulation and begins when a pair are nest-building or earlier, when they spend much time flying together, with wing-tips often touching and tails fanned, in slow flight.

When the female starts to hunt at about the time the young are over two weeks old, food passes from the male to the female usually become less frequent. Prey may be dropped to the young at the nest by either parent. As the brood grows older still some males may cease to bring them prey and after they are fledged it is usual for the female to become the greater provider, but this is variable. At one Galloway nest the female disappeared long before the young were fledged and the male reared them on his own. The female may have been killed or died. If this happens before the chicks are able to tear up prey themselves they may starve while the male continues to leave prey at the nest but does not feed it to them. A particularly good male will take over the female's role and rear young on his own. Elsewhere I write about polygyny – when a male is mated to more than one female. The chapter 'A hide at a forest Hen Harrier nest' tells how a less-favoured female may cease to be provided food by the male and some or all of the chicks may die, especially in prolonged wet weather, which makes hunting more difficult.

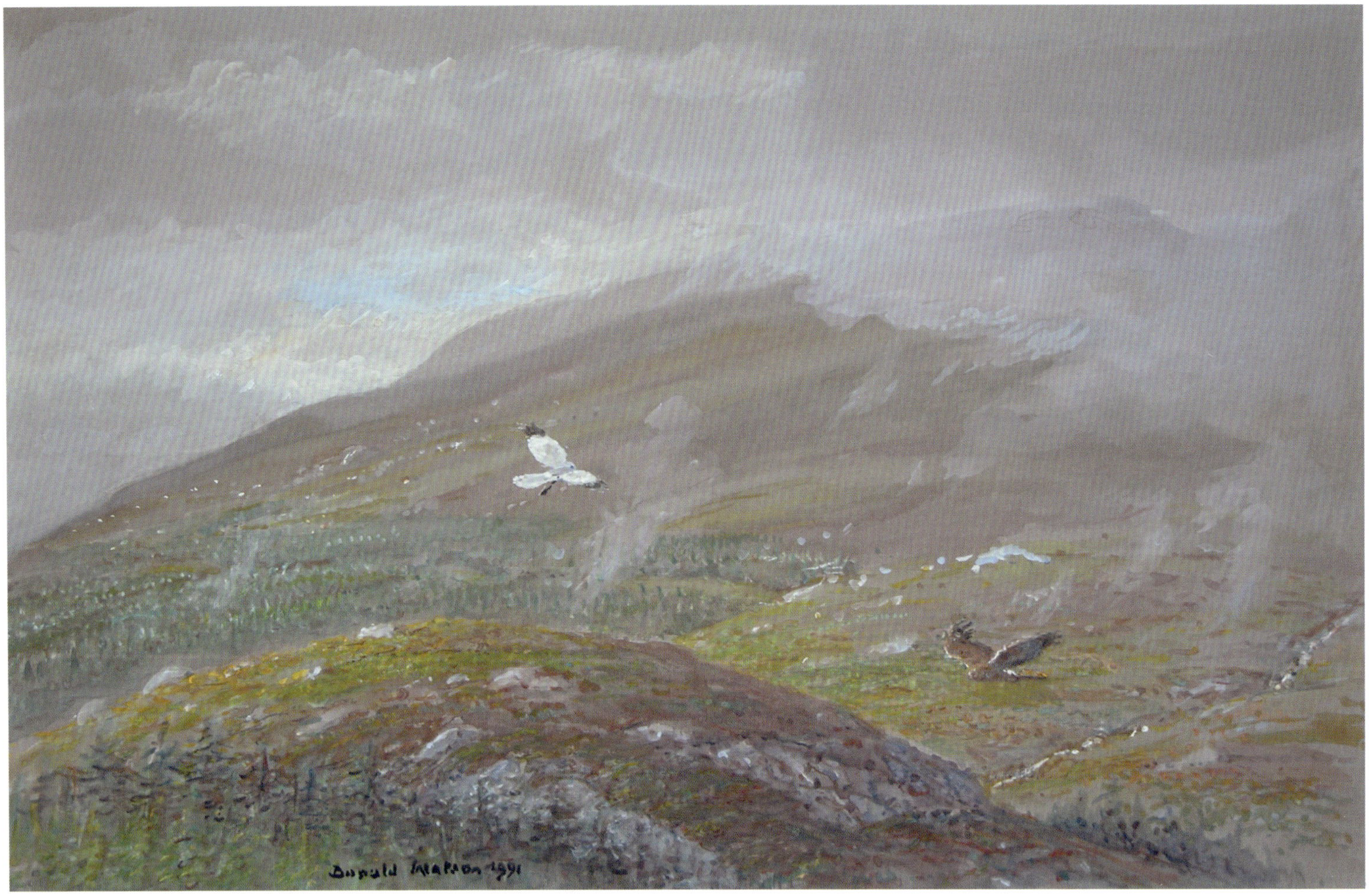

Concerning polygyny in the Hen Harrier

Polygyny in Hen Harriers has been studied in detail by several authors: Balfour and Cadbury, and Picozzi in Orkney, Simmons and others at Tantramar Marsh in New Brunswick, Canada. Although some ornithologists, including Fran Hamerstrom, considered that there were sufficient grounds for recognising the Northern Harrier of North America as a distinct species from the European Hen Harrier, Simmons and others concluded that the two should continue to be classed as the same species.

Here I only mention some of the most important points in the papers published by the above authors.

Polygyny – a term used when males are mated to two or more females – was first recognised in Orkney in 1931 by Nethersole Thompson. Since about 1950 such associations became frequent there, although the incidence of polygyny in recent years has declined alongside the general decline in the population in Orkney. Polygyny in Orkney was closely studied by Eddie Balfour from 1967 until his death in 1974.

He found that most first-year birds which bred were monogamous. Females aged 2–6 years old were often polygynously mated to adult males. Much of the reported increase in the Orkney breeding population around this time was considered to be due to a large increase in breeding females while the number of males remained fairly stable. By 1970, there were about 70–80 breeding females and about half that number of breeding males. It was considered that the holding capacity of mainland Orkney for males remained at about this level while females had to be polygynous if they were to breed at all. There was little evidence of the whereabouts of any non-breeding males which may have been excluded from the breeding population.

Perhaps the greatest insight to the causes for polygyny comes from the New Brunswick study. Here Simmons found that polygyny was linked to the abundance of the harriers' most important prey, voles, whose numbers fluctuated cyclically. In the best vole years the frequency of polygynous mating was highest, and it was lowest in poor vole years. Simmons showed that the intensity of male display (sky-dancing) and the frequency of these display flights were greater in food-rich years and less in food-poor years. He concluded that the frequency and intensity of male display flights, linked to greater provisioning of food by males early in the breeding season, was a key factor in determining the occurrence of polygyny. Ultimately many of these polygynous females were not able to breed successfully as later in the breeding season the male concentrated provisioning on his first mate, or 'alpha' female. Presumably for the other females there was some selective advantage in joining a polygynous group where there was some chance of breeding albeit with poorer success than the 'alpha' females, rather than remaining unmated altogether.

The link between food abundance and the incidence of polygyny is further reinforced by evidence from the changing situation in Orkney. Here the population has declined markedly in recent years, and this decline is thought to be linked to reduced food availability caused by changes in land-management practices. In parallel with this, the incidence of polygyny has similarly declined.

Where harriers breed more sparsely, polygyny is much less common, although it does occur occasionally. An example is described in my chapter relating to polygyny, where a nest in Galloway was watched from a hide. The female in this polygynous group (three females with one male) was under-provisioned by the male and may only have been able to rear her single chick because of the extra food items provided by the watchers.

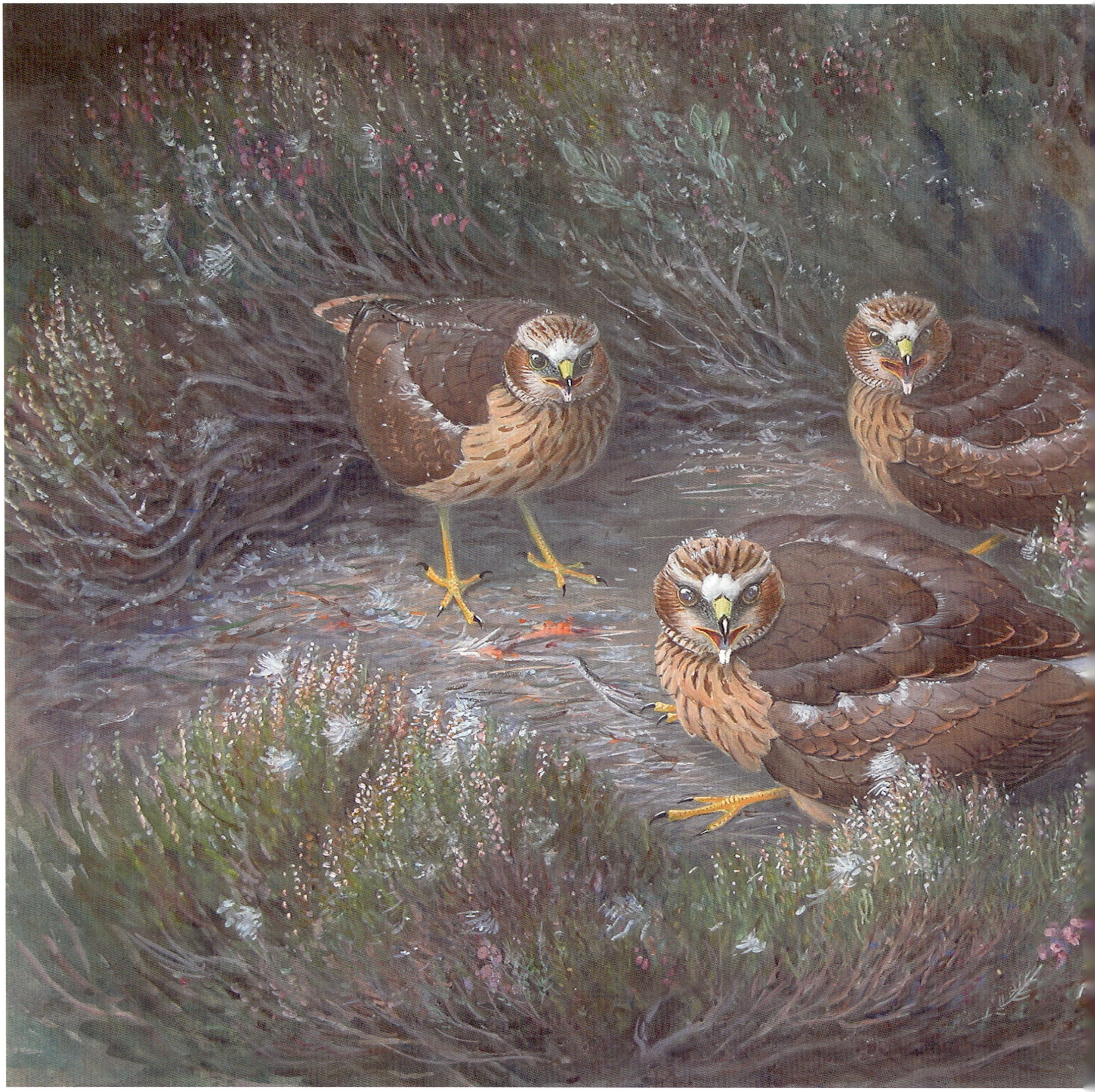

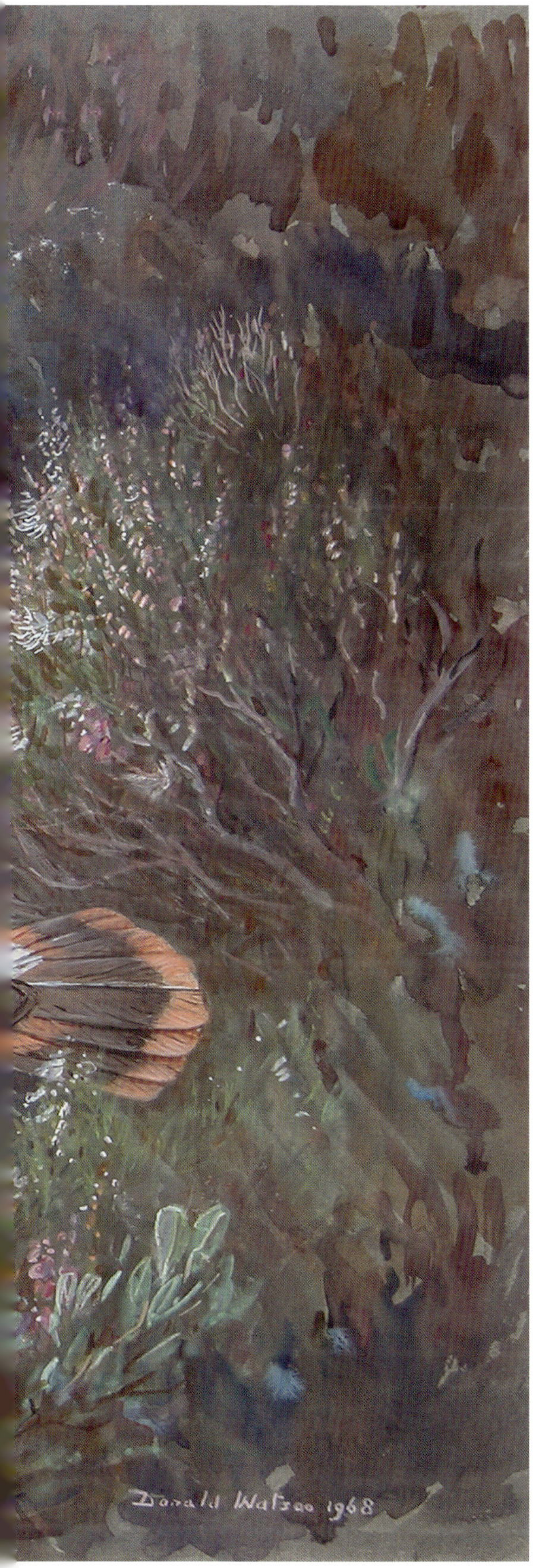

Young Hen Harriers in a nest, 1968

It is more than 30 years since I last saw this picture. The nest was at Auchencloy, not far from Loch Stroan. The forest was still young, planted in 1953, and this was the only nest I ever saw at that end of the forest. It has now been clear-felled. It was also quite near a long-established harrier roost-site. In 1968 Red Grouse were in large numbers with plenty of good heather among the young trees. The harriers brought a fair number of young Red Grouse to their nests in that year. There was of course no grouse shooting interest in the forest. It was always when the young harriers were well grown in the nests that grouse became a major prey. No gamekeepers would have seen this forest nest.

1968–70 were peak years for birds in the young forests, which still had abundant heather. Meadow Pipits, Grasshopper Warblers, Whitethroats, Willow Warblers, Whinchats, Stonechats and Redpolls were all plentiful, and in some years Crossbills too, which featured among harrier prey at a nest. One of the four pairs of Golden Eagles which then nested in Galloway reared a chick on a crag in the planted area in 1965 but moved to a tree-site later when they were disturbed by forestry work. The eagles were often mobbed by Hen Harriers and Merlins and on 27 May 1968, John Young and I found a freshly dead adult female Hen Harrier with a wound on its belly which was most likely made by an eagle's talon when the harrier was sparring with it. I had ringed this harrier as a chick at a nearby nest in 1965.

There was a lek of up to 30 Blackcock at the forest edge. The field vole population was high and I once saw a Kestrel rob a Short-eared Owl of a vole it had caught. The owls had a good season. Five or six pairs of harriers bred among the young trees. They no longer nested on the open heather site where I had found the first nest. The three or four pairs of Merlins nesting within the vast extent of young forestry bred on unplantable rocky ledges.

The three Auchencloy harrier young fledged successfully late in July – one of them was very dark-coloured as a downy chick and was probably melanistic.

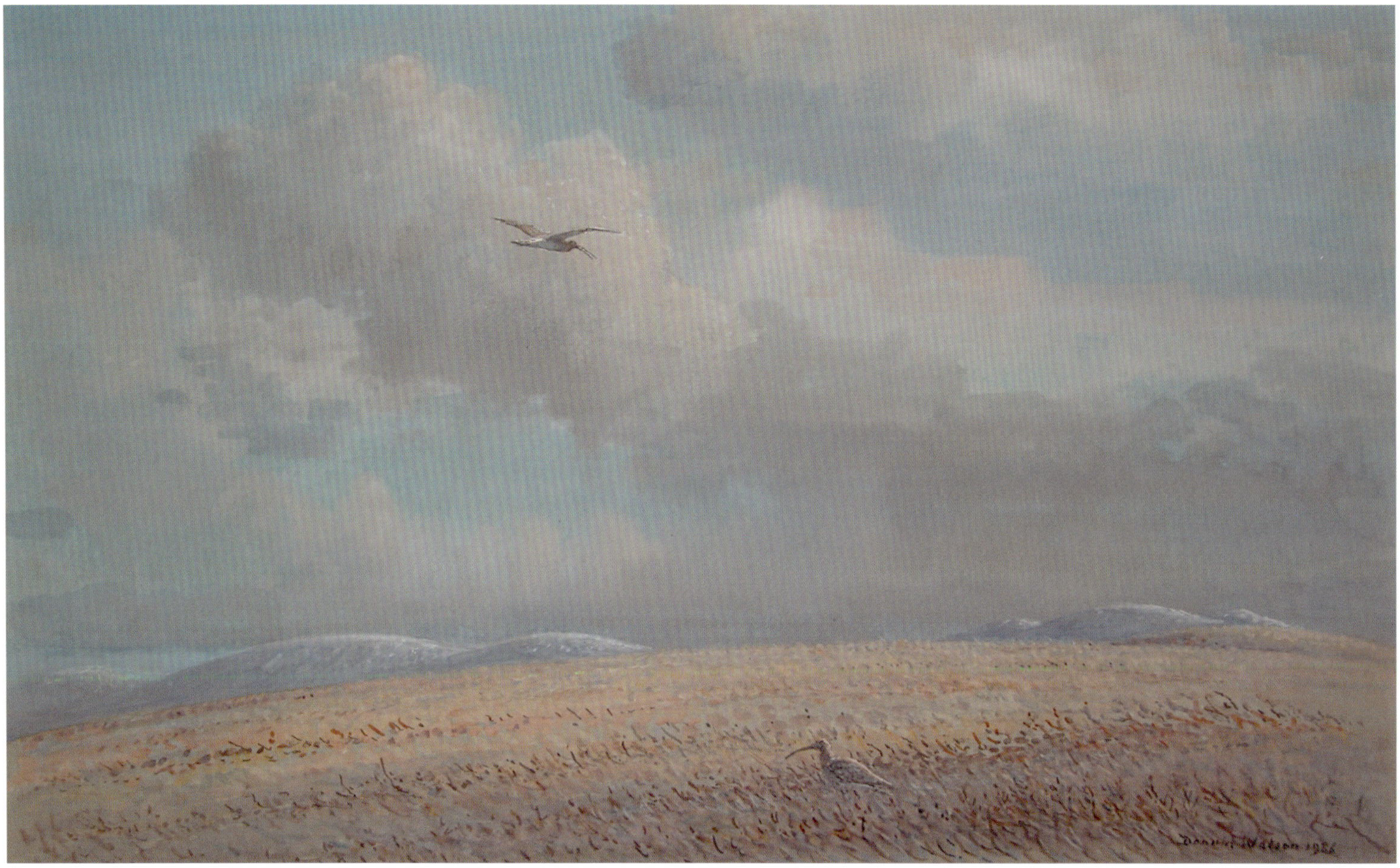

Curlews (Whaups) displaying on suitable Hen Harrier breeding ground.

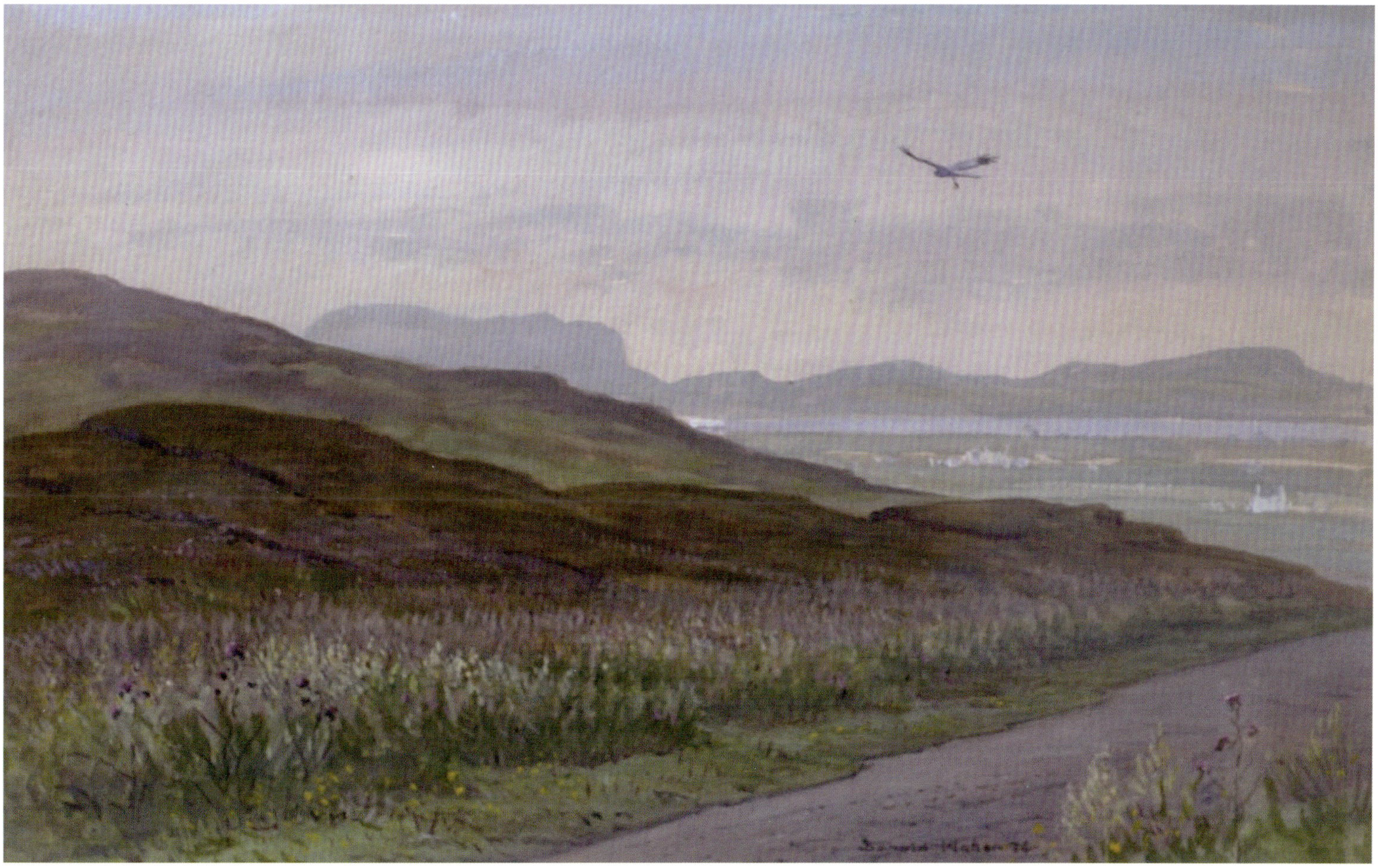

Male Hen Harrier over the Lyde Road in Orkney

The Lyde Road was one of the best viewpoints for seeing Hen Harriers in 1974. Sunniva Green, Eddie Balfour's co-worker on harriers at that time, told me that the male in this painting had a 'gammy leg,' although most people would have thought that his hanging leg, seen from afar, meant that he was carrying prey in a foot. I certainly thought he was.

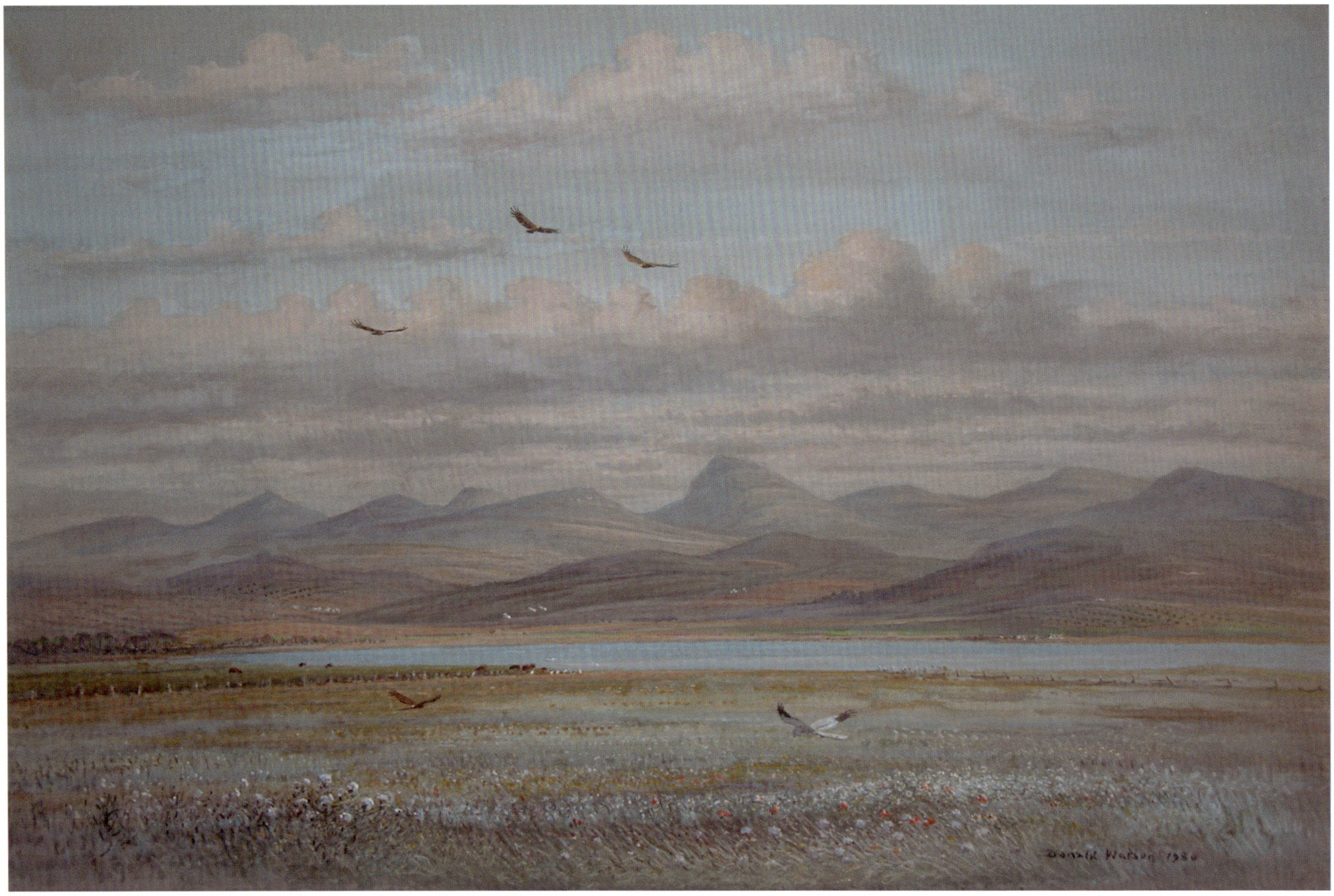

Hen Harriers in Kintyre

Dugald Macintyre, the gamekeeper naturalist, wrote of Hen Harriers being 'on daily view' on a moss in Kintyre 'in his early days,' while in March 1919 he saw 'a couple' on the same moss. 'His early days' were presumably at about the beginning of the 20th century. One day he saw three males hunting Snipe 'in the bog' and one attacking Partridges, but he never saw one kill a grouse. He seems then to be writing of 1919. He is perhaps the best authority for claiming that Hen Harriers never disappeared from Kintyre. I must add that I cannot understand his statement that young males in the nest were assuming 'the blue plumage.'

When afforestation was well established in Carradale – the first nests were in 1950–51 – the numbers of breeding Hen Harriers became quite remarkable, peaking on Cnoc na Gobhar, 'the Deer Hill,' which was kept for deer, at nine pairs in 1958–59. In the Carradale Hills around there 18 pairs bred at that time. Joe Eggeling and George Waterston ringed large numbers of young in Carradale. A number were recovered in the following winters, widely dispersed in Scotland, England and Germany, and one first-year bird was found in a trap in Les Basses Pyrénées, having travelled about 1,000 kilometres.

When we went to Carradale in June 1975, the Deer Hill had patches of brilliant flowers of rhododendrons among the 25-year-old conifers, and deep heather covered the unplanted highest slopes. A few pairs of harriers still found nest-sites there, but the youngest plantations, then about five years old, were in South Kintyre Forest.

From the forest gate I could see a cock harrier hunting over the very young trees. Very soon he had caught a vole which he took to a female for a food-pass. Peter Strang had said that most nests were towards the bottom of grassy slopes, still quite open among the small trees, and I quickly found a nest with six tiny chicks in exactly the situation Peter had described. With Peter we were allowed to drive into the forest. All afternoon Hen Harriers were within view and we were soon watching a second pair. The nest proved more difficult and it would have taken too long to find its exact site. The nest obviously had young. I had the impression that South Kintyre Forest must have had the densest population of nesting harriers I had seen. Hen Harriers, Short-eared Owls and Buzzards were in sight all the time. Peter Strang had been a forest ranger for 23 years. He told me that in earlier years Meadow Pipits and Skylarks were among the commonest prey, but a surge in vole numbers had superseded this. Some pairs of harriers on the nesting grounds in spring disappeared and failed to breed in the older plantations by 1975. Much of Saddel Forest seemed to have nesting possibilities, but the number of harrier pairs was down from four in 1974 to one or none in 1975. Polygyny was rare in Kintyre. Peter Strang only once found a male with two females.

Brian Turner in 1973 estimated that there were 20 pairs in southern Kintyre in June but some did not appear to be breeding – he only saw one nest and no young. In 1981 we saw a few harriers in Kintyre but the date was too late in the summer.

An intensive study of Hen Harriers in Argyll in 1993–94 has resulted in Michael Madders' PhD thesis, 'The Effects of Forestry on Hen Harriers.' One of his study areas was in Kintyre. He found that harriers benefited most when forests were on grassland, although some harriers bred in post-thicket forest, near which there was no useful foraging habitat.

When I read his conclusions I could not help thinking back nearly 40 years to when I wrote a short paper for The Scottish Wildlife Trust. The paper was to some extent about the Hen Harrier breeding in Galloway, pleading for the retention of enclaves of open ground to be left in the forests. It cut no ice with the foresters at the time, ostensibly for economic reasons. Now at last this is happening, as forests are being re-structured and large areas are clear-felled. As Michael Madders has written, second-generation plantings do not have nearly such high numbers of Meadow Pipits as first plantings but voles can be abundant. To date there have been few records of Hen Harriers nesting in the second plantings.

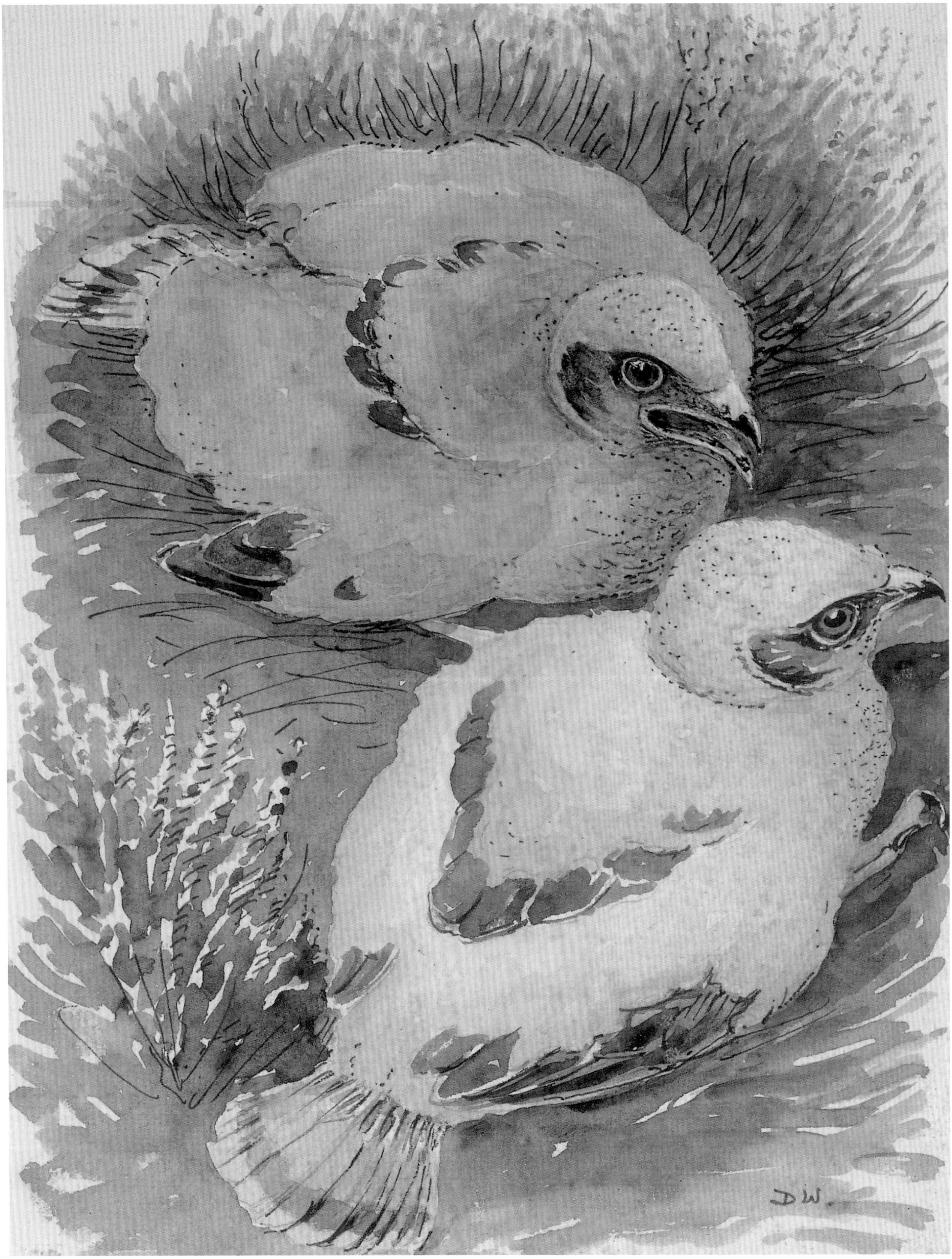
DW.

Albinistic and melanistic Harriers

The only harrier in which albinism is known is the Hen Harrier. In 1974 Eddie Balfour said that he had seen 'about 12' birds in Orkney with 'a large amount of white' in their plumage. None was a pure albino. Occasionally almost pure white birds have been recorded elsewhere in Britain and Ireland. Most were shot and their skins ended up in museum collections and were often displayed as mounted specimens. I have long hoped to see such a bird in life but have never done so. White claws are a feature that appears in all these birds.

In Montagu's Harriers melanism is much commoner, making up about 5 per cent of populations in Spain and Portugal, similarly in their winter range in West Africa. They have long been recognised as 'dark morphs,' some males being almost black. In eastern parts of the Montagu's range the dark form is much rarer. Even in Norfolk, where Vincent saw hundreds of birds in his time, he never saw a dark morph.

Melanism is rare in Hen Harriers, there being no regular dark form comparable to that in Montagu's. David Clugston and friends saw a brood of young Hen Harriers in North Wales in 1968 which had one (male) chick which was melanistic in down and when fledged had no white on the rump.

In Galloway I have twice seen a chick which was much darker in its down than others in the brood but this was less obvious when they were feathered and the most that could be said was that it appeared partially melanistic.

On 16 January 1991, a melanistic adult male Northern Harrier was identified by several observers about one mile northeast of Gray Lodge Wildlife Refuge, Glenn County, California. It was watched for 20 minutes at ranges down to 50 metres in good light. Particularly striking was the absence of the white uppertail-coverts band. Size, shape and behaviour were much as nearby male Northern Harriers. The following is taken from a full description recorded by the observers in Western Birds. 'The flight feathers showed the basic pattern of a typical male Northern Harrier though the contrast was somewhat diffused by the overall dark (mainly sooty grey) pigmentation. At a distance it could have been simply passed over. It was still present in the same area on 18 February 1991.'

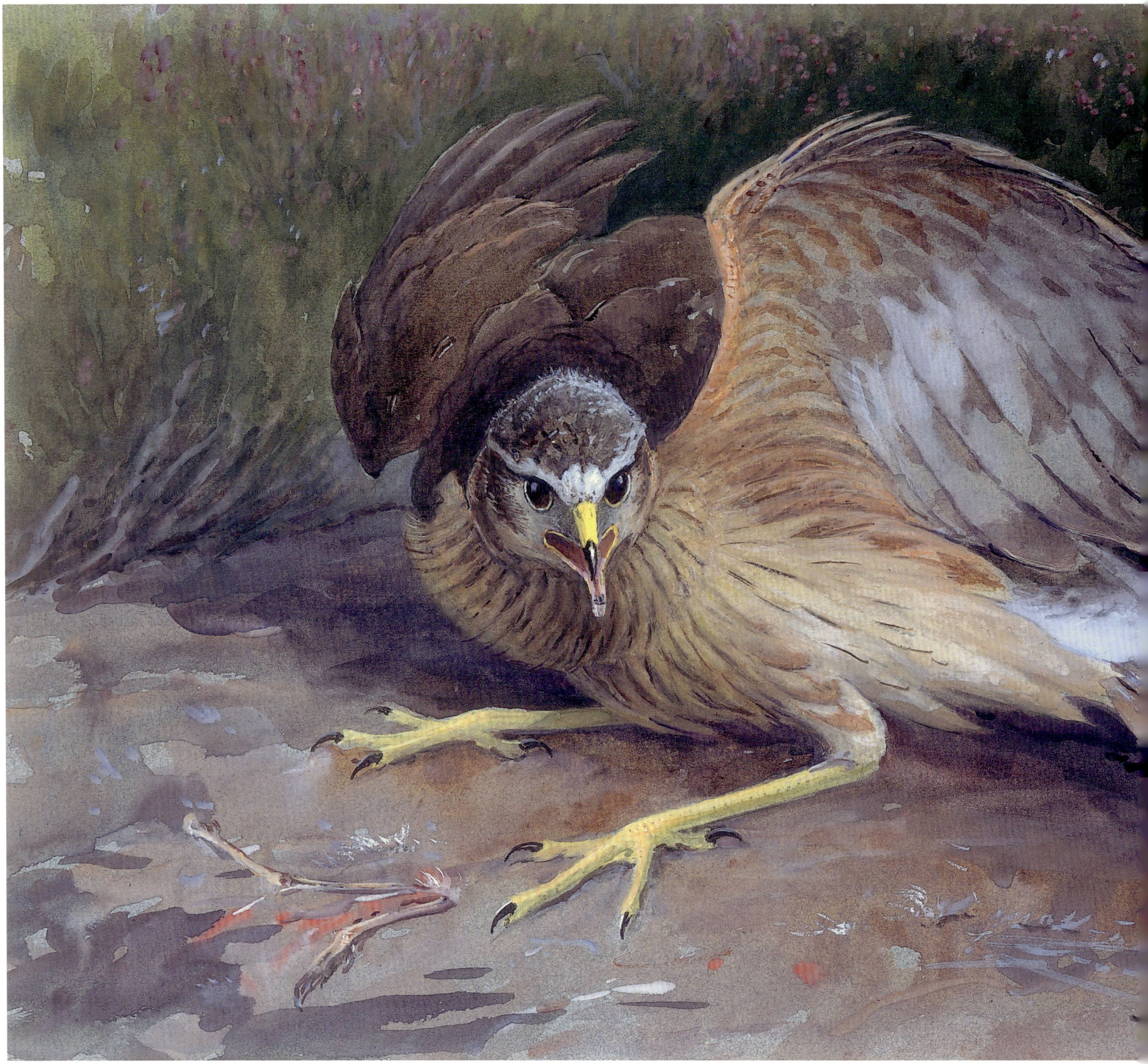

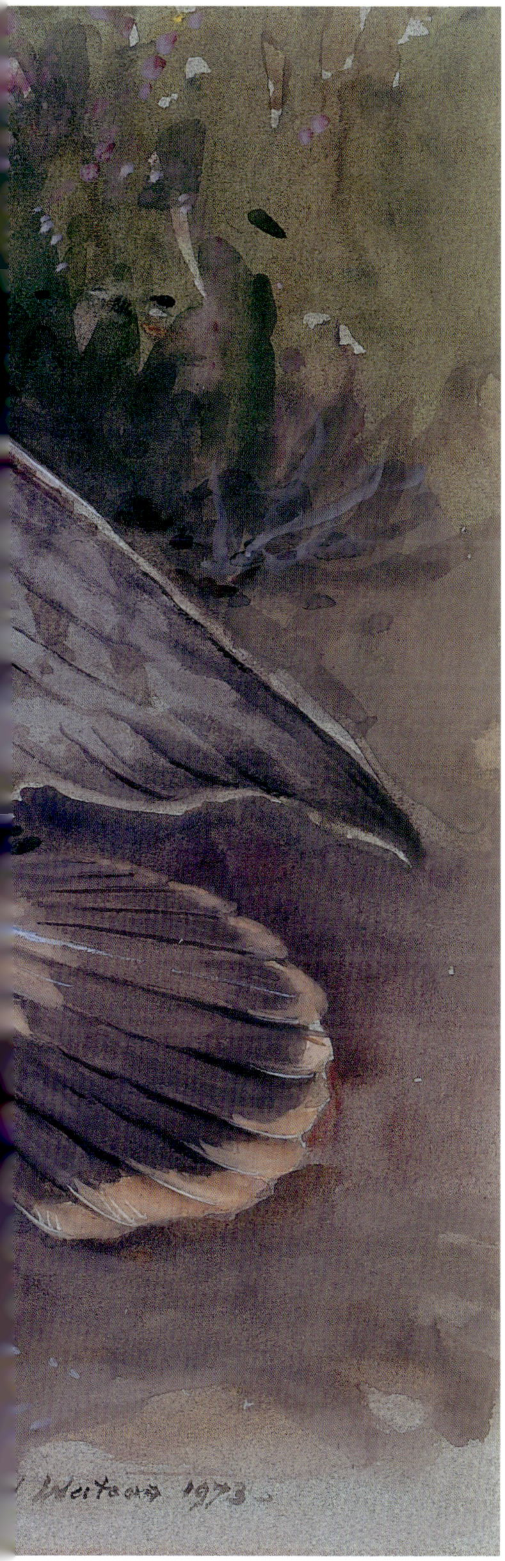

A study of a single chick
about to fledge.

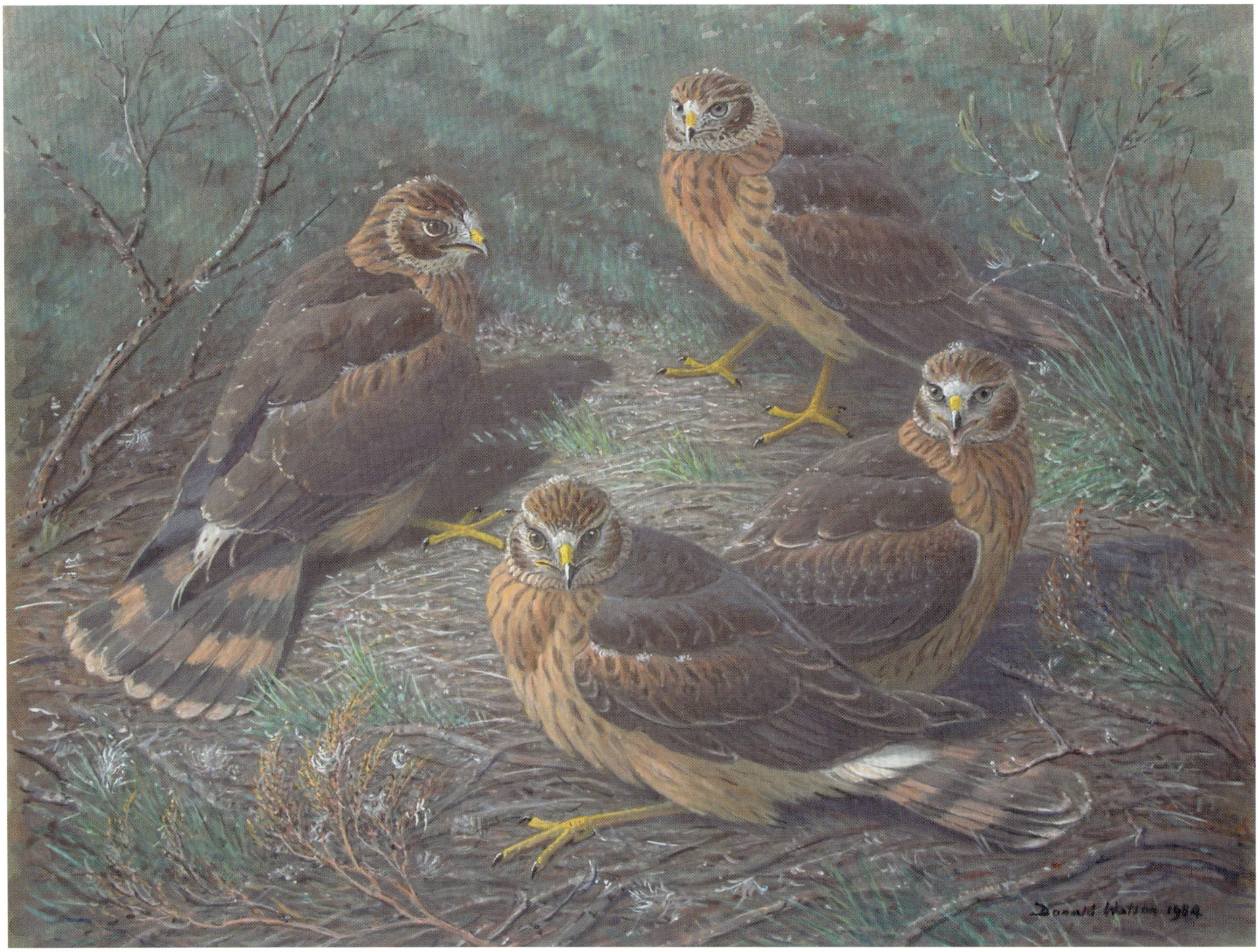

The story of 'Blind Eye,' a young male Hen Harrier, 1984

In June 1984 I found a Hen Harriers' nest in a Galloway forest with six young. It was an extraordinary nest-site, in plantation forest 24 years old. The nest was in a small gap among the trees, no more than 2 metres across, where a tree had not grown. On 18 June I realised I was close to the nest, the female coming close overhead 'whickering' furiously, but the forest was very dense and I failed to find the nest. The trees were Sitka Spruces and were at least 20 feet tall. On 18 July I made another attempt in company with Derek and Jeanette Ratcliffe. We had watched a food-pass from a long distance, but it was impossible to see where the female had gone down.

When I led the way among the prickly sitkas I was far from confident that we would find the nest. It was a dull overcast day with light rain falling. I was lucky that the still partly downy young caught my eyes as a light patch ahead of me. Approaching, we could only see five young, but on a later visit I found that the sixth must have escaped into the bog myrtle, which was the only ground cover among the conifers. The brood was five males and a female. We found that one of the males was blind in one eye. When Derek photographed the nest, of course it showed only five young.
I wondered how long 'Blind Eye' would survive. When I returned a few days later with Geoff Shaw, we found

and ringed the whole brood. The trees were so close together that the adult female could not dive right down on us, although she was aggressive.

When I next visited the nest area I found that three young were flying quite strongly but Blind Eye was staggering about on the forest roadside and the smallest young was clearly not thriving and seemed underweight. I decided to take Blind Eye and the youngest to Frank McGhie, the forest ranger who was already caring for a beautiful young Red Deer stag destined for the forest deer park.

The youngest died in the car but Frank, living by Clatteringshaws dam, said he would keep Blind Eye for a few days and feed him up. After almost a week he was much stronger and I took him back to the nest area, where the rest of the brood were flying.

I already had some food for him at home, domestic cockerel chicks which I got from a hatchery where they were killed and put out with the rubbish in big sacks. I released Blind Eye near the nest and left him five or six chicks in case he could not fend for himself or might not get food from his parents. In a couple of days I found that he had taken two of the chicks but was not flying very strongly. I still doubted whether he would ever be able to catch prey for himself.

The end of the story came about a month later. He was found dead on the Cumbrian coast, at Mowbray, near Silloth, on 15 August. Remarkably he had flown 63 kilometres, a feat which I had supposed would be far beyond him. The ringing report did not give any cause of death – he may have been shot or might have died from exhaustion or starvation.

The summer of 1984 was a good season for Hen Harriers in the Galloway forests. There were at least three successful nests and may have been others. The one which Jeff and I found in Laurieston forest proved very difficult and we only succeeded when Jeff watched from up a tree. This nest raised three young and the site was unusual to me in Galloway, being in an open space where two rides met; the conifers in that part of the forest were planted in 1960, so this was another very closed-up forest. The three chicks evidently fledged, as a family of five harriers were seen together, at dusk, by Dougie Craig over Grobdale, not far from their nest-site, on 31 August.

While I was watching the male from Laurieston forest hunting, over a kilometre from his nest, on 27 June, I saw another adult male harrier approach him from the west. This was a much slimmer bird with more pointed wings and I was fairly sure it was a Montagu's Harrier. Sadly the two males were too distant for positive identification, but I clearly saw the smaller male driven off by the territory holder, which flew below it in typical 'escorting' flight. I never saw the probable Montagu's again.

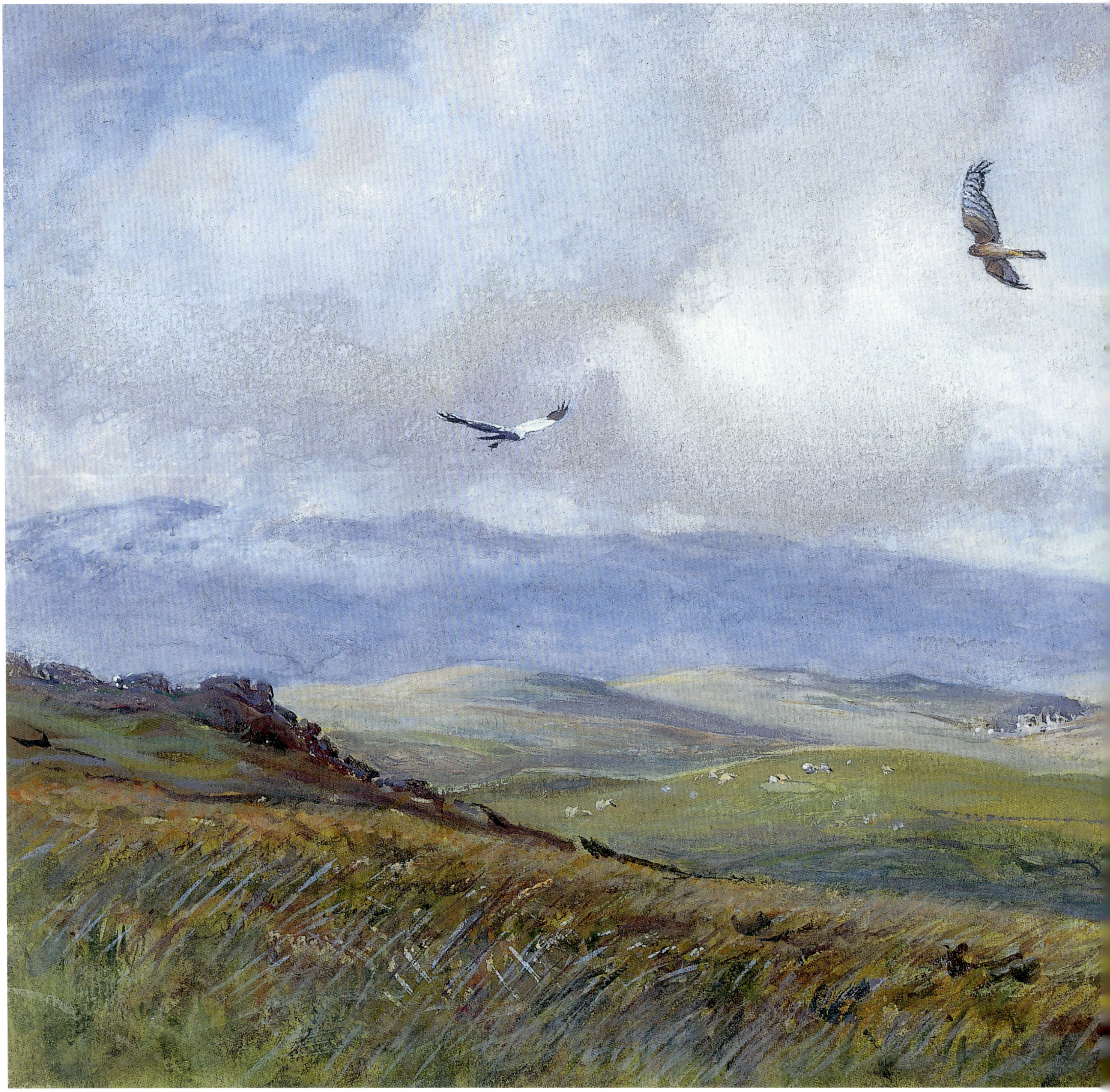

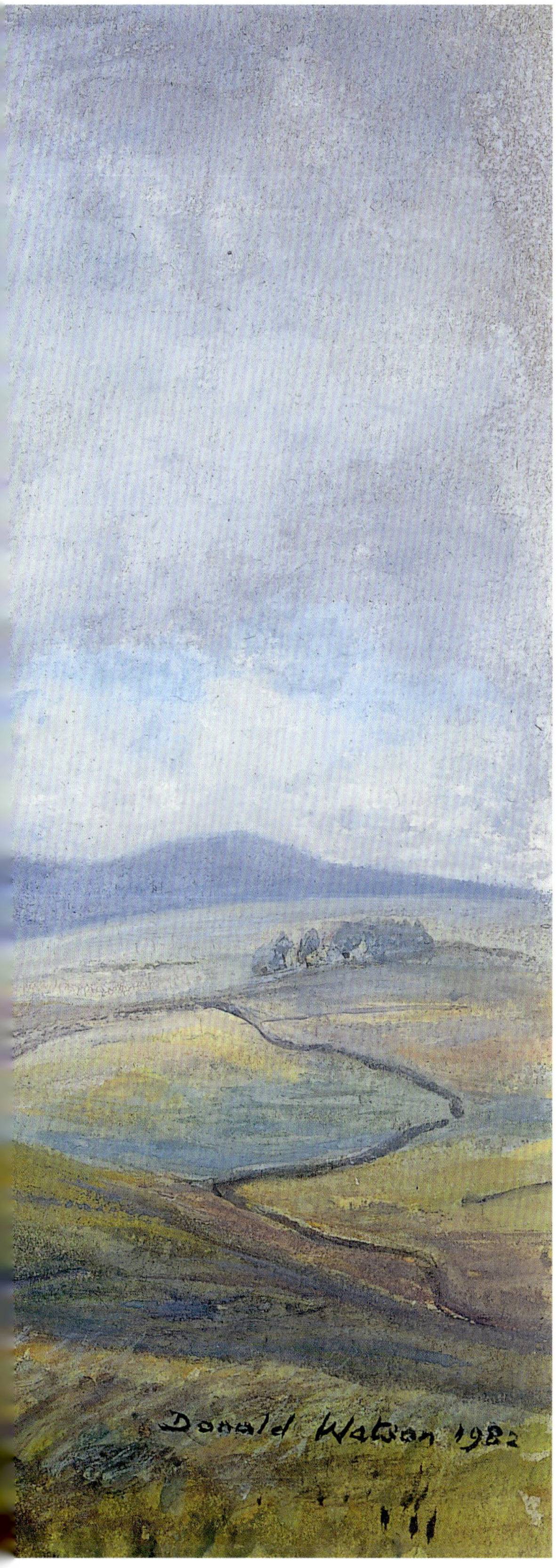

Hen or Montagu's? Ayrshire, 1960

In June 1960 a pair of Montagu's Harriers was said to have nested in Ayrshire, near Muirkirk. It seemed likely that the nest was found by egg-collectors and the clutch taken. Identification was far from certain, and when I visited the area with Joan later in the month we found a pair of Hen Harriers which clearly had a nest. It happened that the male of this pair was a 1-year-old bird and was mostly still in brown plumage. I eventually found the nest close to the Garpel burn, in a lush mixture of tall heather and bracken. Bearing in mind the claim that there had been a Montagu's nest, although this was unconfirmed, the problem was could I be sure that this nest was a Hen Harrier's, not a Montagu's? The male not being in full grey plumage initially raised doubts. Obviously a Montagu's nest would be a much more exciting find.

The only positive nesting by Montagu's in southwest Scotland had been by a pair in Galloway in 1953. In his fascinating papers in Forth Naturalist (1976, 1977), Edward Blake has referred to the Kirkcudbrightshire nest, mistakenly giving the date as 1952. The 1953 nest failed and I knew the story well. A part-time keeper working for the Forestry Commission had set a gin-trap in the nest and killed the female on eggs. When this was reported to the Forestry Commission Conservator, J. A. B. Macdonald, he was furious and gave orders that what had been done would not be tolerated again. Since then forestry workers have generally been protective of harriers. When Blake found Montagu's Harriers breeding successfully in Perthshire in 1952, 1953 and 1955, these were part of a range expansion by this rare species in Britain. In the same period a few pairs were nesting in Durham, where my friend Carol Greenwell had studied them, and they were continuing to flourish in parts of southern England, especially in Cornwall, as described by Bill Robinson in Bird Notes. The female killed at the nest in Corriedoo Forest, Galloway, in 1953 had been ringed as a chick in Anglesey. Blake suggested that the later decline was most likely due to agricultural pesticides, both in their African winter quarters and in the breeding grounds in Britain. He also mentioned the hazards from shooting on their long migration journeys.

I returned several times to the nest in Ayrshire. The site was just below the massive and beautiful heathery hill of Cairn Table. A fine brood, clearly Hen Harriers as they developed feathers, fledged successfully. I showed them to an elderly gamekeeper, who thought they would do no harm. Sadly, as the harriers increased, subsequent keepers began killing them, as their employers wanted. It is only now, in 2003, that there is real hope that the killing may cease. Landowners and keepers have agreed to the start of a new regime, initiated by the RSPB and Scottish Natural Heritage, and Special Protection Areas are being set up in the most important nesting areas in Galloway and Ayrshire for Hen Harriers.

In the painting, a large gouache, I took the liberty of making the male a grey bird, in fully adult plumage, for obvious reasons.

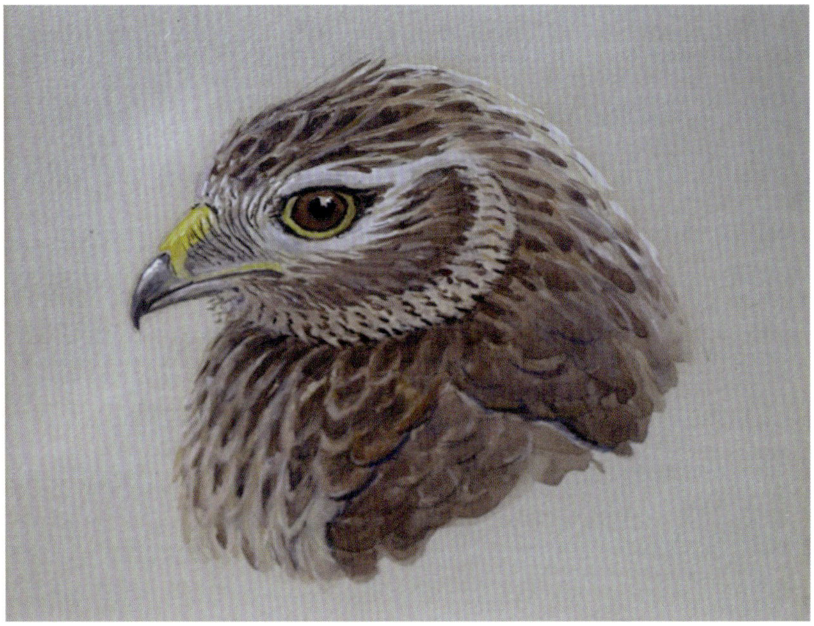

Study of a first-year female Hen Harrier, Orkney, 1974

A small proportion of Hen Harriers breeding in Orkney at this peak time of numbers were one-year-old birds. This one was mated to a first-year male. Eddie Balfour, the acknowledged expert on Orkney harriers, knew from his great experience that catching the breeding birds for ringing, weighing, measuring and wing-tagging would not cause desertion of a nest with young. This pair already had a brood. Eddie and his assistant, Sunniva Green, brought the bird down to the car and I made a pencil sketch of its head on the bonnet. Later I painted a colour sketch and gave it to Sunniva. Their method of catching the harriers was to set up a net at the nest with a stuffed Snowy Owl as a decoy. I confess I watched this with some misgiving but I soon realised that there was no need to have this. Hen Harriers at that time were more successful in Orkney than anywhere else, thanks to a great extent to Eddie Balfour. Jeff and I stayed for a week with Eddie and his wife, visiting Sunniva and Martin Green many times and getting much hospitality.

Nest-sites of Hen Harriers in Orkney were mostly in long spongy-damp vegetation, often in a mixture of heather and rushes. At one nest there was a clump of rushes growing in the nest. At another, meadow-sweet grew tall. Neighbours were frequently Curlews, Golden Plover, Merlins, Wheatears and Twites, with Red-throated Divers and Mergansers on lochans. A pair of Fieldfares had bred that year. Vegetation was so lush that harriers had a great number of options for nest-sites. The absence of sheep on the hills was important, while the widespread peat-cutting did not deter harriers from finding nest-sites. Rabbits abounded. They and the large Orkney vole were major prey for the harriers. Bird prey included Starlings and House Sparrows. Eddie Balfour agreed that the presence of old nest-sites encouraged nesting in the same area.

When the sun shone fleetingly, distant Hoy was clearly outlined behind pearly green fields and sunlit farm buildings. On a visit to Stromness museum I drew and later painted a stuffed specimen of a partial albino female Hen Harrier, dated 1937. Eddie Balfour said this bird only survived a few weeks before being 'collected.' There were also two specimens of mature males (dated 1912) which showed how the plumage differed from that of males 1–2 years old, which are quite dark-coloured on the back. Reflecting on the grey males I had seen at Galloway roosts, I realised that a high proportion are not more than 2 years old, which could mean that the life expectancy of males is not high.

Since the 1970s Hen Harriers in Orkney have declined markedly, although there has been a recovery in the last year or two. The reasons for these changes are still unclear, but it appears from current research that a changing landscape has greatly reduced prey and the extent of damp moorland for nest-sites.

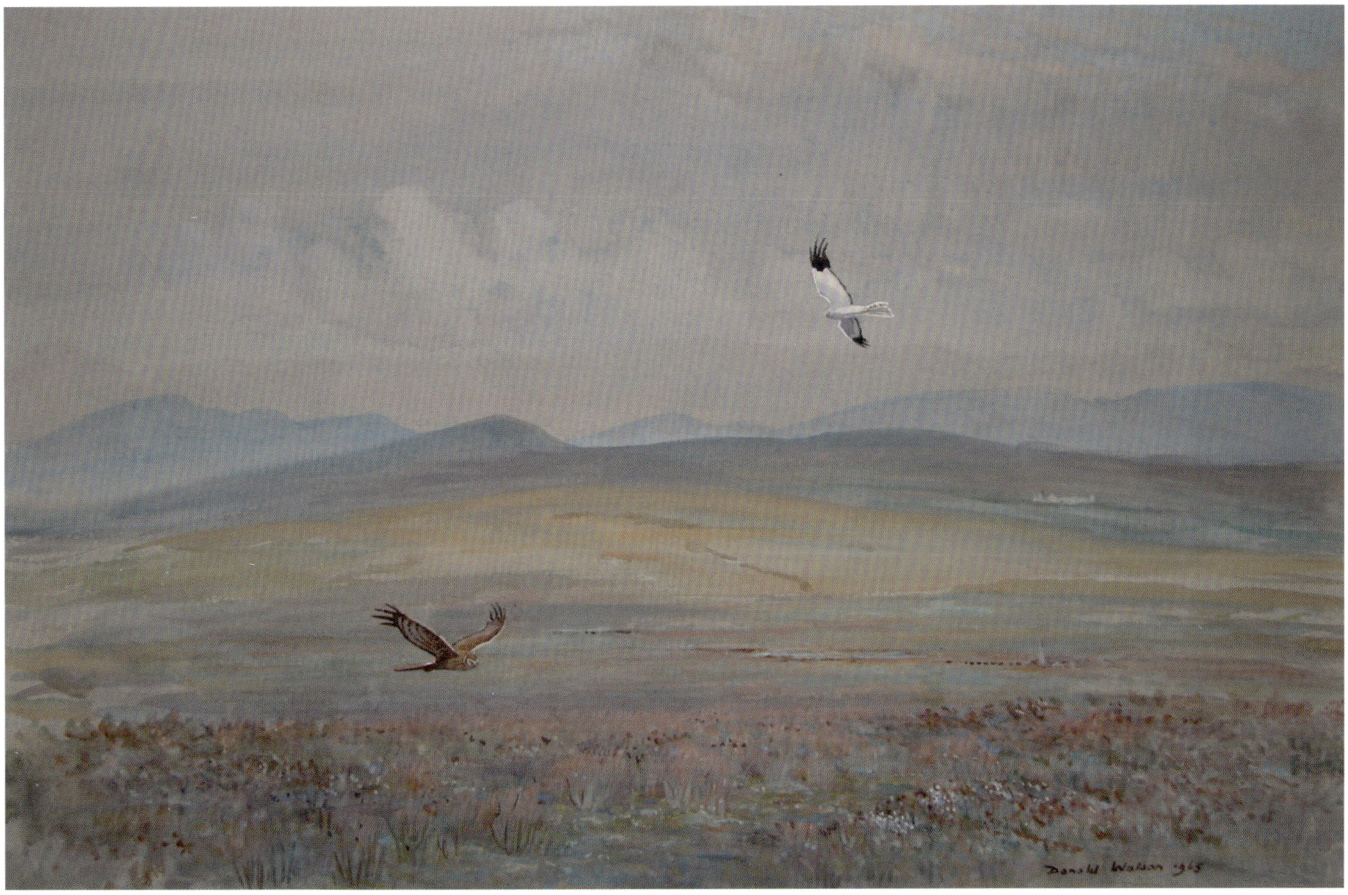

Pair of Hen Harriers on Stair estate, Wigtownshire, 1965

At the present time, the gamekeeper on this moor does not destroy harriers. Back in 1965 the then head keeper said he regarded Hen Harriers as 'his worst vermin,' although they were legally protected. They had attempted to breed on this moorland for some years previously. The keeper said that he was angry that a pair had escaped him that summer and this was probably the pair in this painting. Joan and I saw them in July, but the same evening we found a pole-trap illegally set in their territory. Looking across the moor we could see two more further away, but it was starting to rain heavily so I decided to drive to the police station in Stranraer. It took a couple of hours to persuade the sergeant to come back with us, when it was already dark and very wet. He agreed to take the nearest trap back to the police station. I had no doubt it was set for harriers but it had caught a kestrel. We were promised that the remaining traps would be collected next morning. When I learned that the head keeper was a special constable I feared the worst. Telephones must have been busy and no more traps were found. The Earl of Stair was the most important landowner in the district. I had a sympathetic letter from Peter Conder, director of the RSPB at the time, but of course there would never be proof of who had put up the traps. I know that we caused a bit of a stir. The fact that the only road over the moor had just been opened to the public after war-time closure by the MoD was surely significant.

When my friend Bert Dickson came to live at New Luce, he kept a close watch on the breeding harriers and they began to have some success. This continues to improve and now the present Earl of Stair has given his support to a Special Protection Area.

In 1965 the Stair moors were known for the large numbers of grouse shot there. In recent years deterioration of the heather has made the habitat much more grassy and no longer a prime grouse moor. I can only suppose that the harriers' increasing numbers rely more on other prey, perhaps voles, pipits and blue hare leverets.

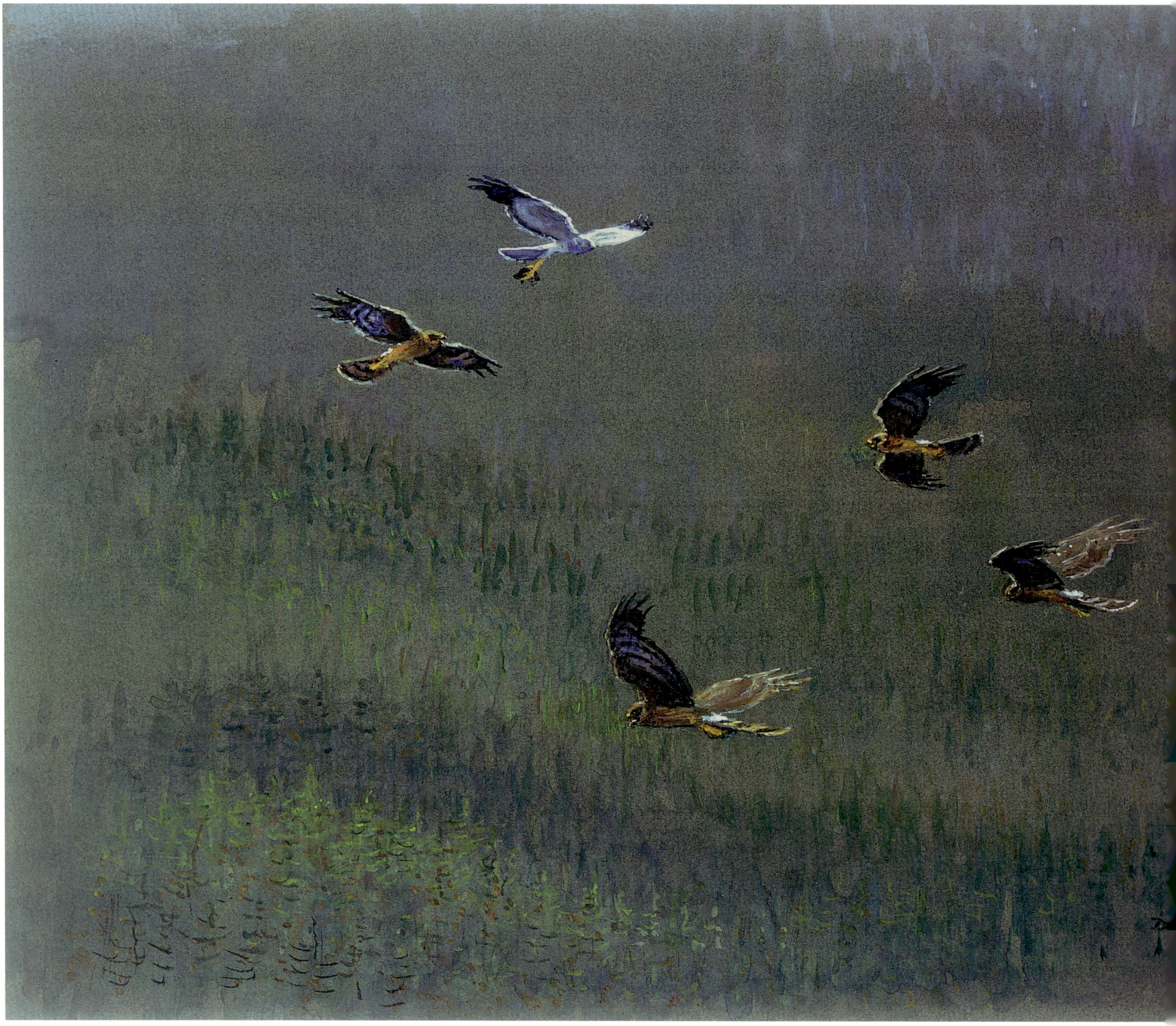

Softly Softly move for rare bird

In the late summer of 1986 a Hen Harrier nest in which a female was sitting on a clutch of eggs was discovered directly in the path of a road to be built in the Clyde submarine base. The sequence of events that followed was remarkable and probably unique. I was one of the people asked to give advice to Andrew Moore, an NCC assistant regional officer, on how to save the nest. The eggs were first removed to safety and replaced with hen's eggs. A pallet, a 4 foot six inch copy of the original site, was built, camouflaged with peat and heather, and placed on the site. The next day the pallet was moved 12 feet up a slope and the Hen Harrier was watched from a distance as she returned to the eggs. This move was repeated daily for two weeks as the Hen Harrier continued to return and incubate the hen's eggs. Young spruce trees were felled to keep the sitting bird's view as similar as possible to her view from the original site. One tree was always left, to mimick the original site, and a red ribbon was tied to it by a surveyor to mark it. On 15 June, after a fortnight, the pallet had been moved 150 yards and the harrier's eggs were replaced in the nest. Part of a stone wall was removed as we thought the bird might not accept her view being restricted. On 29 June the eggs had begun to hatch. The nest was successful.

This story was covered in an article printed in *The Times* newspaper of 22 August 1988, entitled 'Softly Softly move for rare bird.'

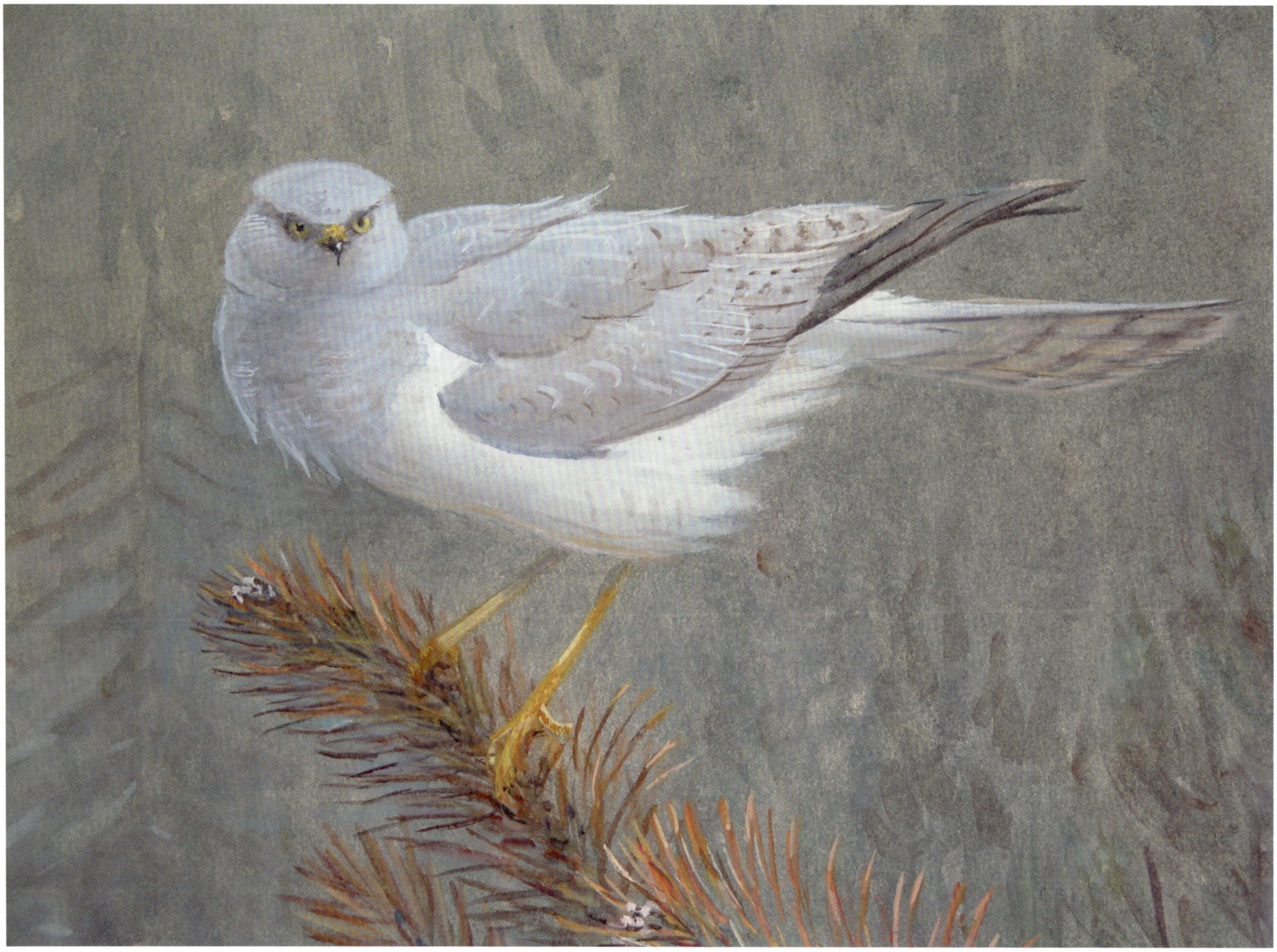

Recolonisation of the Loch Lomond area by Hen Harriers

John Mitchell summarised the Hen Harrier story in the hills around Loch Lomond in *The Western Naturalist* (1980). Hen Harriers are believed to have become extinct there in about 1868, when a keeper shot a female off its nest and put a foot on the eggs.

John Mitchell wrote of the ruthlessness of gamekeepers in the district. They were advised not to shoot females on nests with eggs, but to wait till the young were half-fledged, when the adults were bringing food frequently. The chicks would then be tethered in two circles, out of sight of each other, and the parents would be trapped easily as they responded to the hungry cries of the young next day.

Quite early in the 19th century, the hills around Loch Lomond were being transformed as sheep became increasingly numerous – they were described as changing from 'dusky' to 'a lively green.' No doubt this may have meant that nesting sites for harriers also became scarcer.

It is not certain exactly when Hen Harriers began to recolonise the Loch Lomond hills, but sightings increased by the early 1940s and in 1953 Meiklejohn and Palmar reported seven pairs in Loch Ard Forest; in 1961 Blake knew of 11 pairs there. Although early plantings by the Forestry Commission were becoming less suitable, large areas were being newly planted apace. Harriers quickly began nesting in these. In a survey in 1973, Geoff Shaw found five pairs and three nests on Forestry Commission land in the Loch Lomond district.

Male Hen Harrier hunting in South Uist, 1974

After Joan and I had supper at Howmore in South Uist I drove down the sound to Gheatry to observe the big valley below Beinn Mhor. A pair of Red-throated Divers was evidently nesting on a lochan not far away. I sat painting between 8.30 and 10.30 in the evening, by which time the sun was setting. The foreground was hummocky heather and it was not long before I spotted a cock Hen Harrier hunting. It was 28 June (my birthday). I had no doubt that the harrier was hunting for prey to take to a nest, probably with chicks. The harrier was a fine grey bird but during the time I was there he never revealed where the nest was. I think he caught a Meadow Pipit once but then sat on a knowe for about an hour until I packed up my painting gear and headed back to Howmore. It was essentially an 'on the spot' picture. Later I gave it to Joan as a reminder of our wonderful times in the Outer Isles. The painting is reproduced on page 18 of my book, *One Pair of Eyes*.

Thanks to Ian Newton's advice on where to look, I did find a nest with well-feathered young harriers, in North Uist, where the female harrier sparred with a pair of Arctic Skuas, and a pair of Black-throated Divers swam nearby on a big loch. The poignant cries of Golden Plover followed us all the way to the promontory close to the loch, and it was no surprise to find that the only prey at the harriers' nest was a Golden Plover chick.

It was not a difficult nest to find, as the female harrier virtually led us to it by her increasingly anxious protests. We had to walk a long way through luxuriant heather and Joan was getting very tired. Our biggest worry was that we had to catch the boat at Newton ferry that evening and we were already cutting things fine.

At the beginning of July 1950 we had made an earlier visit to the Outer Isles, on our honeymoon. Apart from two nights at the Lochboisdale hotel – thanks to a generous cheque, a wedding present from Archie Bryson, an old friend – we stayed in a tent on the flower-rich machair at Griminish, Benbecula. We had no car and the days were spent exploring Benbecula and South Uist on foot. There was then no causeway to North Uist. The post van drove over the machair to deliver our mail. I had an introduction to Donald John Mackinon, the keeper on Benbecula. At least in those days keepers did not kill Hen Harriers on those islands. We found Donald John and his wife very friendly and helpful. They allowed me to keep my finished paintings in their house and I was able to use an abandoned croft to paint in on wet days. On one memorable day Donald John led us on a long walk into the wild moorland across on the east side of Benbecula, visiting many lochs, Black-throated Divers nesting on one. Donald John was mightily impressed by Joan's walking prowess, saying that the walk 'would have killed' the shooting tenant. Hen Harriers nested on the moors, hunting mainly over the low machair ground in the west. Sometimes we would see one within sight of our tent. Before we left home we had called in at MacNicols gallery in Glasgow and persuaded him to have an exhibition of my work in the autumn. So I knew that we would have a working honeymoon, as I had promised to bring back many pictures from the Outer Isles. It was a very wet summer, even by Western Isles standards. Our crofter neighbour was hardly a keen worker and once remarked, unforgettably, 'more rain, more rest, bad weather is the best.'

Anyone who knows the bird life of the Uists recognises them as having the best numbers of breeding waders in Britain. Coming from Galloway, where many waders were already declining by 1974, the abundance – especially of nesting Lapwing, Ringed Plover and Dunlin – was a revelation. Most of the Lapwings had their fledged young on the wet fields by July, but the tiny Dunlin chicks ran ahead of us everywhere among the machair flowers. Redshanks were also in great numbers and Golden Plover plentiful on the peaty moors.

We took the car to the south edge of South Uist, where there were two pairs of Eagles. Buzzards had increased since 1950 and Merlins were not scarce. I had a good talk with Mr Snow, the keeper at Askernish, who had a lot of information about the birds on his beat. He liked Hen Harriers as much as Donald John Mackinon did and told me that many wintered in the islands. There would certainly be a winter roost somewhere. Probably nobody had looked for one. He thought that the harriers were increasing. He told me of nests in chest-high willow and heather scrub up the Hornary glen, where he would go Woodcock shooting in February.

The absence of breeding harriers on Harris and Lewis is believed to be due to lack of voles there.

The recent sad decrease of breeding waders in the Uists and Benbecula is due to the misguided introduction of hedgehogs, serious predators on eggs and chicks.

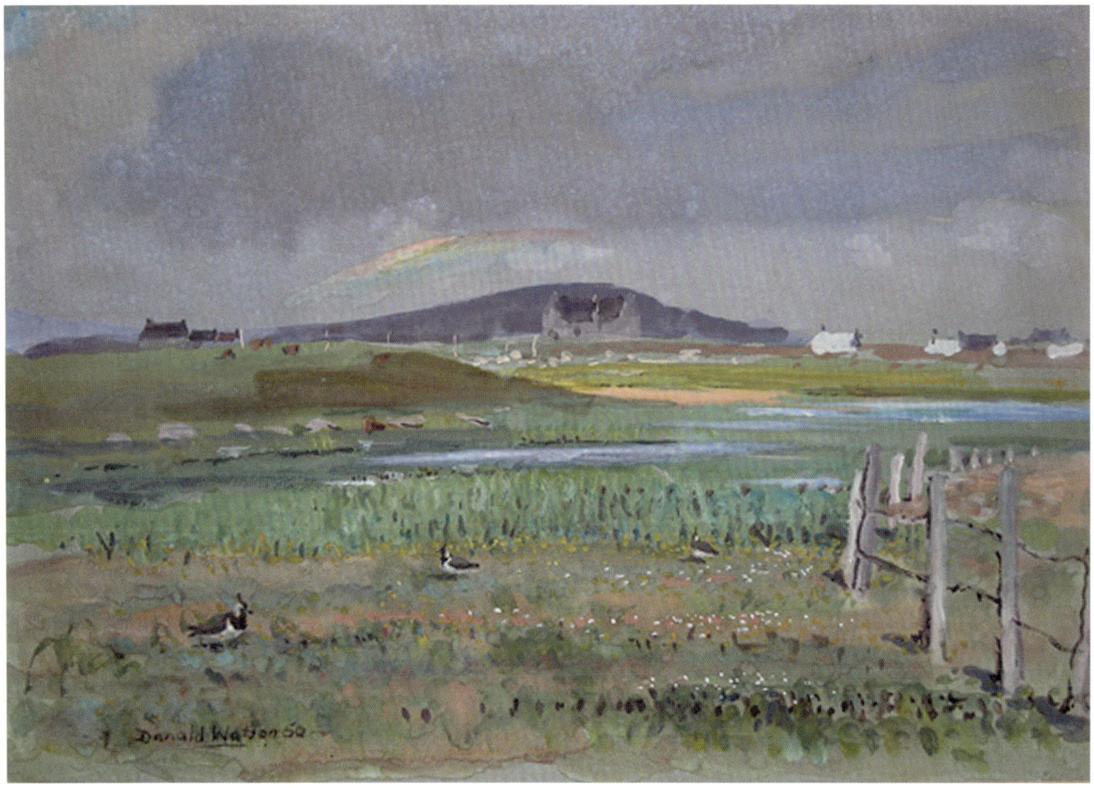

Rainbow over Benbecula
Lapwing fields, 1950

This picture was painted in 1950. The fields were just over the road from our tent, on the machair. Tiree in 1957 and 1992 could almost rival the Uists and Benbecula for abundance of nesting Lapwings. This 1950 painting is typical of its date, an 'on the spot' picture painted very quickly. In July the young Lapwings were mostly already fledged, flocks beginning to form, many still in family parties. Perhaps the Scots name 'Pewee' or 'Peewit' is more apt.

An American friend thought that it was one of the most beautiful of British birds. In the States it is a rarity, only reaching there when a flock is blown across the Atlantic by a gale, as happened in 1927.

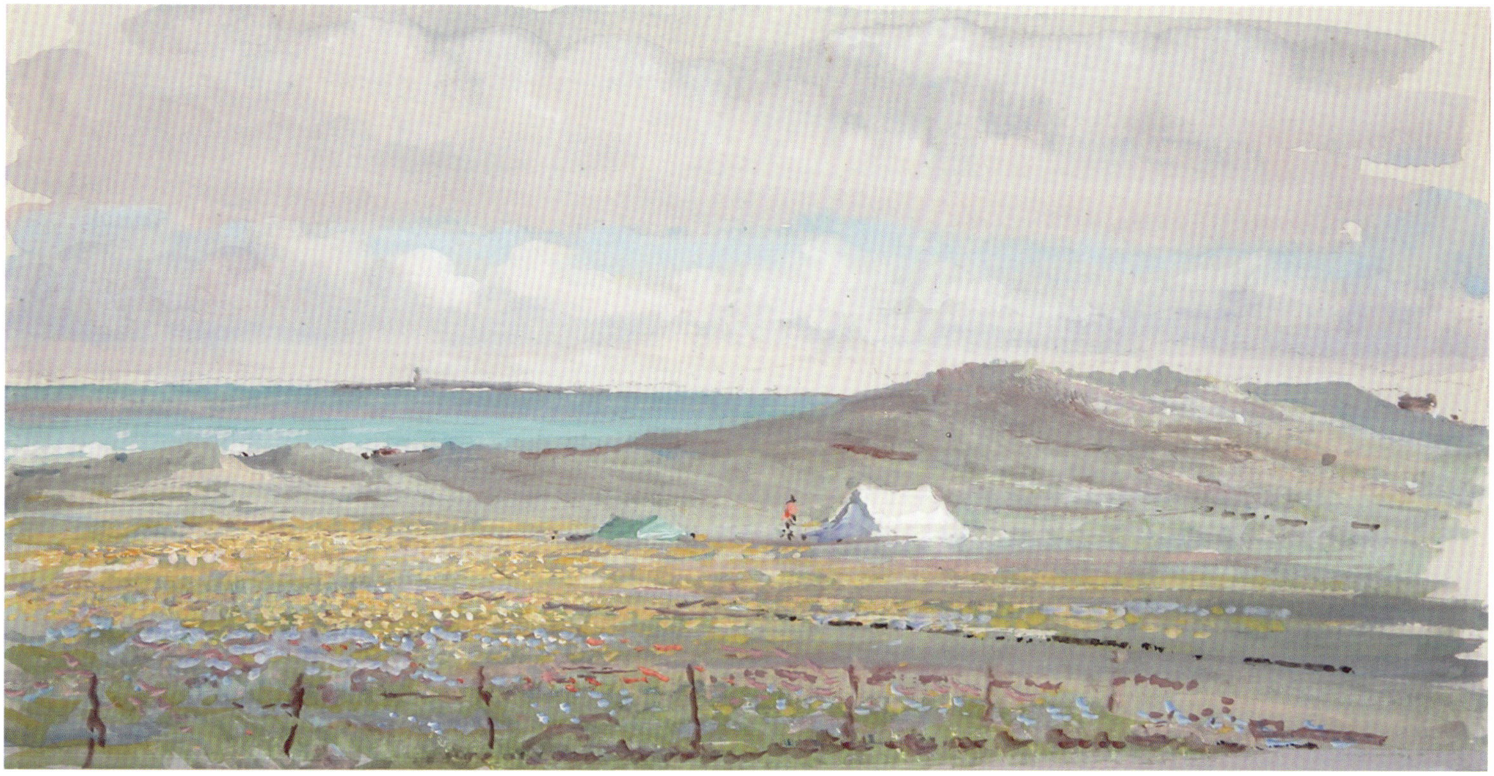

Joan at the tent

The sketch of my wife Joan at our tent, in her red anorak, was done from a distant memory, years later. We certainly had our fair share of gales on that 1950 visit. The tent was almost blown away on some nights.

I painted a picture of the Atlantic breakers with an Eider duck and its ducklings which still hangs in our house. It was also painted on the spot and was criticised by our crofter neighbour for having a fence closer to the sea than he thought that anyone would have put one.

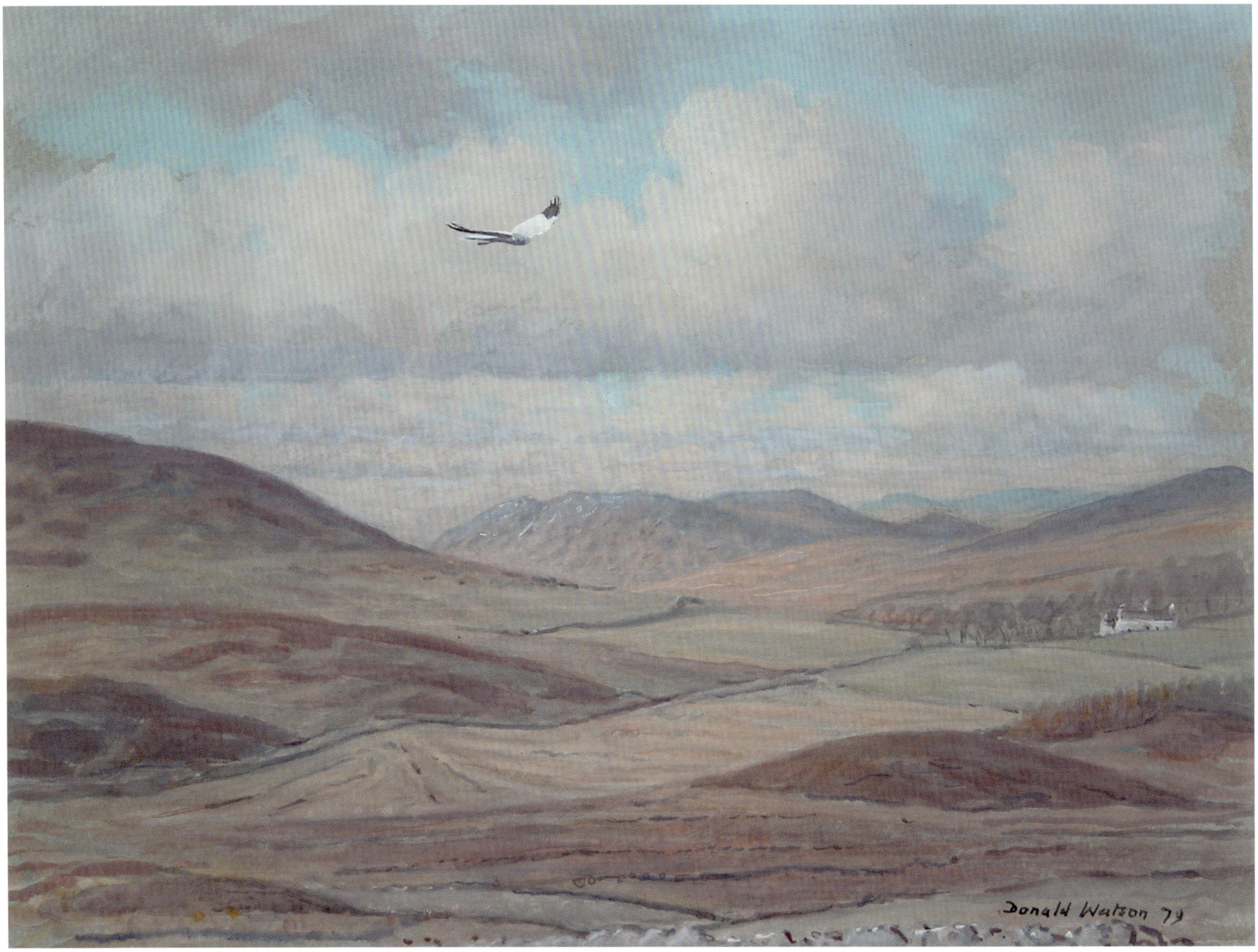
Donald Watson 79

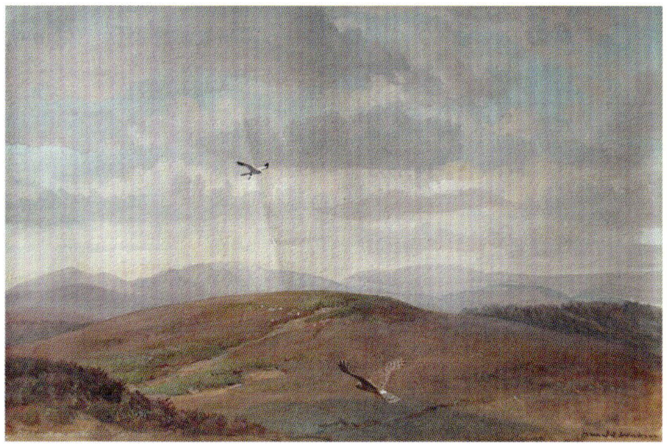

A pair of Hen Harriers at Benmeal and Merlins in the Galloway Forest Park, 1980

My nephew, Roger, and I failed to find the nest of this pair of harriers. I tried again with other companions but with no success. This is not the painting I would have wished to include for this subject but I was unable to trace the owner of my 1980 painting. I could never fathom how the nest eluded us. We saw the male arrive with prey several times and sometimes saw the female come up and take a food-pass. We realised that the nest must be among dense conifers on the lower slope of Benmeal but even an exhausting search through the dense, prickly forest was fruitless. Towards the end of July, a fledged young bird was flying above the trees. Then I abandoned the search.

When ten years later I was told by Don Scott of Hen Harriers nesting successfully high up in conifer forest in Co. Antrim, Northern Ireland, and I went over to see one of these, I half-wondered whether we had missed a tree-nest in Galloway. But I do not think so, as the Benmeal trees were much younger and a tree-nest would have been obvious. At first it was assumed that the harriers were using old nests of Crows or Sparrowhawks but Don Scott found that the harriers had built the nests themselves. To date it seems that no Hen Harriers have taken to tree-nesting in Galloway and probably nowhere else in Scotland or England. The Spotted Harrier has long been known as a tree-nester in Australia. It might have been a ground-nester long ago and possibly took to trees to avoid ground predators. I am not the only person who has thought that the Hen Harrier might have avoided much persecution by taking to nesting high in conifers in Britain. Certainly they sometimes roost in such situations in south Germany, where Goshawks can be a threat to them at ground roosts.

Roger and I watched mostly from near the unplanted top of Benmeal. From there we had an unrivaled prospect of the big range of mountains to the west which are in the painting. Our viewpoint was above the planted lower slope. Somewhere among these trees the nest had to be. The male harrier would come towards us with long glides and flaps, but as he got near he would disappear from view among the trees below us, and we could not identify the spot where the female rose. We saw and heard the arrivals of a pair of Merlins when prey was brought to downy young in their nest among rocks and boulders. Merlin nests we found in those days were always 'ground-nests,' some on low cliffs in the forest park. These sites were abandoned as the forest matured, when most became tree-nesters. It was not certain how much the numbers declined, as the tree-nests in the depths of forest blocks were much harder to locate, but Merlins always depended on open moorland country outside the forest for most of their hunting.

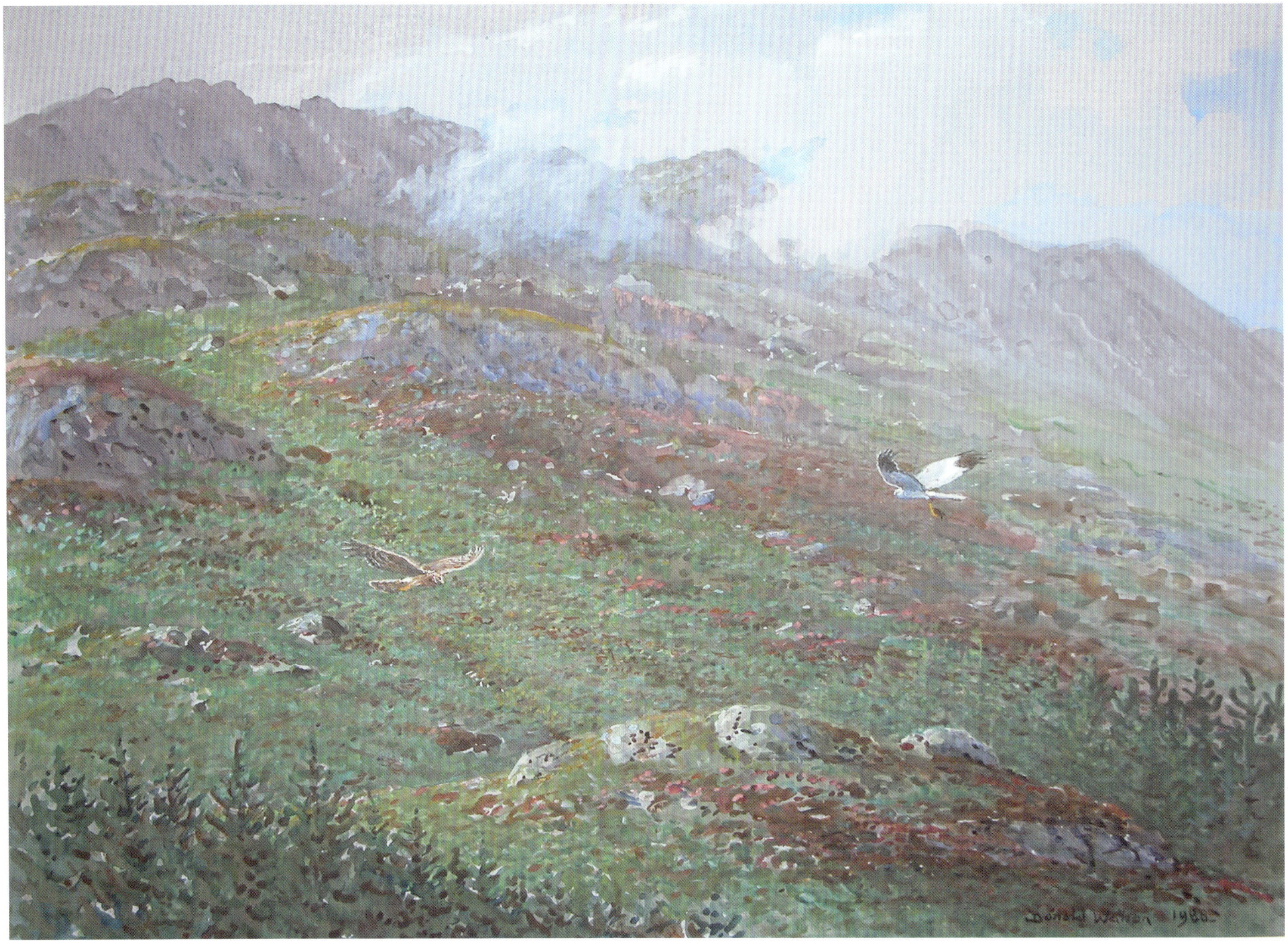

Pair of Hen Harriers food-passing over the open hill (Cairngarroch near Craigencallie), 1988

This painting was of the pair which chose the open heather and bracken slope above the forest, in 1988. I think the rich colours of dark heather and green bracken helped to highlight the birds. Far up the hill the burn was in spate, drawing the eye there. Silence would sometimes be shattered by the staccato barking of a Roe buck as it made its way up the hill. When it was near the harrier nest with young, the male harrier would dive at it, calling excitedly, its 'whickering' alarm much lower-pitched, more reedy sounding than the female's.

When they left the nest, the young did not go far but waited on the hillside for the female to bring prey to them and would fly up to her and try to catch it in a food-pass, not always successfully. The male was no longer bringing prey at this stage, when I watched with Robin Shillcock, one of the artists who travelled abroad with 'Artists for Nature' to paint. I think that was the year that they worked in the wonderful marshlands in eastern Poland.

Young Hen Harriers in Britain usually stay fairly near the nest for about three weeks after fledging. In Wisconsin, U.S.A., young carrying radio transmitters have been tracked for long distances after leaving their natal area. Once when a bird was flying near Milwaukee, the trackers followed a signal which turned out to be not from the harrier but from a radio ham in a house in the city. The Wisconsin young harriers left the nesting areas individually, making long migrations southwards.

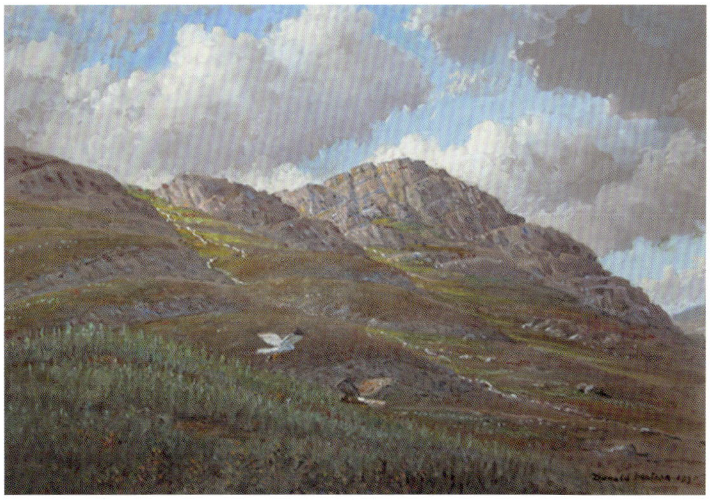

Hen Harriers nesting in the pylon line and on open heather and bracken slopes outside the forest, 1985-93

As more of the forests in Galloway approached clear-felling, Hen Harriers began to find that the blocks of trees offered fewer and fewer possible nest-sites. They did not start to nest high in the conifers, as some did in Northern Ireland. In Galloway there was far more ground cover than in the Irish forests I saw, so it was perhaps not surprising that they continued to nest in this, where they could find enough of it. By the mid-1980s the forest south of the New Galloway–Newton Stewart road was mostly too closed-up and lacking in good secondary cover for harrier nesting. After 1985 nesting apparently ceased in Laurieston and Kitterick–Round Fell areas and the birds moved north of the road. At first I was surprised they were nesting in the fairly narrow strips of unplanted ground where the electricity pylons stood. They were evidently not deterred by the very steep slopes in most of these, but they found good nest-sites in abundant heather, bracken and lemon-scented fern. Nests in 1982–88 were in this and were very successful, though finding them was not easy. I watched a male hunting up the pylon line disappearing from view many times, when dense trees obscured my view. There was certainly a nest in the pylon line in 1985 but the site was never found until the young were flying. Even in 1993 there must have been a nest in the pylon line, in tall bracken in the Tonderghie Glen, where Joan Howie and I watched a pair for a long time but failed to find their nest and could never be sure that any young fledged. In 1986 prey at the nest included a leveret, probably a blue hare.

In 1991 Roger Clarke, watching with me, first realised that there were two grey males, one food-passing to a female towards the north end of the pylon line, the other doing the same at a nest up the heather and bracken slope on the open hill well above the forest. Of these only the pylon-line nest was successful, a fox or possibly a dog accounting for the two young on the open hill. There had been successful nests in a mixture of heather and bracken up the hill in 1989 and 1990. The pylon-line nest was in tall bog myrtle.

The remarkable 1980s nest-site in dense trees was probably exceptional and has never been repeated.

The risks of nest-predation by foxes were demonstrated again when an entire brood of six was certainly taken by a fox from a nest among bog myrtle in the pylon line in July 1992.

The last nest I have seen in central Galloway was in a surprising site, a few yards from a road in long heather near Loch Grannoch. It was found after a long search by Charlie Park and Chris Rollie. Three young were fledged in July 1992.

So no nests in this area were among the trees in these years. Looking back at the dates of nests within forest blocks it is clear that these are generally only suitable for Hen Harrier nesting for a finite period of not more than about 15 years. As there has been no indication that the Galloway harriers have yet nested in the young 're-stock' trees, the future for nesting harriers here is not promising.

The painting is of a pair over the heather and bracken slope up the hill. This was a superb site to watch from a distance, having great landscape painting possibilities, with colours changing according to weather.

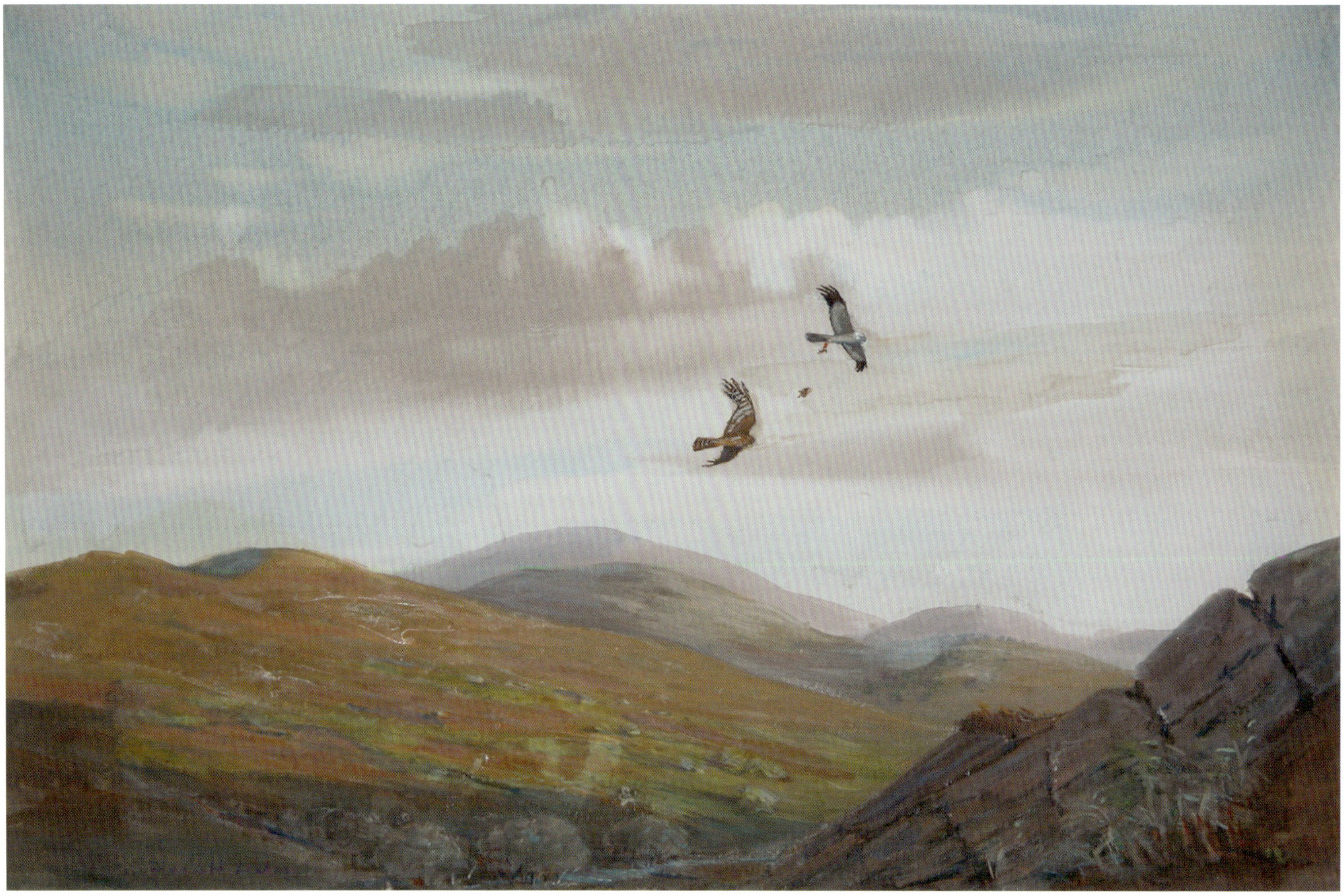

Hen Harriers in front of the Merrick range

The mountain range which stands on the western side of Kirkcudbrightshire includes several of the highest hills in the southern uplands. Merrick, rising to just under 1,000 metres, dominates the skyline in the west. The 711-metre Cairnsmore of Fleet is the highest summit south of the Newton Stewart road. Seen from Wigtownshire the Merrick range makes a fine panorama, only rivalled in Galloway by the Rhinns of Kells viewed from the southeast.

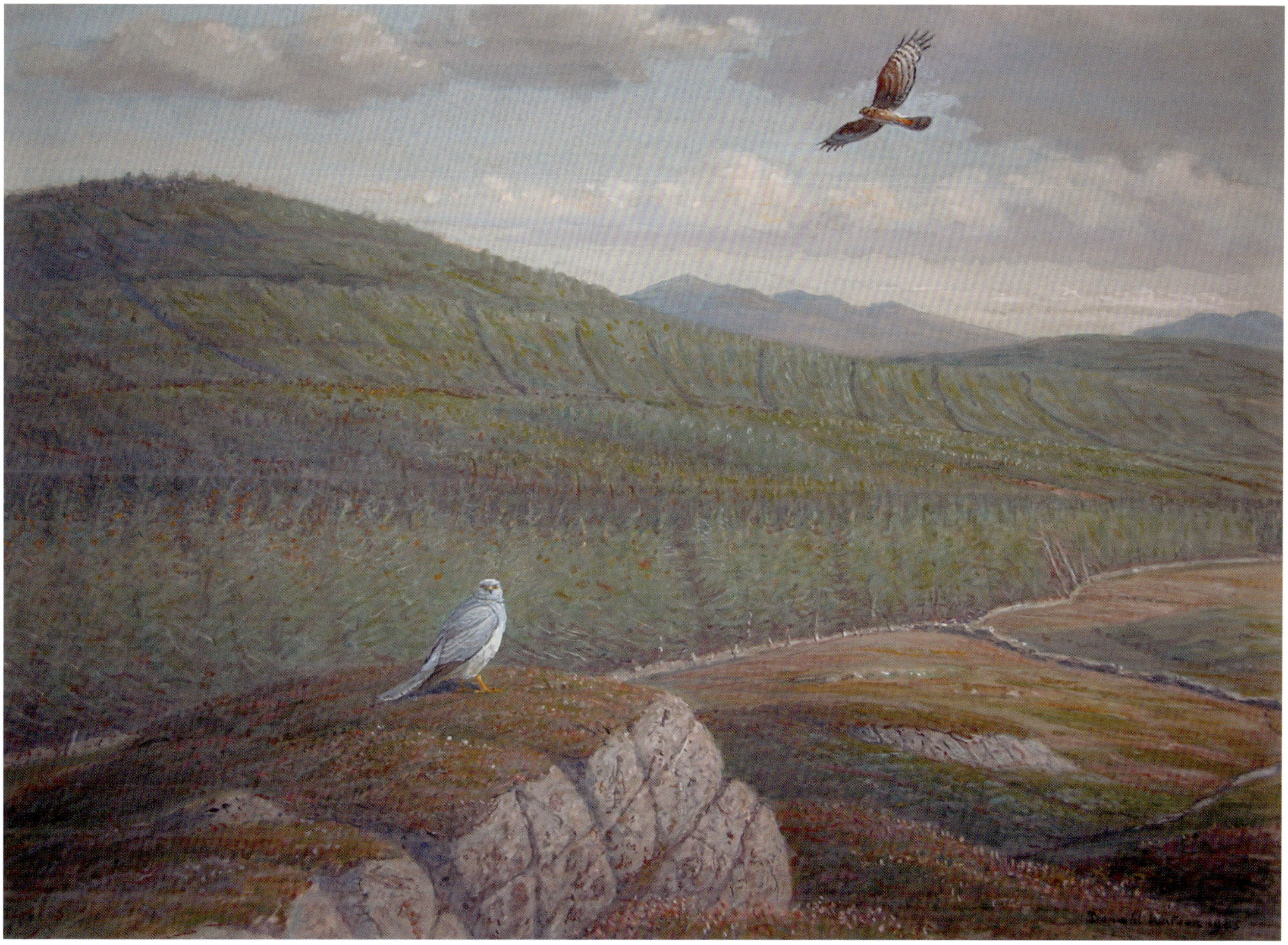

Might Hen Harriers nest on Airie Flowe?

Airie Flowe looks as though it could in its drier parts make a possible site for a nest. I have not known this happen here but I have been told that a nest in England was successful on ground that had for years been a winter roost-site.

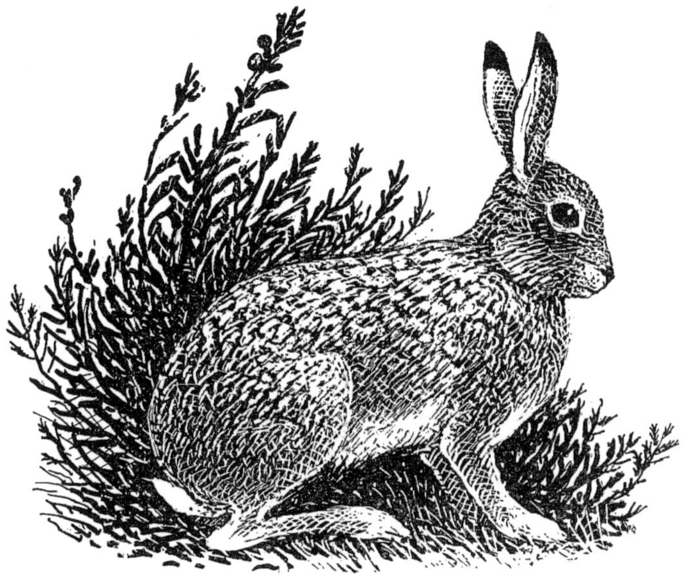

Winter roosts

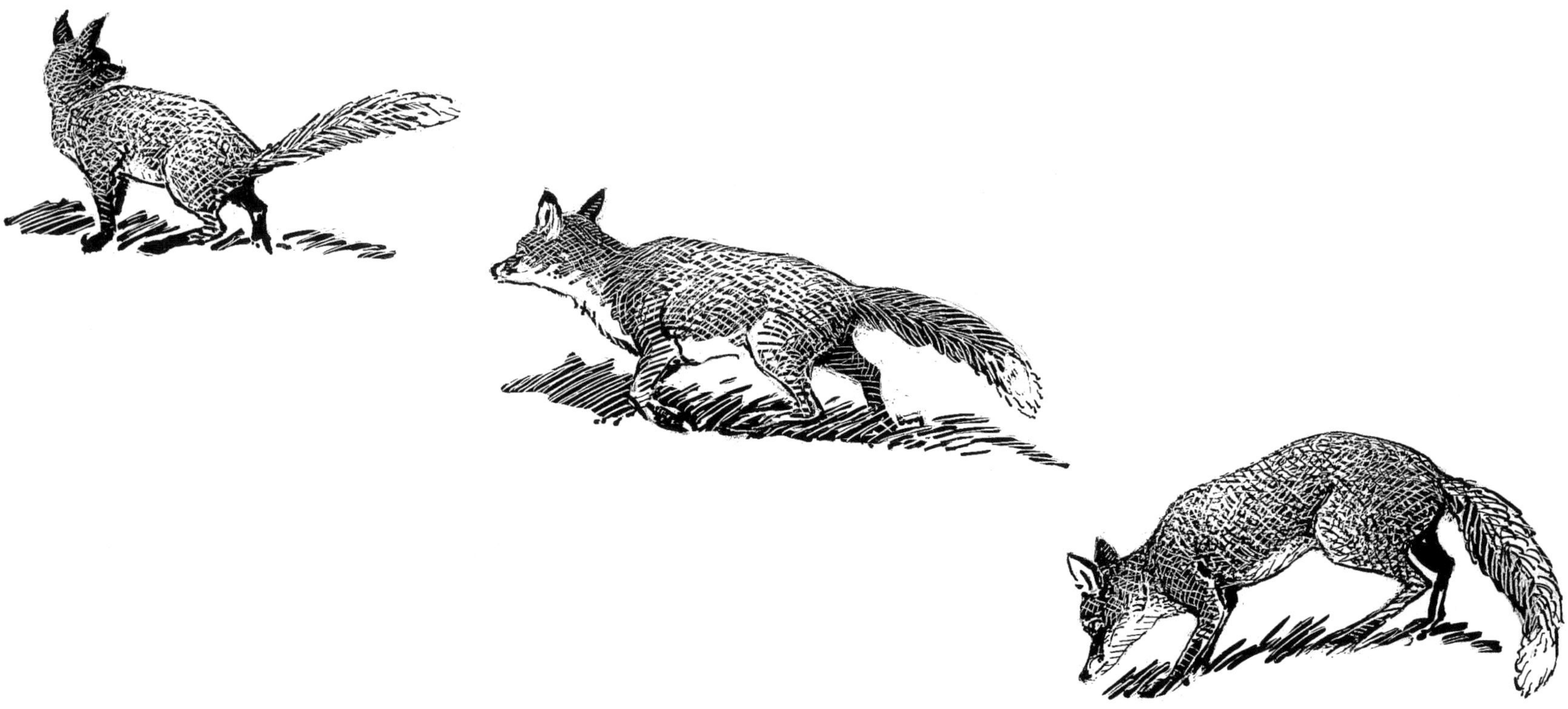

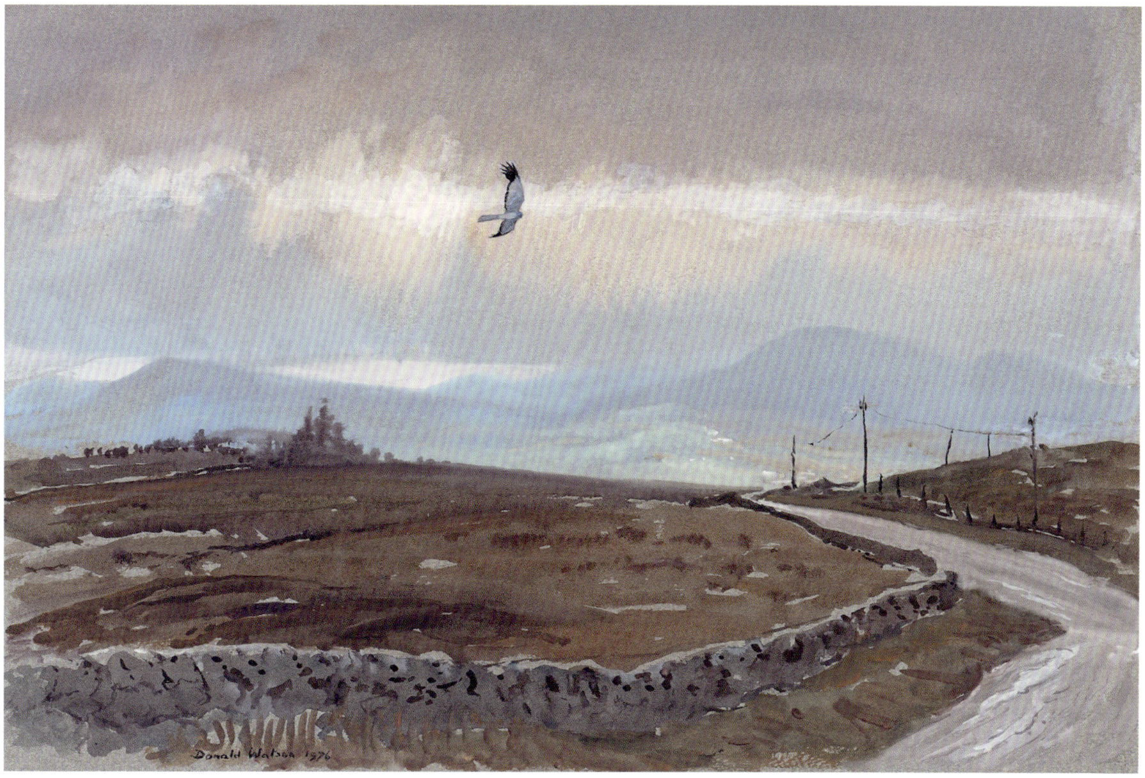

Male Hen Harrier crossing the Moniaive road, 1974

Many years ago, before Galloway farms had combine harvesters, cornstacks were scattered around in cut fields and there were two of these stacks close to the Moniaive road, not far out of my home village, Dalry. I used to drive up to a good viewpoint for watching the birds which gathered there on winter afternoons. Most were finches and buntings, the majority Chaffinches and Yellowhammers. There were quite a few other birds, including Grey Partridges, Wood Pigeons and Pheasants, but I especially enjoyed the Blue Tits attracted by the corn. Nowadays there are many silage fields and the huge black sacks of cut silage are clumped at the edges of these fields. As more and more people in the villages put out food for birds, many small birds have been attracted by this to feed in gardens in the winter. One or two Kestrels or Sparrowhawks and the occasional Merlin would come to the stacks I watched in search of prey. I never saw a Hen Harrier make a kill there, but male Hen Harriers were particularly attracted by weedy turnip fields, where finches were found in numbers. The harrier in the painting would probably be travelling between a roost and known sites for prey. When travelling a distance it would fly fairly high, and was easy to spot against the sky. The highly decorative Red-legged Partridge, reared on shooting estates, has replaced the native Grey almost completely in Galloway. I have even seen a Red-leg crossing the lawn behind our house, which I never saw a Grey Partridge do when Greys were plentiful in the fields near the village.

When I was watching the birds at the stacks, I would often hear the distant, but far-carrying bubbling of Blackcock at the lek near Lochinvar Loch. As the cocks challenged each other they would also make a sound rather like an explosive sneeze. In those days parties of Black Grouse in spring fed on larch buds in the forest which was then growing rapidly beside the Moniaive road. Later, in the 1970s, a forestry ranger told me that he had seen fledged young harriers in this forestry where I had never found a harrier nest, although one year I had seen an unmated male displaying and even starting to build a nest among the young trees. It had spectacular aerial tussles with Short-eared Owls.

The finches always flew away to roost in the conifers long before dusk while Robins, with their large eyes, could continue feeding till or even after dark. Driving homeward for a couple of miles along a forest road I would sometimes flush eight or nine Robins in the darkness.

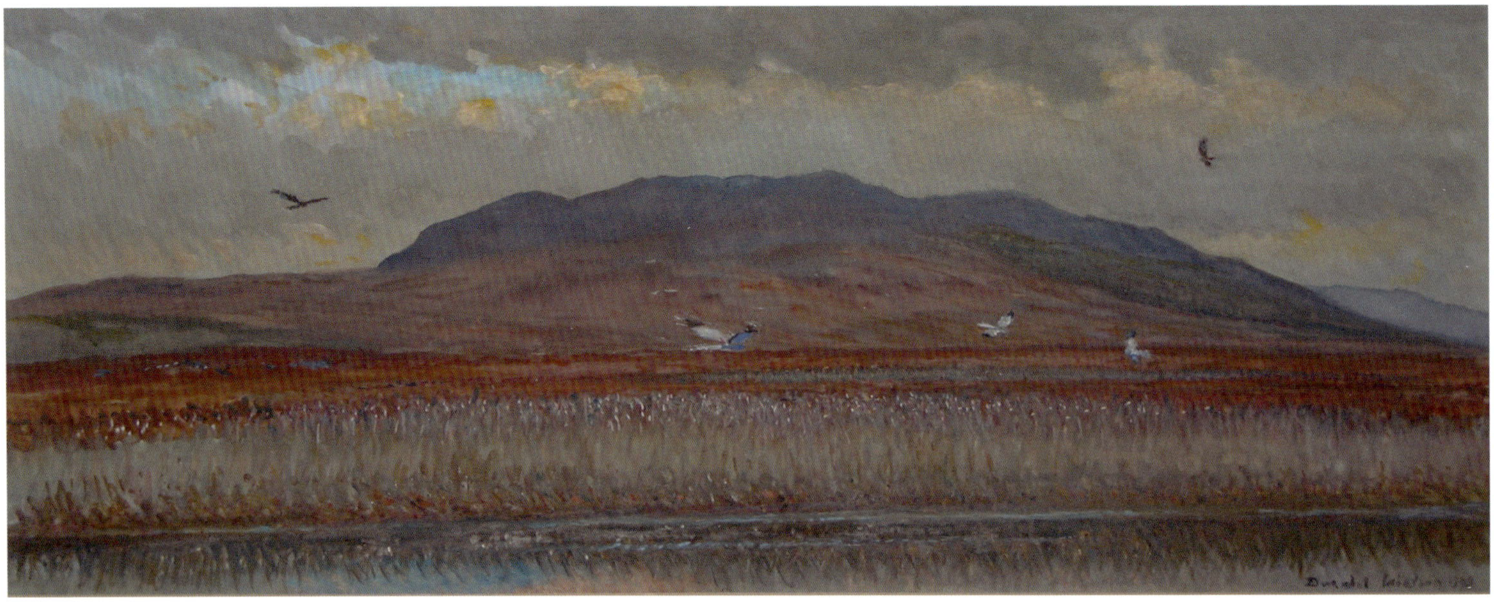

Hen Harriers at Airie Flowe roost, 1969

The five harriers in this painting were by no means as many as would sometimes be seen at this period. The best numbers could be 20–30, occasionally over 30. Once one female, which had been flying low over the roost, crossed the river to attack me, diving very close to my head. I was inclined to believe that it must have been a bird that recognised me from when it had bred at one of the Galloway sites that I had visited in the summer, when it had been very aggressive at the nest. It made the 'whickering' calls that are usually made when a nest is approached. Several other harriers came briefly out of the sky to join in the attack, but soon returned to the roost area. This was a time when the numbers breeding in Galloway were at their peak, and many of the birds coming to the winter roost doubtless included birds from the local breeding population and their young. Harriers from distant nesting places certainly made up a proportion of those wintering in southwest Scotland, as a few had wing-tags which marked them as coming from much further north. There was never any evidence that any were immigrants from continental Europe, which might have been a possibility.

The greatest numbers of birds at the roost were most often seen on windy, mild evenings. Very cold nights produced low counts, or none at all, especially in hard frost. A high count could be followed by a very low one if conditions changed rapidly. It seemed that freezing weather deterred harriers from roosting in this partly water-logged site, as ice could result in frozen legs, or even wings, trapping the birds. There was also the risk of predation by foxes.

It is clear from this painting that the sky was overcast and rain was not far away. Some of the highest counts occurred on really wet nights when it would be difficult to count birds and particularly testing for accurate observation.

When I first found this roost-site I had no idea how long it had been in existence. It may have had a long history but would hardly have been much occupied during the long period when intensive persecution made the Hen Harrier a rare bird over most of Scotland. It is likely that a recent increase in persecution on many grouse moors is an important factor in the reduction in numbers of them at many winter roosts lately.

Walking into Airie roost in daytime was quite treacherous, as some parts of it were so wet that water would come over the tops of Wellingtons. I paid a few visits to collect pellets and found a number of them. The forms made by the roosting harriers were easily spotted from the trampled vegetation and splashes of white droppings surrounding them.

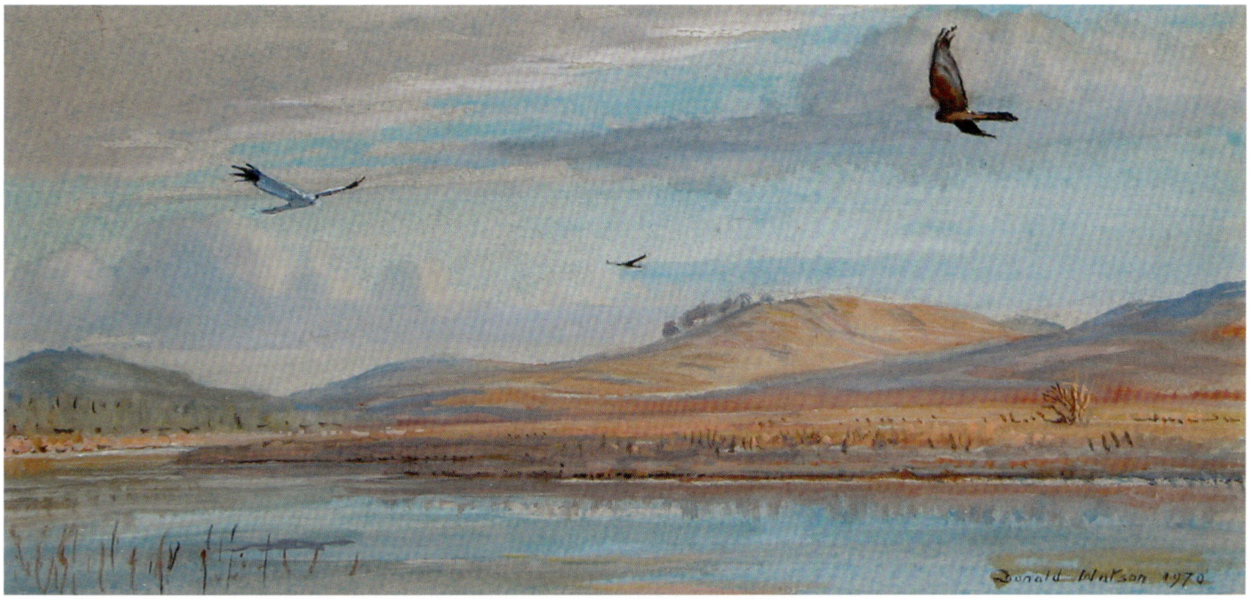

Hen Harriers at Airie roost

This painting treats the subject simply, concentrating on the birds. Airie Hill is in the background, under a cloudy sky with perhaps a threat of rain. Certainly a mild evening, when at that time, many more than are shown here would be expected in about an hour's watch. The flowe is mainly painted thinly with a large watercolour brush in a single wash of mixed colour on a light grey paper, allowing this to somewhat neutralise the yellow-brown molinia. I found that using a toned paper was useful, helping me to get the unity of effect I wanted. The small willow bush on the right middle ground was a familiar landmark in the roost area, for which I would have used a smaller brush. I had to avoid detail on this to convey that it was some distance out in the flowe, but it needed to be a long way in front of the background hill. In a painting like this, it was essential to get the 'tones' right. Strictly, the medium is gouache, not pure watercolour, allowing the birds to be overpainted on the landscape. Obviously it is a fairly windless evening, and I have suggested cloud reflection in the foreground to help the distance to go away. The few sprigs of vegetation in the foreground, probably rushes (juncus), with a slight indication of reflection in the calm water, may be a balance to the nearest-incoming female harrier.

As the most important features in the painting, the birds had to be painted with care, the flight postures aiming to make them instantly believable as harriers flying in at different distances. Harriers have a distinctive wing-shape and rather long tail, which make them easily distinguished from Buzzards or falcons. Using opaque white very sparingly gives the contrast between the light males and the darker brown females, though the shadowed underside of the male against the sky looks quite dark. Although the sky is grey and cloudy, it is still the source of light and a flying bird always looks dark against it on the underside of its wing.

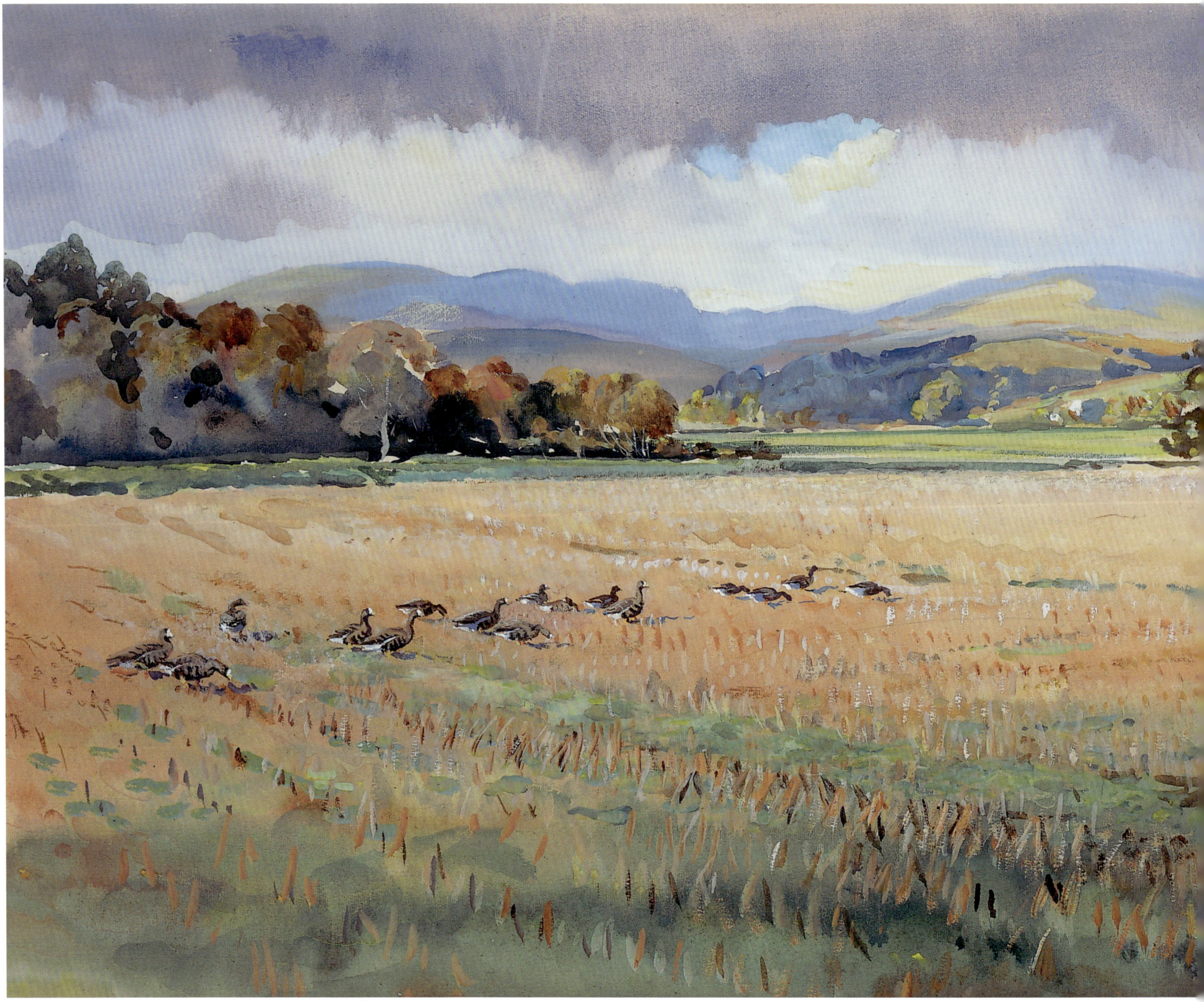

Greenland White-fronted Geese feeding at Kenmuir Holmes in the Ken Valley, near Donald's home, before going off to roost at Loch Stroan.

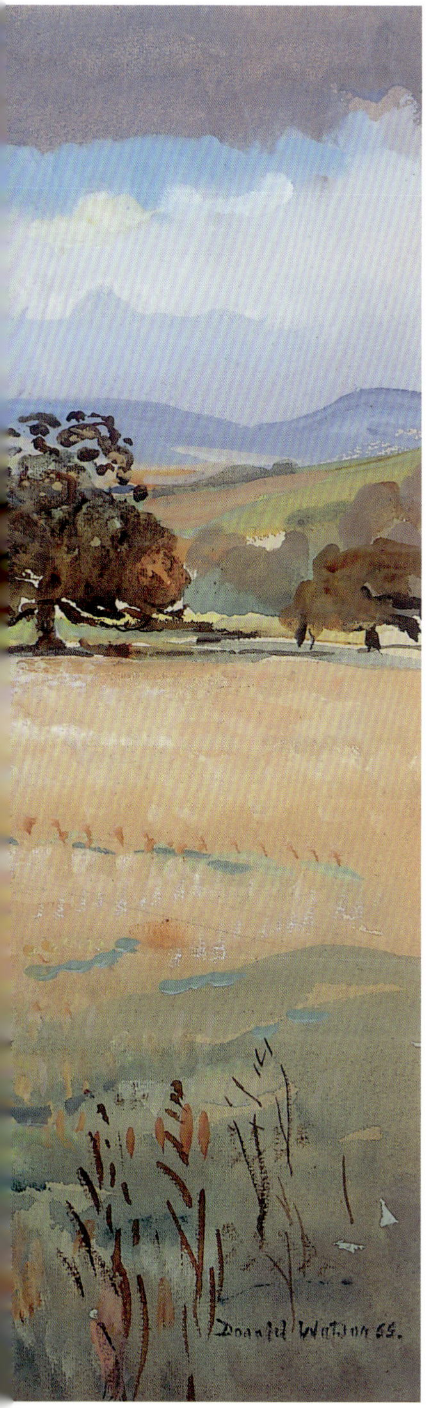

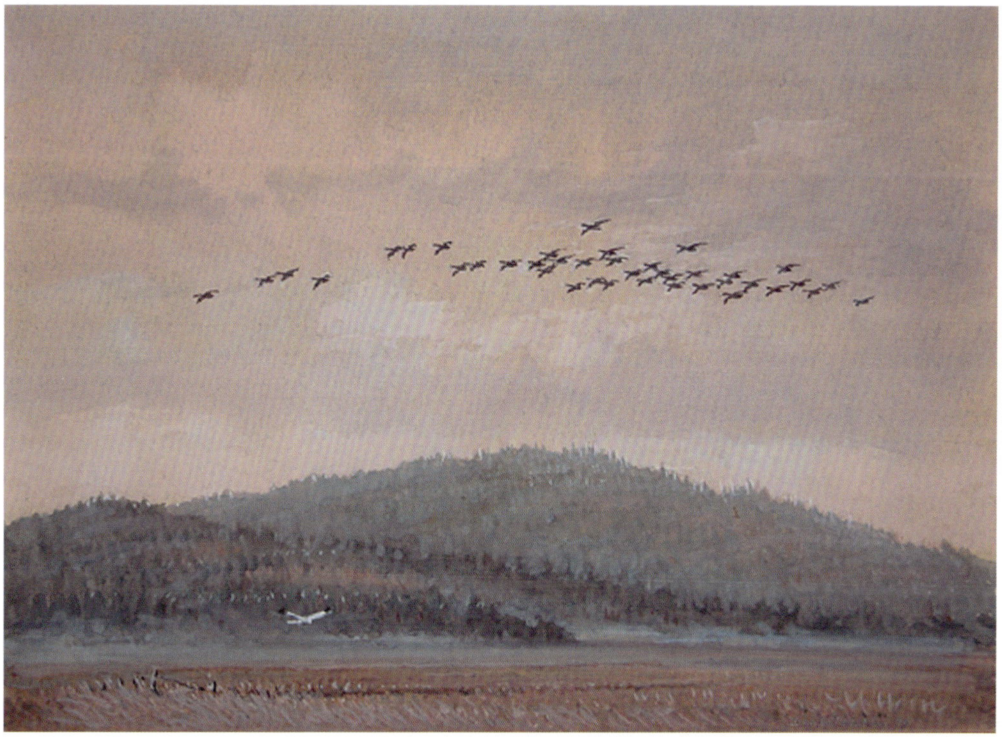

Dawn at the Black Water of Dee

Here comes a skein of geese – they have to be Greenland Whitefronts heading for their feeding grounds in the Ken Valley. Looking at this little picture I am reminded of their calls, always heard before the flock is seen, the pleasantest of all goose music; in the distance they remind me of happy children's laughter. When the flocks flew northwest in April, I would often see some leaving their winter haunts in Galloway at the start of the long flight to their breeding sites in the east of Greenland. Hugh Boyd, an authority on goose migration, thinks it possible that some of these Whitefronts fly direct to Greenland from Britain or Ireland, but so far he has no certain proof that they do not all break their journey in Iceland.

My main object of an early morning watch at the roost was to find out when the harriers flew out and in what direction. On 24 December 1990, the first bird, a male, was airborne at 8.05 a.m., when there was only a glimmer of light in the sky. Some early risers could easily have been missed, especially ringtails. I could not spot any birds as they rose from the ground. By 9.10 at least seven birds had left the roost, heading in different directions. A few days later, John Wykes, out after deer early, saw three grey males flying in line across the flowe but said that some harriers 'hung about' over the roost for more than an hour. The small flock of geese flew away from their roost at about 8.30, when the sky was very bright.

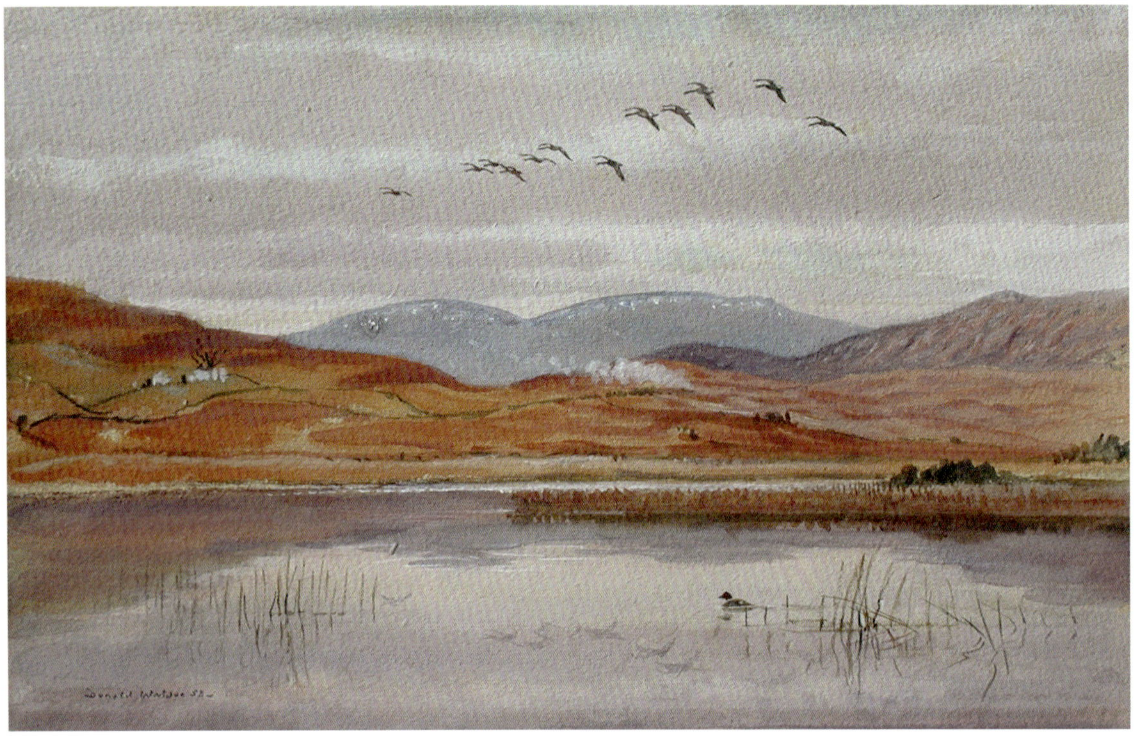

Loch Stroan

This painting was done long after the railway which used to cross the viaduct was closed down. Nowadays quite a few people walk along the disused railway as far as Loch Skerrow or beyond to where the Big Water of Fleet viaduct still stands. The railway track is a good place for butterflies in high summer. In addition to the commonest species (Small Heaths abound), Common Blues, Large Skippers, Small Pearl-bordered Fritillaries and in most years Painted Ladies catch the eye, and it is much favoured by Small Coppers. It is also a haunt of Adders. The painting shows a small skein of Greenland White-fronted Geese in flight. At times in the winter a large flock settles on the loch and I have seen them come down further up the Black Water of Dee to bathe and converse merrily. In mild winters the old railway attracts many small birds like Stonechats, Reed Buntings, thrushes and tits. No attempt has been made to keep the track open as a walkway so in many parts it is much overgrown with trees and bushes. Loch Stroan, lacking islands, does not have Common Gulls nesting as they have done for many years at Loch Skerrow, though lately in declining numbers.

When watching the Hen Harrier roost on Airie Flowe I used always to hear the yaffling of Green Woodpeckers from the remnants of hardwood among the conifers at Nether Gairloch, but as the plantations have grown up there the Woodpeckers may no longer find nest-sites.

I once saw two duck Goosanders quarreling over a nest-hole in an ash in Nether Gairloch wood. Goosanders visit any of the lochs in the vicinity, but Loch Skerrow is probably the nearest where they breed. The spread of feral Greylags continues.

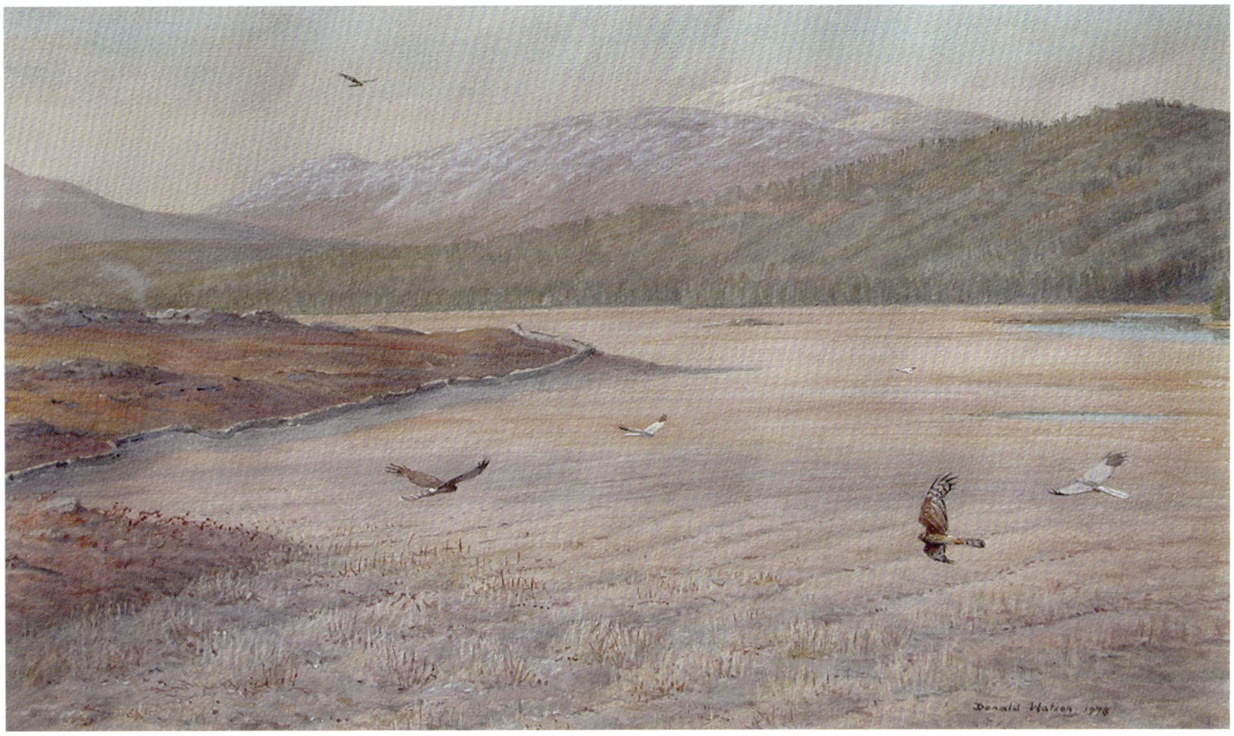

Loch Stroan

A friend, seeing Loch Stroan for the first time, was reminded of Finland. As you drive down towards the loch along the Raiders Road, the conifer forest can look almost natural. On a calm evening the large amount of low-lying unplantable ground at the far end makes a welcome break in the forest. The Black Water of Dee snakes through this to the loch, most beautiful when the distant mountains are reflected in the water. The treeless gap is orange-coloured on a fine autumn evening. The harrier roost is almost out of view from here, but approaching birds often came from this side having spent the day in the Ken Valley or further to the east. At the car park there is a plaque in memory of Charlie Parley, who was head forester here for many years. When he was a boy at school the teacher thought he was pulling her leg when he gave his name as 'Charlie Parley' and he got the tawse for cheek.

The railway across the viaduct at this end of Loch Stroan (note the train in this painting) was closed down by Beeching in 1966, when we took our young family on its last run to Stranraer. There used to be a pair or two of Golden Plover nesting on the heather between the railway and the loch. There are still Curlews nesting on the molinia ground alongside the harrier roost. A reed-bed now has Great-crested Grebes breeding, and in autumn the Swallow roost there can be very large.

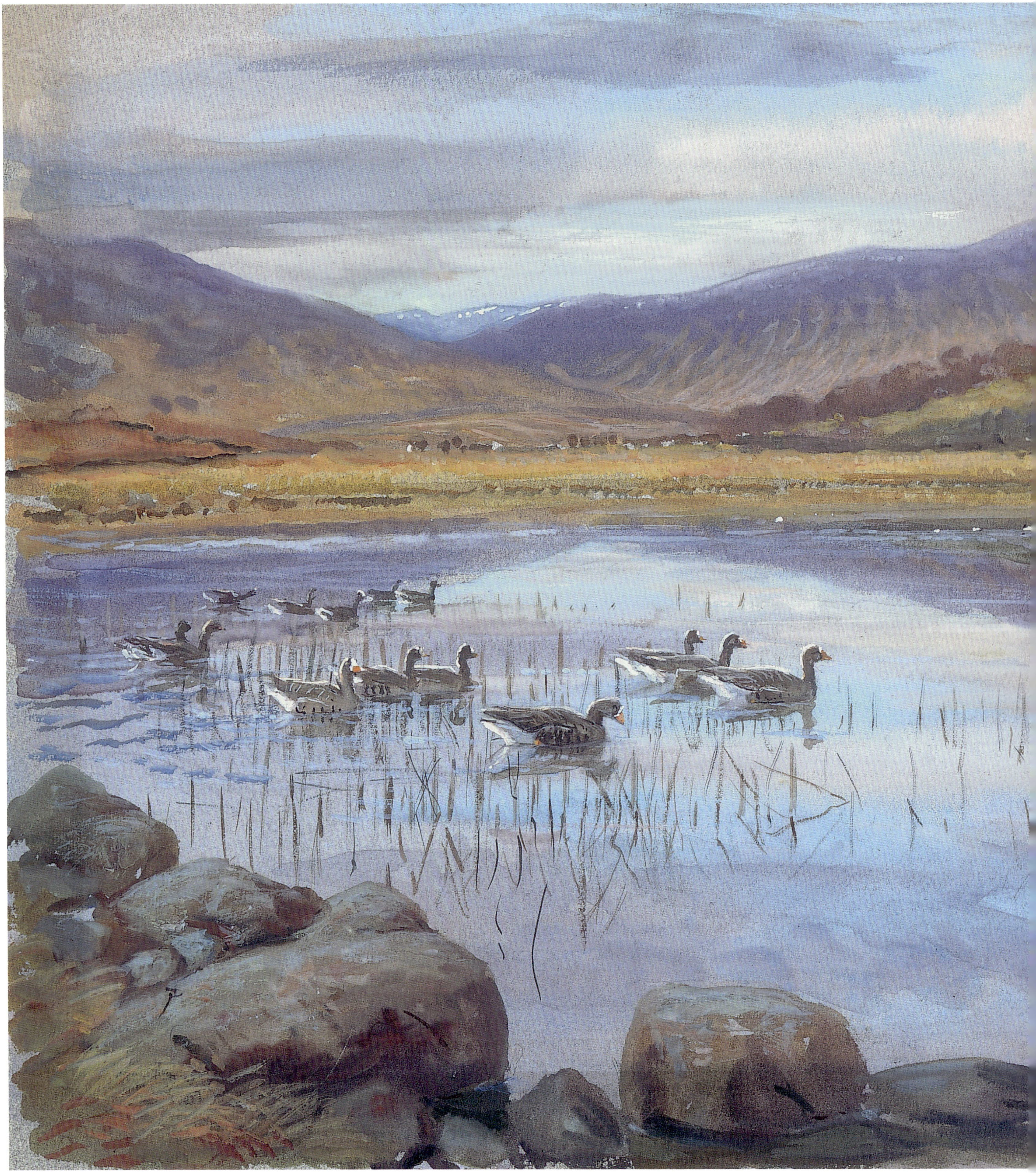

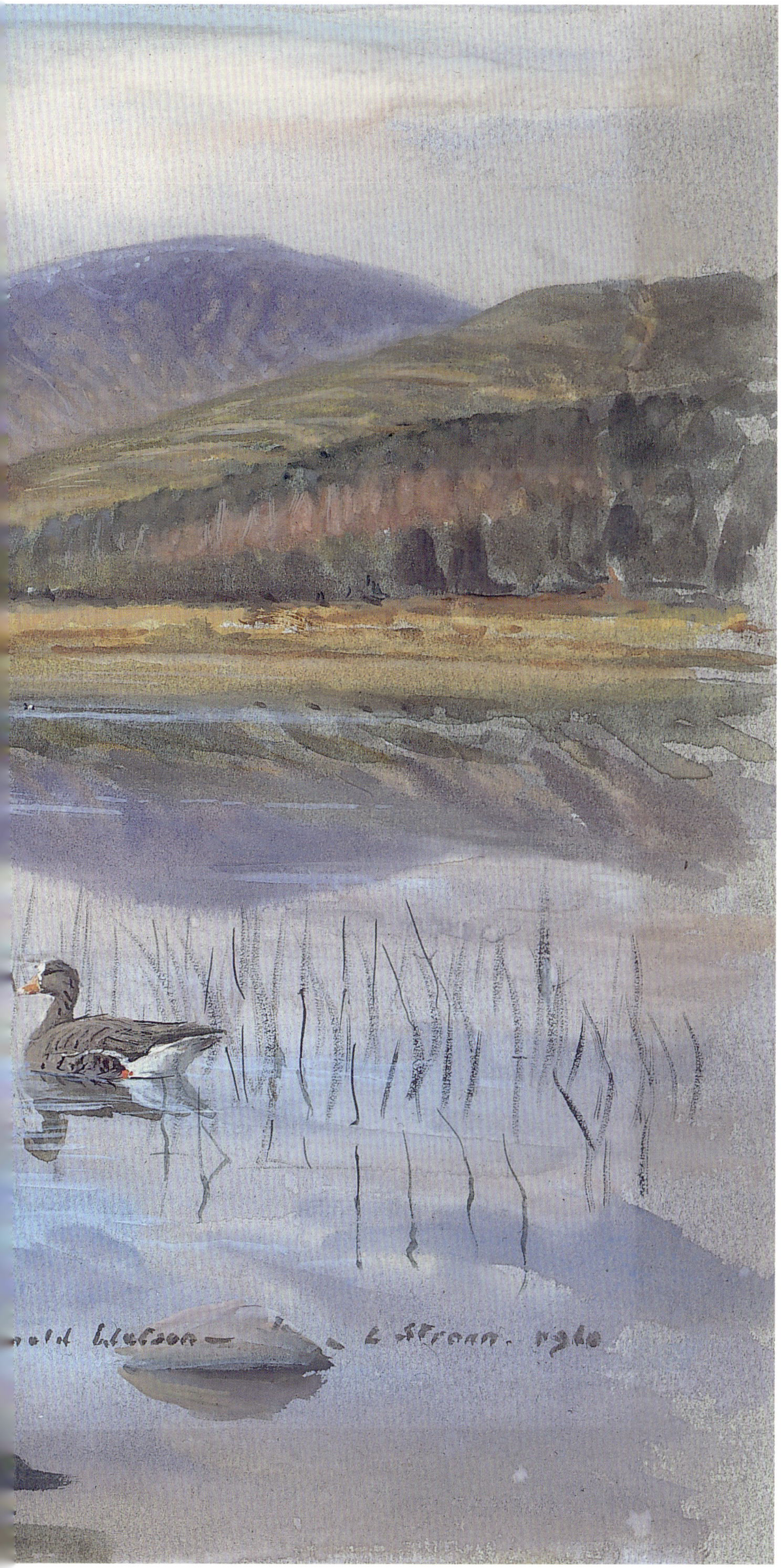

Greenland White-fronted Geese roosting on Loch Stroan.

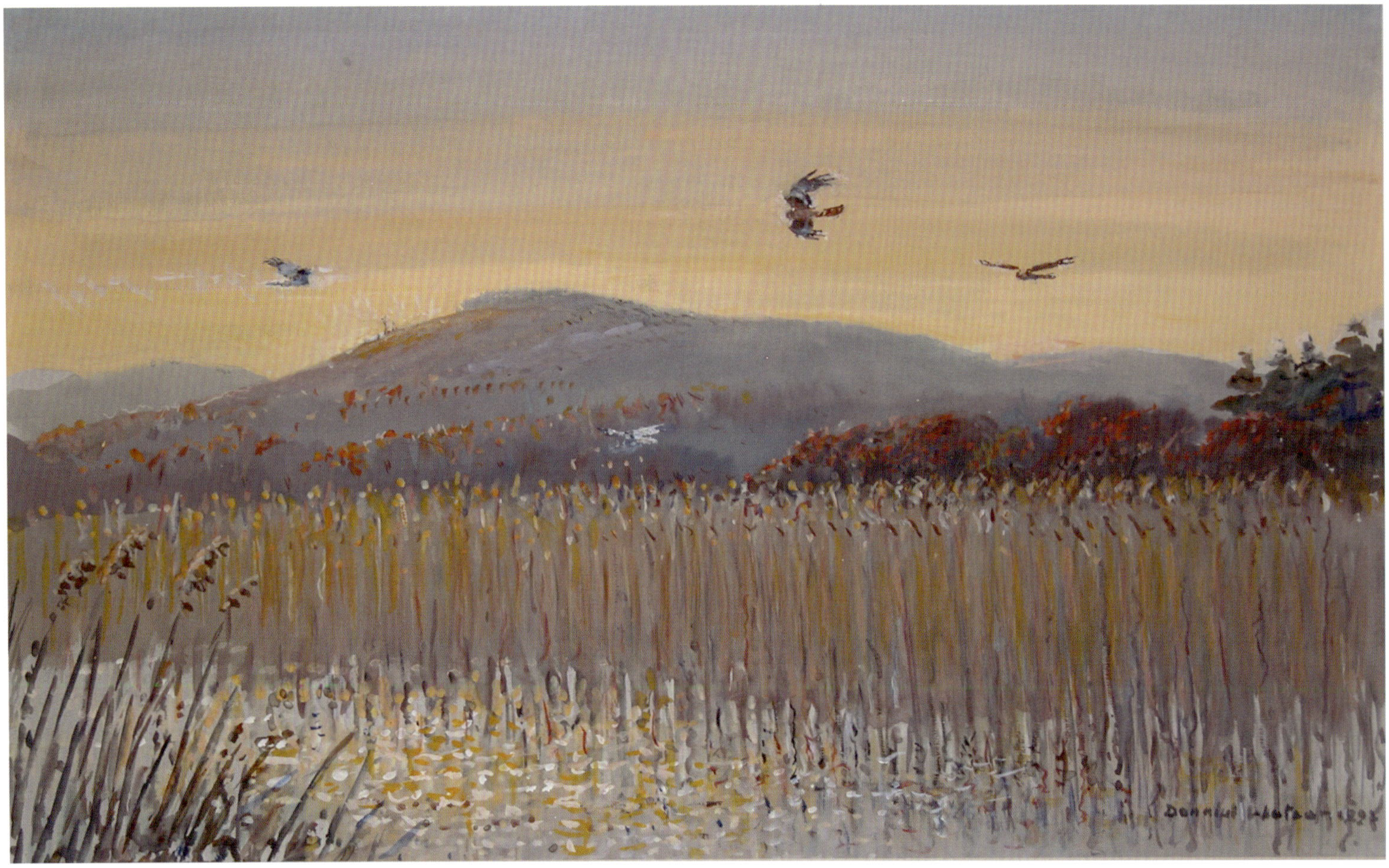

Hen Harriers at Airie Hill, 1991

It was not unusual for males to be the majority of harriers coming in to the roost-site on the flat Airie Flowe in October. In this painting, the impressive mass of Airie Hill looks dark and brooding, setting off the light-coloured adult males to great effect. On some evenings, quite a procession of them would fly in along the riverbank, following the same line, keeping to a low level just above the stand of pale creamy-yellow Tufted Hair Grass rising tall above the riverbank. The 7 October 1991 was an exceptionally good evening, a count of 12–16 being recorded, very high numbers for recent years. Typically for October, adult males outnumbered ringtails by 10–13 to 2–3. The highest counts are nearly always made on windy mild evenings. There is no doubt that the harriers make use of the wind when hunting or travelling. On cold, still evenings, it seems that most stay to roost on their hunting grounds, avoiding slow and tiring flights to a communal roost, and there they may roost singly or in small groups.

Many times I have seen an Otter, occasionally two, on the river when roost-watching. On one unforgettable evening, many years ago, with Dr Grace Fleming, one came onto the bank where we were standing and passed within touching distance before diving into the water with a loud 'plop.'

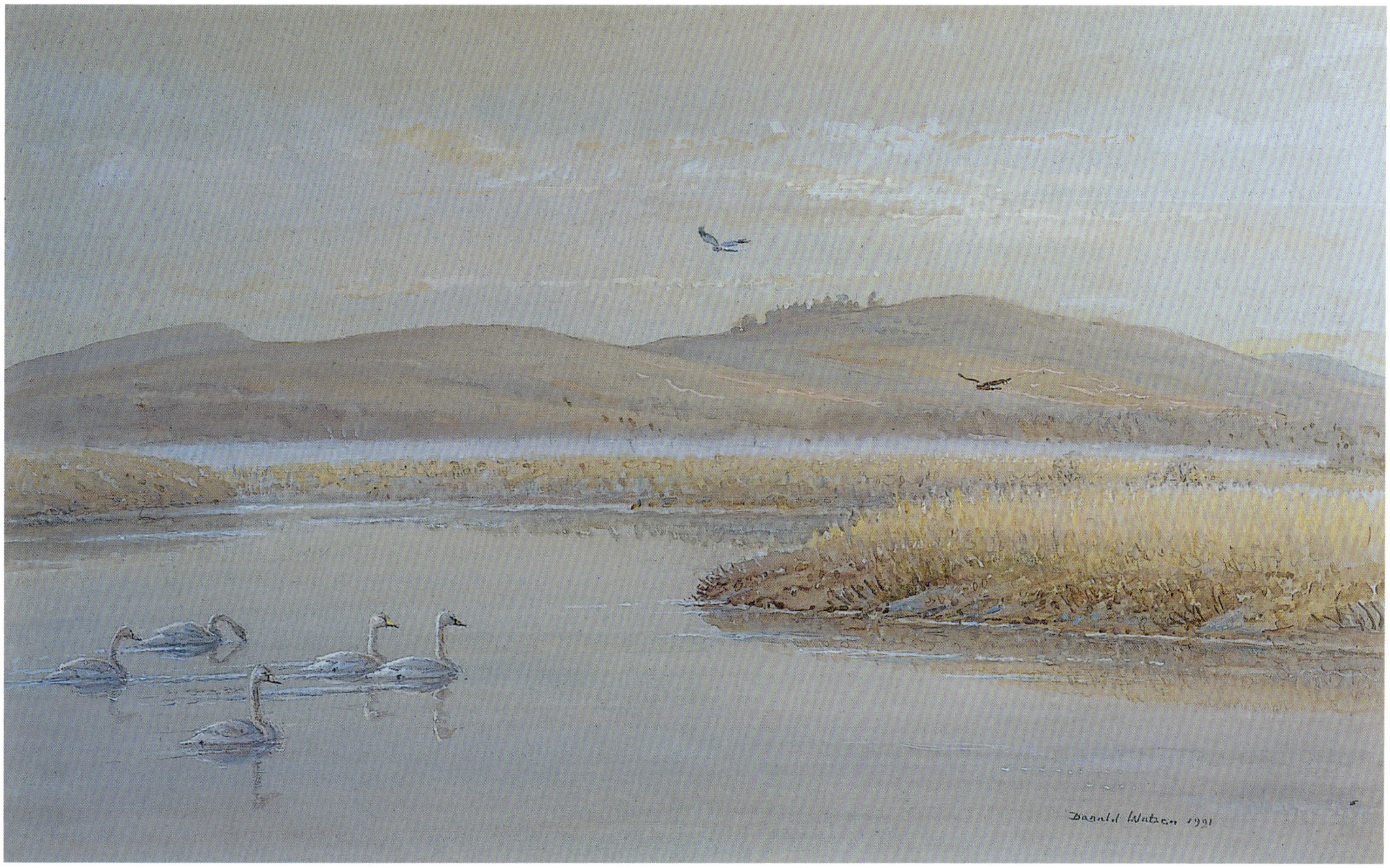

Whooper Swans and Hen Harriers near Airie Flowe roost

The soft trumpeting of Whooper Swans is one of the most evocative sounds that I have heard when watching the long-established harrier roost on the flowe beside the Black Water of Dee. This is surely the most beautiful landscape setting for a harrier roost in Galloway. It is only now and again that a flock of Whoopers add their special charm to the scene. They would have flown up river from Loch Ken. The background in this painting is looking down river.

To the west and north it is more dramatic, with a range of higher mountains taking the eye to distant Cairnsmore of Fleet. On a fine evening, shafts of eye-dazzling sunlight can make the harriers flying to the roost hard to follow. Once the sun has dropped behind the mountains, the birds are much easier to see, until darkness slowly makes it impossible to continue watching. All the harriers apparently come in before dark.

Whooper Swans. A regular visitor to Airie Flowe.

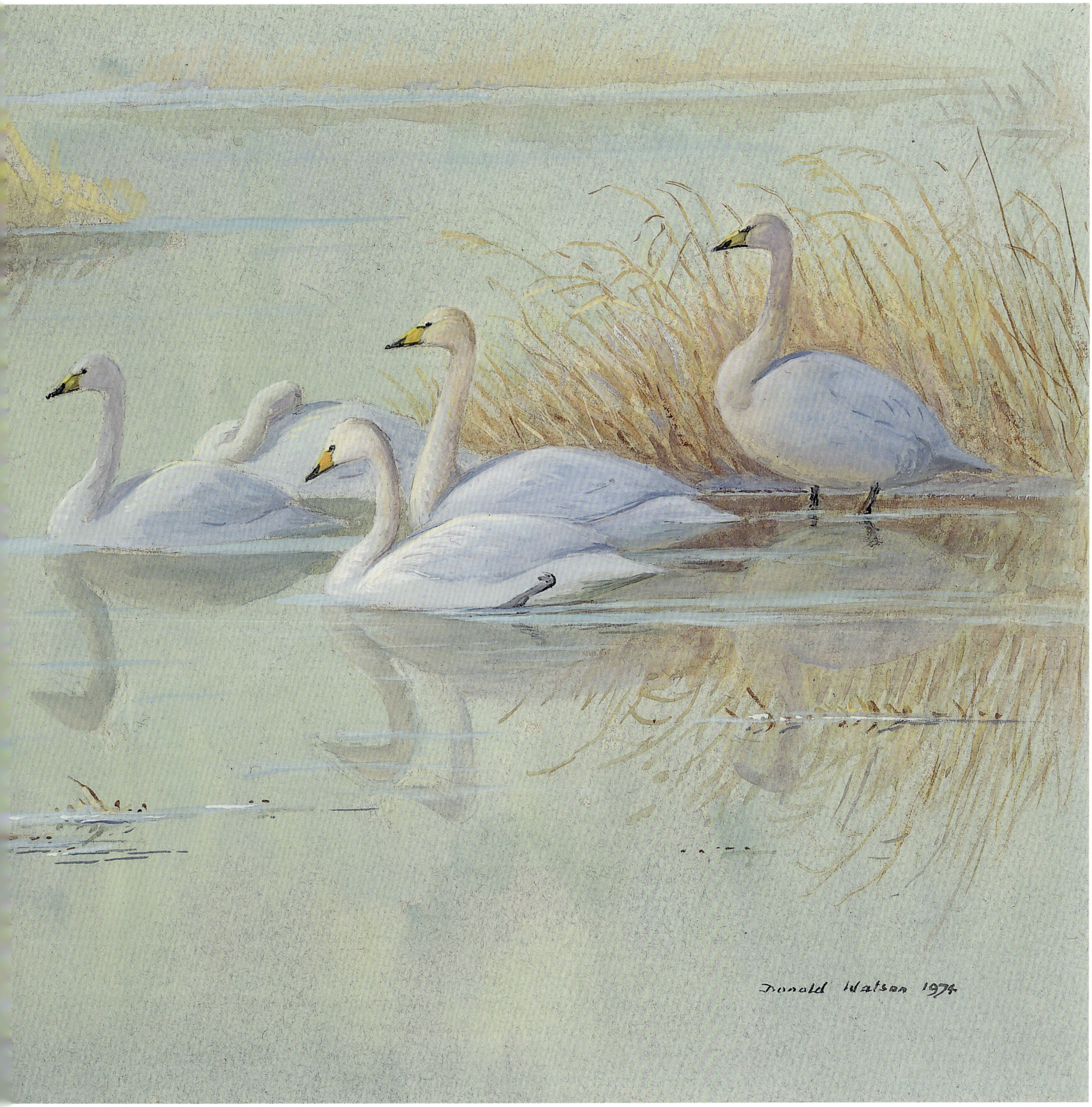
Donald Watson 1974

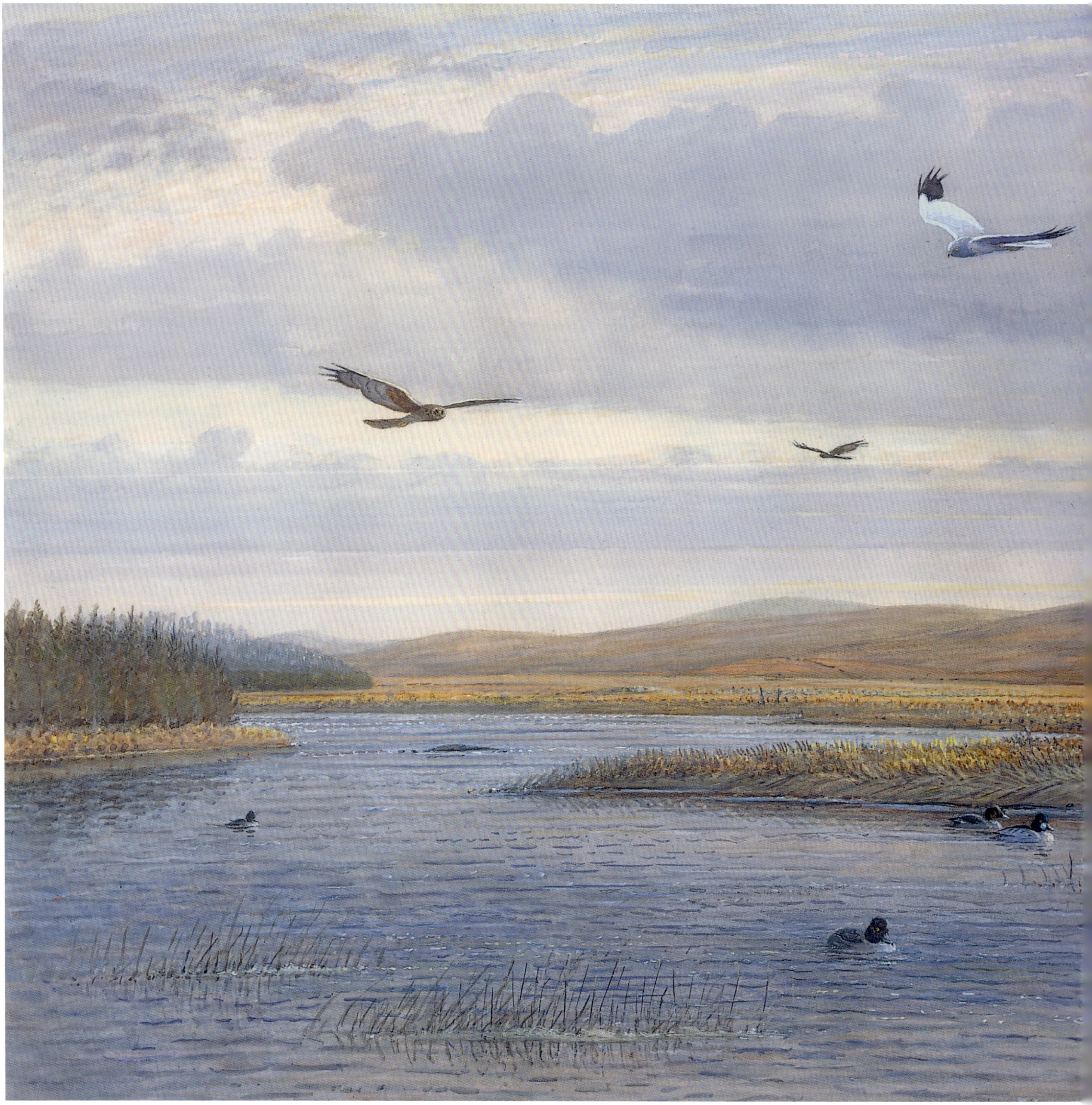

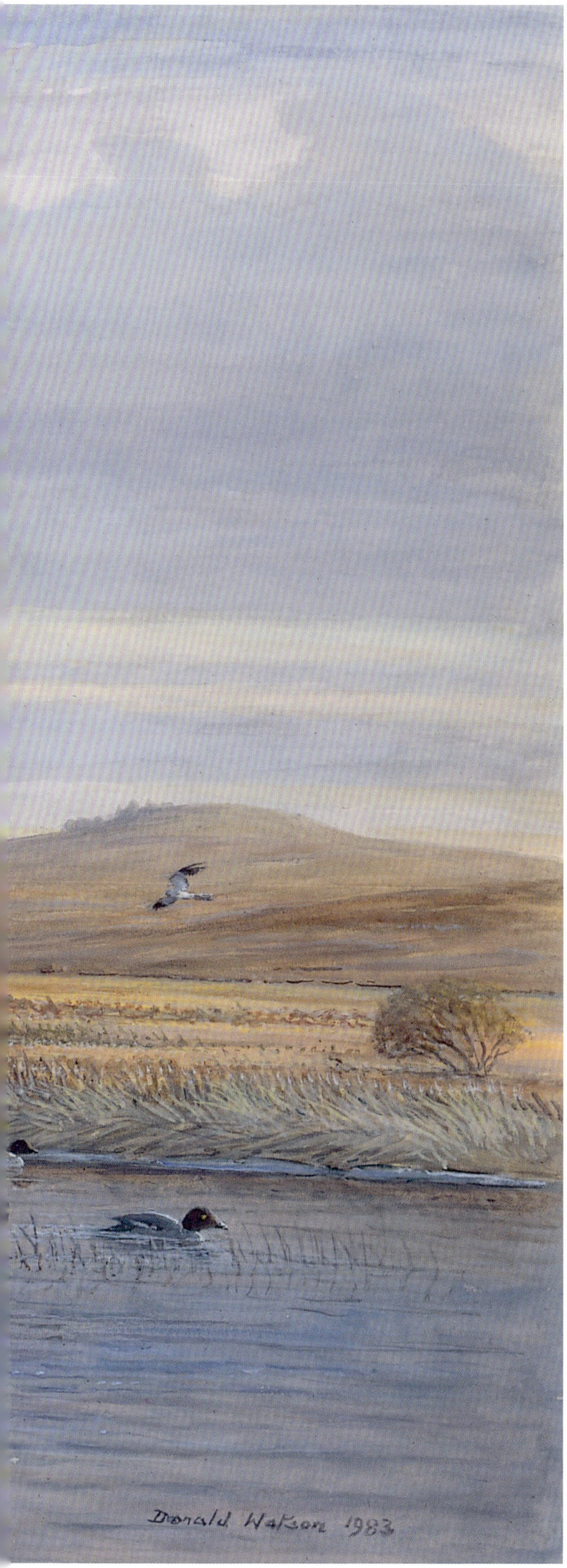

Goldeneye and Hen Harriers

Even when no harriers come to Airie roost there are always waterfowl to enjoy on the Black Water of Dee: pairs of Teal or Goosanders, Mallard returning to nest as spring advances, and, most interestingly, the small parties of Goldeneye which tend to frequent the river around Baddon's Isle. They do not often appear before the end of October, although some are on Loch Ken earlier. They seem quite unbothered by harriers flying close above them. The drakes may display to the ducks before Christmas, throwing their balloon-shaped heads back over their shoulders and scooting over the water in sudden rushes. In the failing light, the green-purple sheen on their heads is not apparent. When Goldeneye are about to dive, their heads are much more sleeked down. An almost circular white patch between bill and eyes is always unmistakable. In drakes their golden eyes are very striking. In flight their pinions make a singing whistle. Goldeneye display postures were well illustrated by J. G. Millais in his *British Diving Ducks* – he was the son of the more famous Sir John Millais, the Pre-Raphaelite artist who became a fine painter of atmospheric Scottish landscapes in his later years. I once read an article about Van Gogh, who surprisingly rated these as his favourite English landscape paintings. One, 'Still October,' is in Perth Art Gallery.

Goldeneye have been breeding in nest-boxes in Scotland since 1970 but none has so far colonised any Galloway nest-boxes. Roy Dennis told me that they were slow to occupy new areas. For a few years I expected them to breed in Galloway when late-staying pairs were often seen in May. Our wintering stock most likely goes to nest in Scandinavia, where both Goldeneye and Smew make use of nest-boxes. For some years in the 1970s, there was always a large congregation (100 or more) of Goldeneye at Loch Stroan in March but I have not seen this recently.

I painted the picture in the 1980s. The Otters on the Black Water, sometimes seen while I was roost-watching, seemed to me to have been possible predators of the Goldeneye, perhaps snatching them from below, unawares.

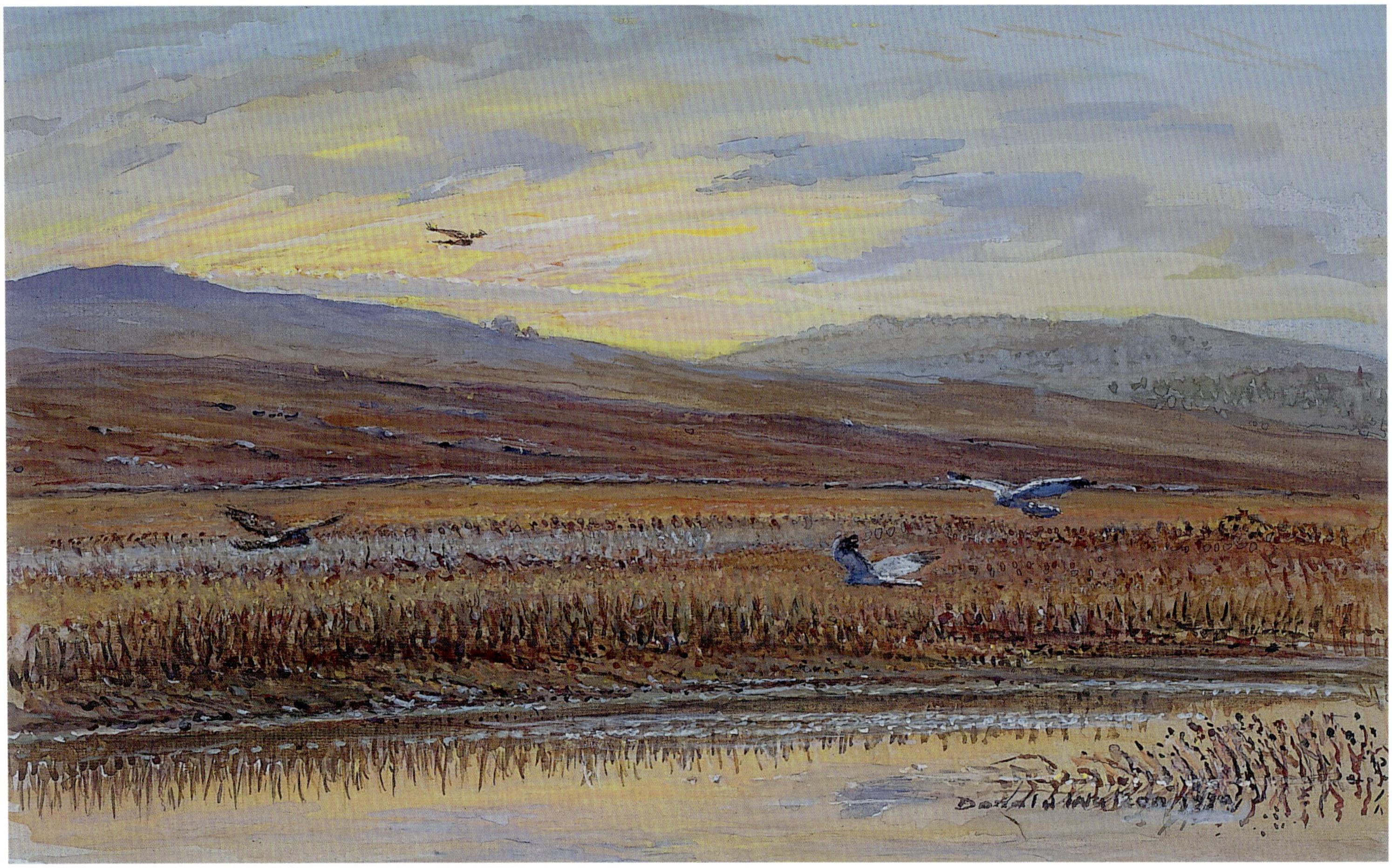

Peregrines alarming Hen Harriers at Airie Flowe roost

In late October–November 1979 Peregrines were sometimes flying over the harrier roost area. Once there was a single Peregrine, and at least once there were two, probably a pair. Flocks of Fieldfares were hunted by them, but most dramatic was the reaction of the harriers to a Peregrine. On 31 October 1979, I was watching with Derek Langslow when the harriers began to show signs of anxiety, but at first we could not see the cause. Soon a Peregrine flew out towards the roost from its hidden perch on a rock. The harriers, some having already settled to roost, left the ground and towered into the darkening sky, trying to rise above the Peregrine. At that time roost counts were not uncommonly into double figures. Some would fly right out of the roost towards Loch Stroan, but most rose high against the forest. There was a fair amount of 'whickering' in alarm. For the most part the harriers rose high enough to keep well above a Peregrine and would not settle to roost until it had moved away. A few harriers, mostly adult males, dived aggressively at a Peregrine when it had landed on a rock. It was difficult to follow all that was happening in the dusk light. Most memorable was the alarm which the presence of Peregrines caused. In spite of looking smaller, the Peregrines had a turn of speed which no harrier could match.

Background noises at this time of year came from the roaring of Red Deer stags at the rut, quite awesome when they were close by in the forest.

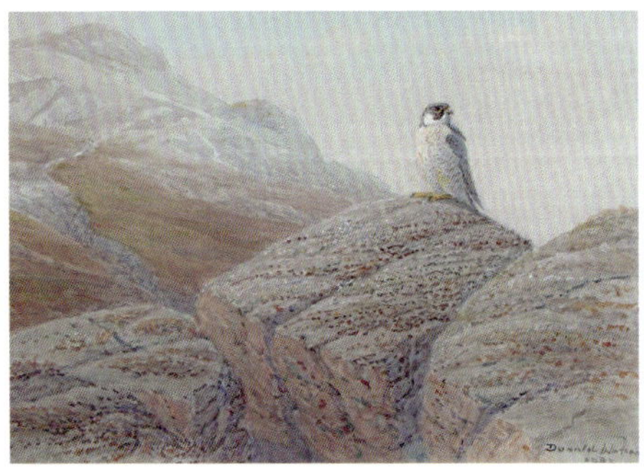

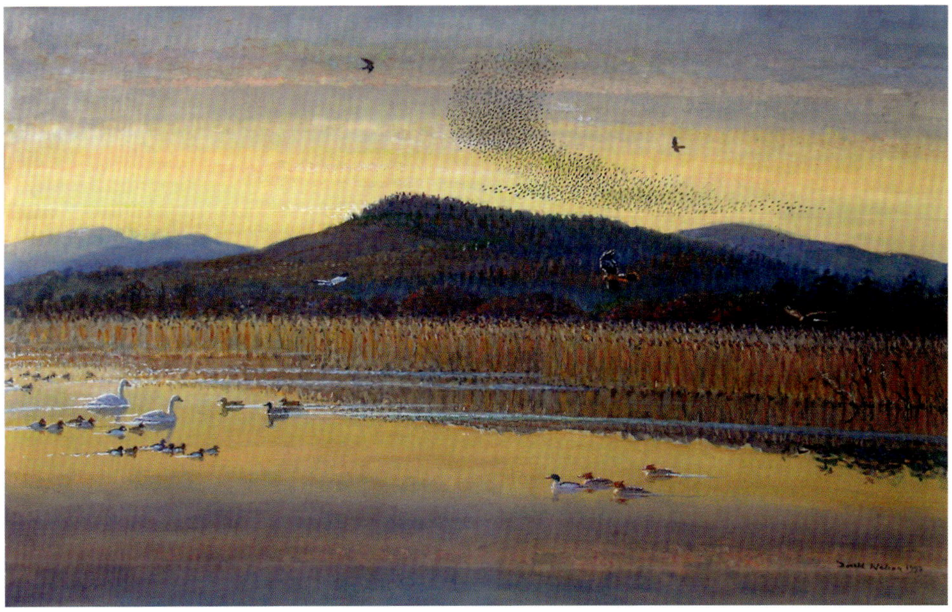

Predators at a huge starling roost and wildfowl at a Galloway loch, 1992

In the 1970s I used to visit this loch quite often. The peat bog near the water's edge was a favourite feeding place for the flock of Bean Geese which then came to Galloway in the winter. They are rarely seen there now, having almost deserted Galloway for central Scotland, where they are increasing. It had seemed to me recently that it looked a likely site for a Hen Harrier roost, but I did not investigate it until 1992 because I thought that shooting in the evenings would have deterred harriers. When this no longer seemed to be happening, I decided that an evening visit might be worthwhile. In January 1992 I went with Joan to look.

Some people may not believe that this painting is a true picture of what we saw on many evenings, but as far as I could make it, it is. Yes, some harriers were coming in to roost and what must have attracted them was the huge flock of Starlings, at times up to 10,000 of them, which came to roost in the reed-bed. They came in, not in one flock, but in a succession of smaller droves, each of a few hundred birds. On many evenings I sat with a companion, Chris Rollie, Ricky Gladwell or Ian Langford, on a slope above the loch, among young conifers, to watch this wonderful spectacle. The Starlings flew in low, almost brushing our heads in a great rush of air. High in the evening sky the big flock formed a dense mass, like a ball, to deter attacks from the predators which were threatening them, the distinctive outlines of two or three Peregrines and Sparrowhawks and sometimes a Goshawk too silhouetted against the sky. Twice a Lanner Falcon, clearly a falconer's escaped bird, was present.

The harriers, never more than 6–8 of them, tended to fly over or near the reed-bed waiting for the Starlings to dive in to roost, when they had the best chance of capturing one. Some of the harriers had been wing-tagged as young at nests. With some difficulty in the failing light the sharper-eyed of the watchers could identify some individuals. Amazingly, two first-year males and a young female came from a nest I had found further north in Galloway in 1991. The young female was recognised again breeding in the west of Ayrshire in the following summer, where Ricky Gladwell found her. Other wing-tagged birds came from Argyll and Tayside. In the foreground of the picture, ducks of several species swam on the calm water, unconcerned by the drama of the predators and the Starlings. Sometimes there was a Smew among the usual ducks. I made an interesting discovery in October 1992, when about 500 Starlings came to roost: there were no predators about, which must have been the reason why the Starlings flew directly into the reed-bed, with no aerial maneouvres, and unlike in the presence of predators, they settled to roost silently.

I have not named this loch because the landowner has suffered from vandals damaging his property. In later winters the Starlings have been very unpredictable, often none coming in at all.

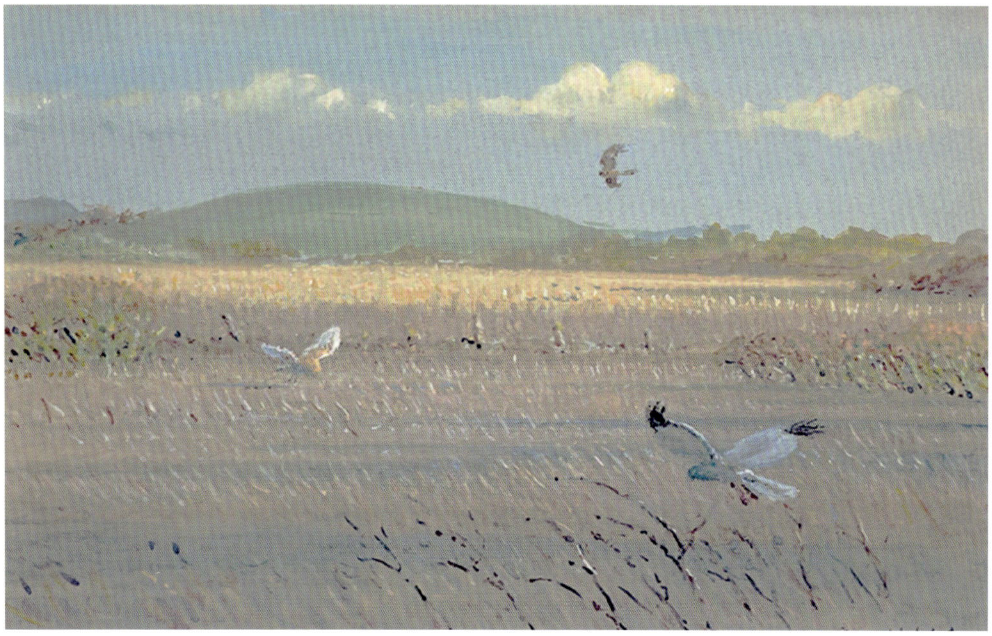

A harrier roost in the Machairs of Wigtownshire

This harrier-roost site is very different from Airie Flowe. A decade ago it was the largest roost in southwest Scotland, but recently numbers have declined greatly. It might be that increased breeding success in the far west of Galloway has been drawing more birds to an old roost which is nearer, although recent counts there have not approached the figures reached at the Machairs site, which had peaks of over 20 in earlier years.

In the Machairs a farmer has allowed Jim McCleary and others to watch from slightly higher ground close to the farm buildings. From there the harriers can be seen much closer than at any other roost I know. A male with some white feathers among the black on the wing-ends was seen for five consecutive winters.

It is the best site for seeing Barn Owls, as many as four hunting where the harriers go down on some evenings.

When I have been there, there has always been a wealth of bird activity with masses of Rooks gathered before roosting, Water Rails squealing from among rushes or sedges, a Merlin flying into the willow thickets, up to three Kestrels in the sky, a cock Stonechat in the foreground gorse bushes, and Fieldfare flocks passing over.

While lacking the dramatic landscape distances of Airie roost, this is a lowland site, with a background of woods, willow carr particularly. Incoming harriers often disappear from view among the trees and may go down there.

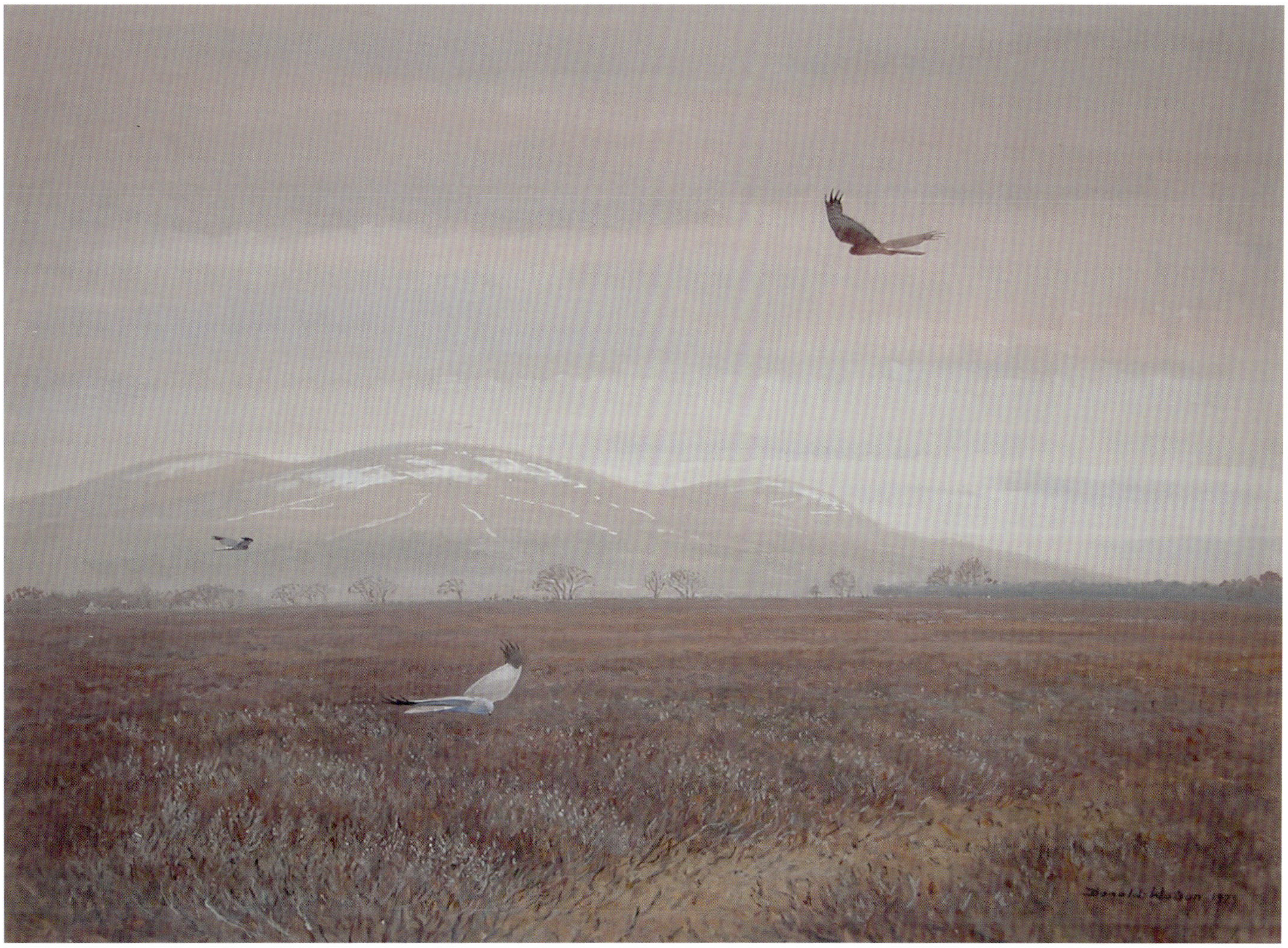

Hen Harriers flying to roost at Moss of Cree

I first noticed one or two Hen Harriers going to roost at Moss of Cree when I stopped one evening on the main road south from Newton Stewart at Balterson Farm. A small number of Hen Harriers appeared to be going down to roost on the rough grassy moor outside the large blocks of conifer forest which had transformed much of the Moss. It must have once been a real wilderness, now mostly long reclaimed. The flat, cultivated fields became a magnet for winter flocks of birds. The huge numbers of Skylarks attracted a variety of predators, especially when inland country was snowbound. Later, with my friend Louis Urquhart, I made quite a few visits and found that the main roost turned out to be in the wide heathery rides within the forest. It was never an easy roost to watch and very hard going on bitter winter evenings, especially for Louis, who was quite old. It was also a long drive each way from our homes in Dalry. I remember finding two Fieldfare kills which could have been made by a Peregrine that also hunted the Moss. There was no high ground to oversee the forest rides where we could be sure Hen Harriers had gone down.

In 1979, after a big snowfall in February, the flocks of birds on the Moss of Cree fields became spectacular, including many thousands of larks, a hundred or so Bramblings among the Chaffinches and many Reed Buntings. A small party of Bewick's Swans had joined the usual Whoopers. There were even a few Corn Buntings, which have since come close to extinction in Galloway. We saw a Peregrine stoop at and miss a Wood Pigeon and there were a few Stock Doves among the masses of Wood Pigeons. Sparrow Hawks were the commonest predators, but there were almost as many harriers, several Short-eared Owls, a Barn Owl and almost certainly a Merlin. Big flocks of Curlews and Pink-footed Geese were feeding in the fields.

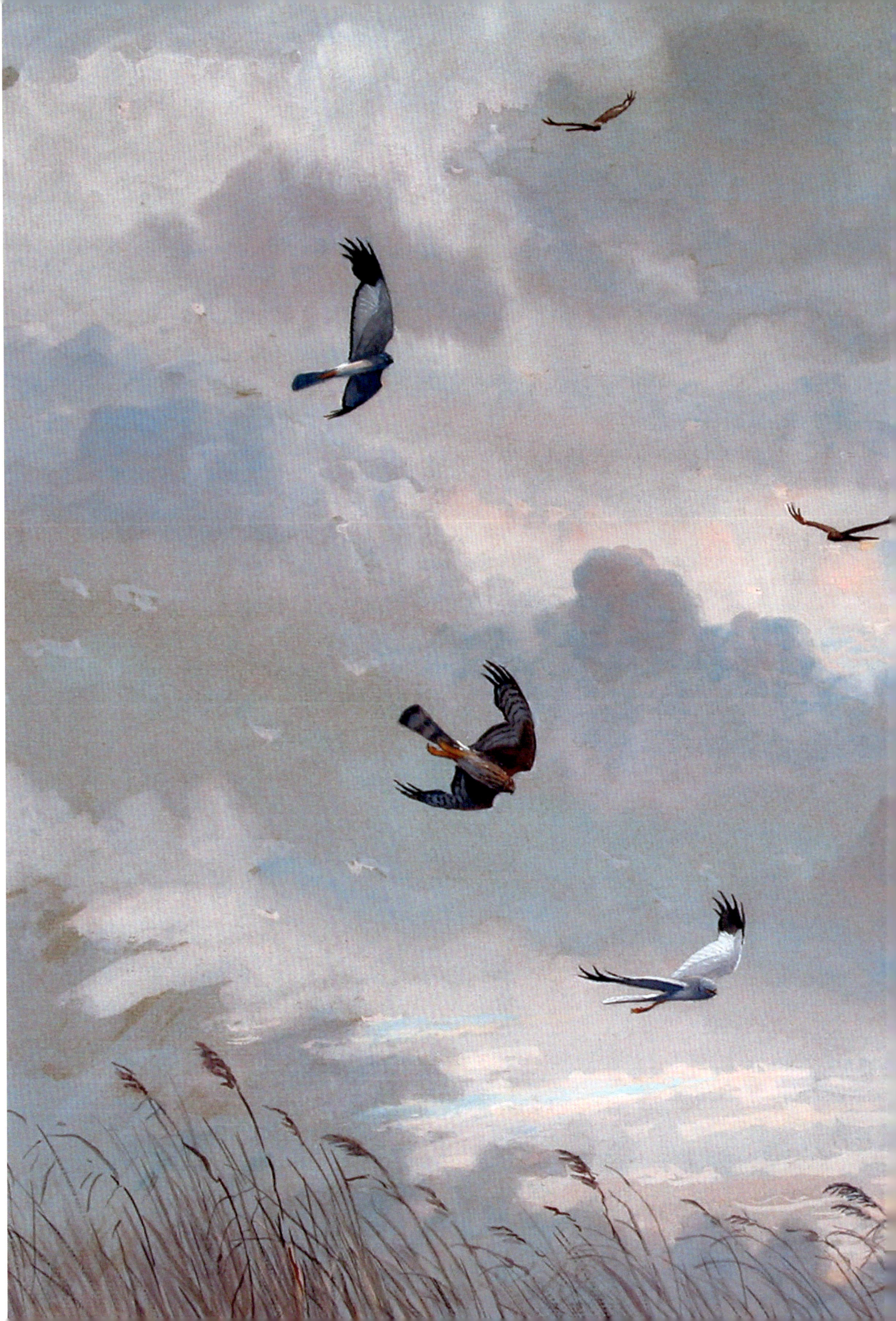

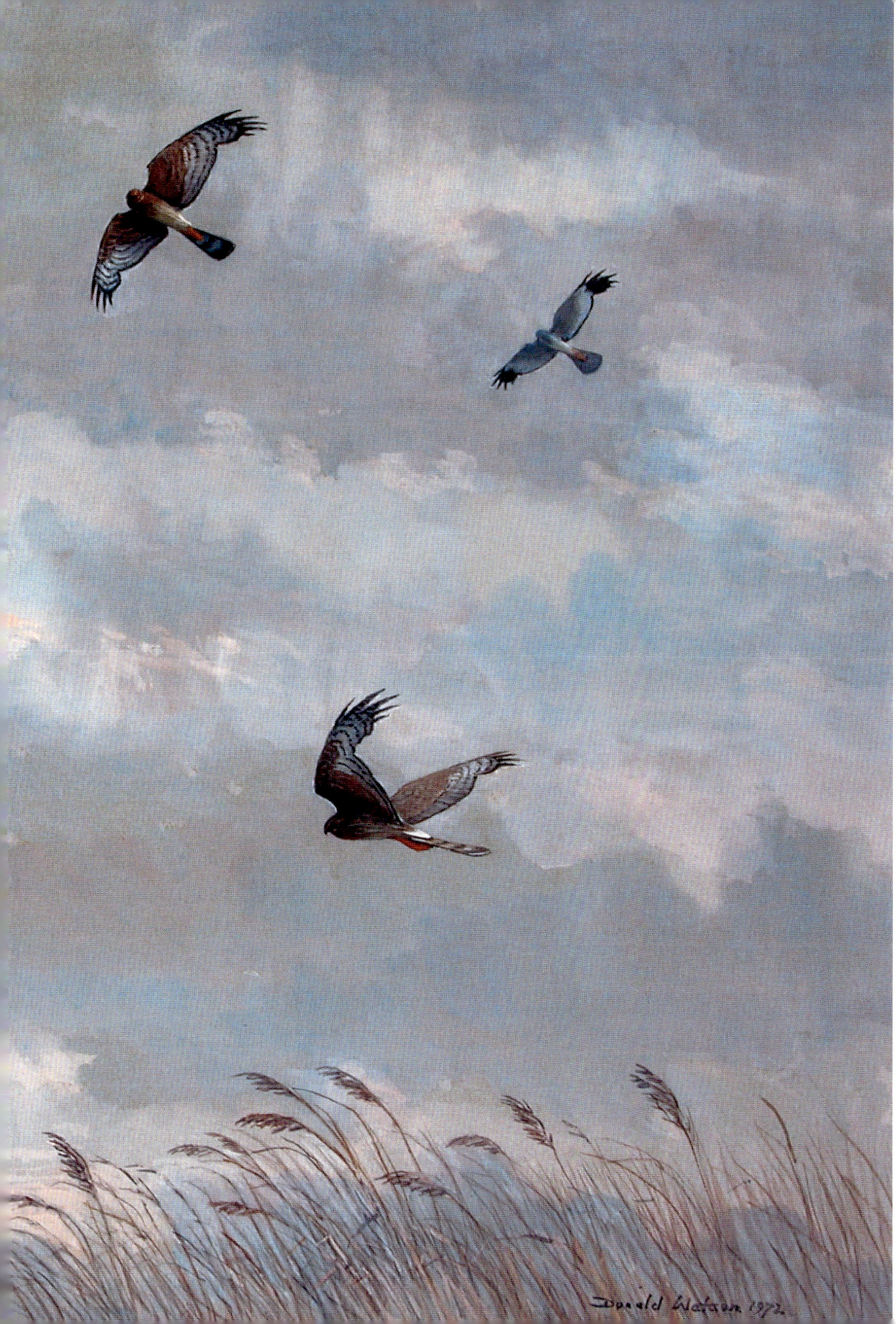
Donald Watson 1972

Hen Harriers roosting at the Curraghs, Isle of Man – the largest roost in the U.K.

In early October 1992, Joan and I flew to the Isle of Man. I was to open the hide that had been built for roost-watchers. Our hosts, Dr Pat Cullen and his wife Nini, as well as a host of people we met, were very welcoming.

Hen Harriers had never bred in the Isle of Man until 1977. For some time it was a well-guarded secret. It was an astonishing discovery that there was a massive winter roost at the Curraghs, in the north of the island. This roost, at times of over 100 birds, still flourishes and it appears that most are from the island's breeding population. It was a great experience to watch it from the hide. We were taken to see many fascinating places and birds. The Isle of Man is of course well known for its Choughs. On our first afternoon we saw over 30 feeding among seaweed at Sandwick and were shown where many nested on the cliffs around Dallby. At that time there was little persecution of harriers in the Isle of Man, there being no driven grouse shooting. It seemed surprising that the Hen Harrier had only colonised the island so recently, as the large number of heathery hills looked ideal nesting habitat. When we walked along the path to the hide at the Curraghs, Royal Fern was growing profusely, as it did formerly in Galloway.

When the harriers began to arrive at the roost, it was soon clear that they were settling over a wide area, dropping into willow and birch cover. Although it was early in the season and maximum numbers were not expected yet, it was going to be very difficult to count them, because the extent of roost ground was so extensive, but even more because of the dense tree-cover. I could see many birds dropping low among the trees and bushes, but to be sure exactly where they landed was a real challenge. It was reckoned that 30–40 birds had positively gone down. This was the highest total I had ever seen at a roost but only a fraction of the biggest counts later. Pat Cullen was also counting another sizable roost and a third roost at the south end of the island was quite big too. It might seem that the scattered sightings we had on outings during the day were surprisingly few and gave no indication that there were such numbers around. I had never seen such a densely wooded site used as a roost before. Long-eared Owls were also seen but I could not say how plentiful they were. I did have the impression that quite a large proportion of the grey males coming to roost had brown backs and were therefore not more than 2–3 years old.

I had an interesting time when Aaron Sampson took me up to the Point of Ayre one day. From there we could see the Galloway hills well. A correspondent in the Isle of Man had told me that he had seen a Chough fly north far out across the sea towards the Mull of Galloway. Choughs that started to breed at a site on the Galloway coast in 1988 had probably come from the Isle of Man population. Unfortunately, they have not increased in Galloway, where they were quite widespread long ago.

Rabbits are an important prey for the Isle of Man harriers.

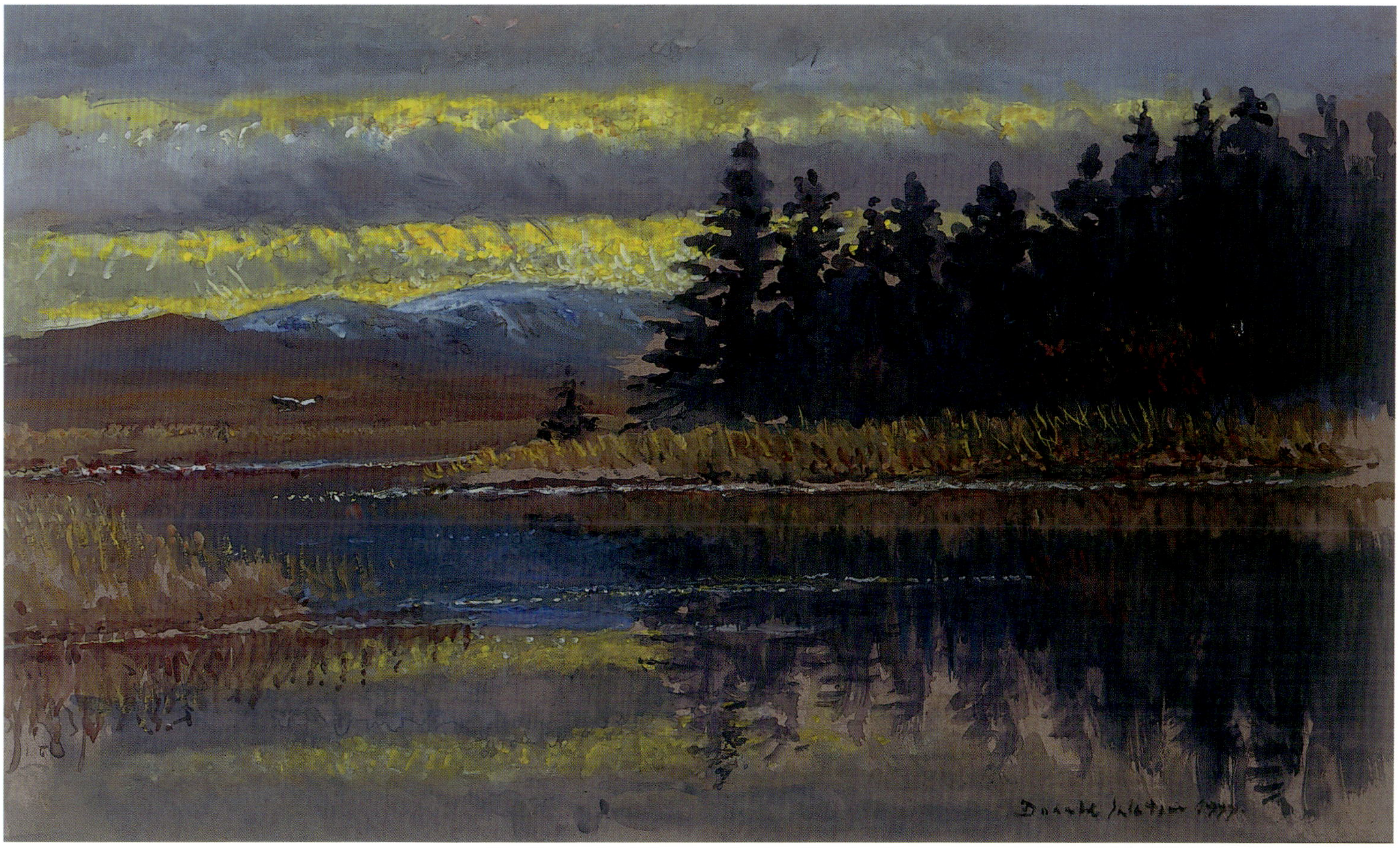

Rain shower approaching Airie Flowe roost, 1989

In the 1980s, numbers of harriers coming into Airie roost were mostly rather low, as in this painting. This was clearly a good evening for seeing them, with only scattered showers. Visibility was excellent, the hills in the background showing up well and making a beautiful setting.

When harriers were more numerous, there was always some displacement of earlier arrivals by those which came later. Most often the more powerful females would displace males, but surprisingly there were times when even a young male could displace a female. Any bird displaced by another would rarely attempt to regain its original site and might spend some time to find another. In earlier years both Black and Red Grouse came to roost among the harriers, always in small numbers. This never led to much interaction. Through all the years a Barn Owl often appeared about dusk and hunted the fringes of the roost area or the river bank, at times flying across the river and passing very close to an observer, looking luminously white, especially when seen against a dark stand of conifers. Short-eared Owls were hardly frequent and the more nocturnal Long-eared Owl only occasional, although a pair has nested not far away. Buzzards, so much increased in late years, now often cross the roost in the early evening. While a Golden Eagle may at times be seen distantly, I have never seen one overflying the roost. A late-hunting Kestrel, hovering in the sky as long as some light lasts, belongs to the early evening. Fast-flying hunters like Merlin and Sparrowhawk not uncommonly pass across the roost, or a Goshawk in recent years. The extraordinary incident between a Peregrine and harriers that had settled to roost is described on page 102.

There are always Carrion Crows at the roost, perhaps finding some pickings, and the deep croaks from a pair of Ravens heading homeward for the night up the river valley are usually to be heard before dark.

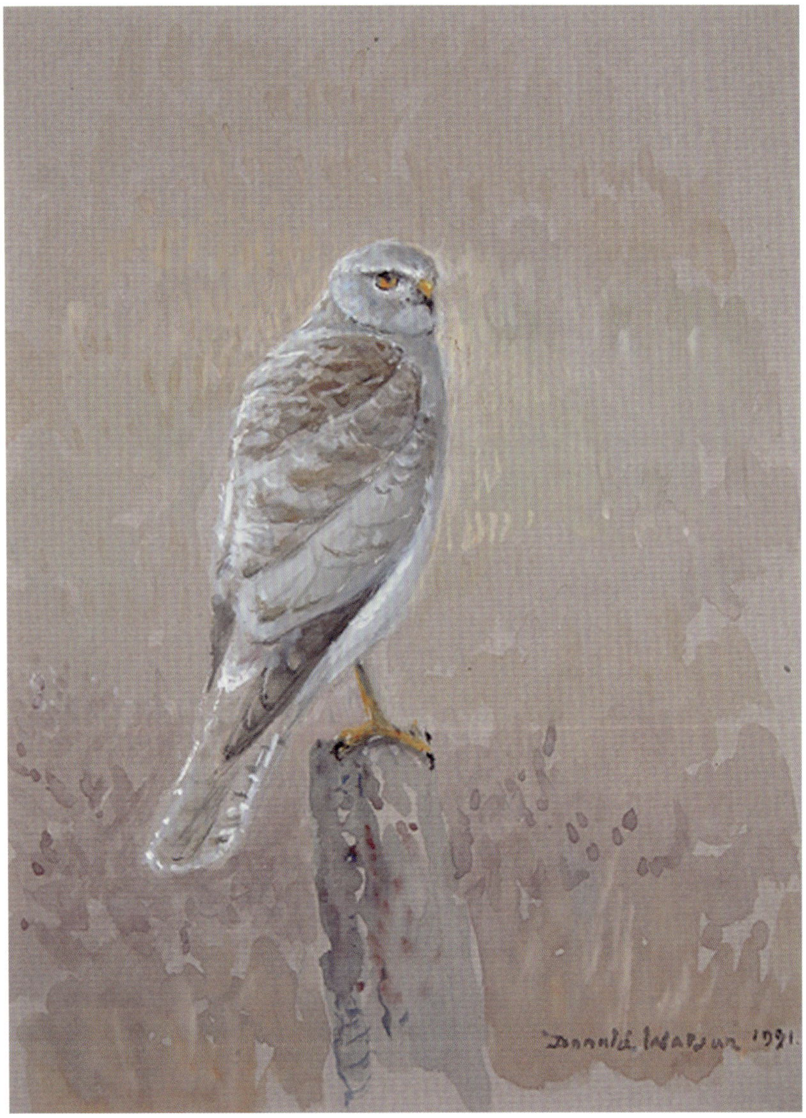

A year-old male Hen Harrier at a roost in Galloway

Males, looking grey, but still showing some unmoulted brown feathers, are seen commonly; in 1960 I was able to see the progress of moult in the male of a pair nesting at Cairn Table, Ayrshire, over several weeks. This was in high summer, but this painting is of a male seen in early March at Airie roost. It was presumably less than a year old but superficially could have passed as a grey bird, especially in flight. It remained perched on a post at the edge of the roost-site for about 45 minutes, a telescope allowing a detailed view of it. As Eddie Balfour said to me years ago, it can at times be difficult to be sure whether a partly grey male is one or two years old. I would guess that the bird in the painting was most likely not yet a year old.

My friend the late Donnie Macdonald reported a full clutch of eggs in the Highlands, laid in early April, certainly an early nest in that region, or even in southern Scotland. Young males from such an early nest might by March in the following year look like the bird in the painting, retaining a fair amount of brown on the mantle and scapulars. Grey males seen at Galloway roosts very often have dark or dusky mantles. Such birds must be one or two years old. In flight they have largely grey wings contrasting with their dark backs. The high proportion of winter roosting males in this plumage seems to suggest that many males do not survive for more than one or two years.

Langford Press – Wildlife Art Series W.A.S.

1 *Rural Portraits*, Polly Pullar,
Illustrated by Keith Brockie
ISBN 978-1-904078-06-7

2 *Further Afield*, Polly Pullar
ISBN 978-1-904078-10-4

3 *In Search of Harriers*, Donald Watson
ISBN 978-1-904078-12-8

4 *In a Natural Light*, Chris Rose
ISBN 978-1- 904078-16-6

5 *From Dawn till Dusk*, Darren Woodhead
ISBN 978-1-904078-19-7

6 *Orchards*, Jonathan Latimer
ISBN 978-1-904078-08-1

7 *Butterfly Landscapes*, Richard Tratt
ISBN 978-1-904078-15-9

8 *At the Edge/Aig an Oir*, Robert Burton/SWLA
ISBN 978-1-904078-18-0

9 *The Great Fen*, Chris Gerrard/ANF
ISBN 978-1-904078-13-5

10 *Cutting Away*, Robert Gillmor
ISBN 978-1-904078-14-2

11 *A life in Detail*, Terance James Bond
ISBN 978-1-904078-17-3

12 *Dance of the Brush*, Ralph Thompson
ISBN 978-1-904078-21-0

13 *Pride of Place*, Carl Brenders
ISBN 978-1-904078-22-7

14 *Between the Tides*, John Threlfall
ISBN 978-1-904078-23-4

15 *Images from Birding*, Michael Warren
ISBN 978-1-904078-24-1

16 *Beneath the Surface*, David Miller
ISBN 978-1-904078-25-8

17 *Arctic Flight*, James McCallum
ISBN 978-1-904078-26-5

18 *Archibald Thorburn*, David Waters
ISBN 978-1-904078-27-2

19 *Fish in Art*, C.E. Jackson
ISBN 978-1-904078-28-9

20 *Pecked and Painted*, Tony Hopkins
ISBN 978-1-904078-29-6

21 *True to Form*, David Bennett
ISBN 978-1-904078-30-2

22 *A Celebration of Butterflies*, Ed. S. Wood and W. White
Various artists
ISBN 978-1-904078-31-9

23 *New Forest Painters*, Gorgina Babey
ISBN 978-1-904078-33-3

24 *Capturing the Moment*, Raymond Sheppard
ISBN 978-1-904078-34-0

25 *Natures Powers*, Carry Akroyd
ISBN 978-1-904078-35-7

26 *Wild in Europe*, Renso Tamse
ISBN 978-1-904078-36-4

27 *There and Back again?*, Various artists
ISBN 978-1-94078-37-1

28 *Wildlife Art in 3D*, Various Artists
ISBN 978-1-94078-38-8

29 *The Un-feathered Bird*, Katrina van Grouw
ISBN 978-1-94078-39-5

30 *Wildlife in Print*, Various Artists
ISBN 978-1-94078-40-1

31 *Beyond the Plough*, R Jefferson and J Davies
ISBN 978-1-94078-41-8

32 *Otters*, David Bennett
ISBN 978-1-94078-42-5

33 *The Winter Hare*, Andrew Haslen
ISBN 978-1-904078-43-2

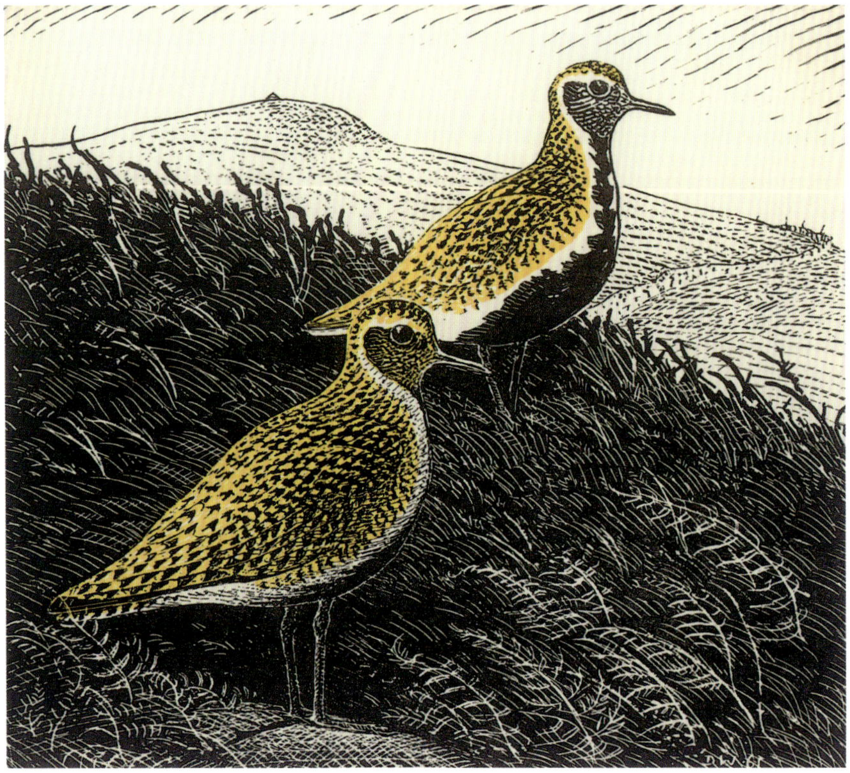